Proceedings of the Second International Conference on Credit Analysis and Risk Management

Proceedings of the Second International Conference on Credit Analysis and Risk Management

Edited by

Pascal Gantenbein, Simone Westerfeld and Beatrix Wullschleger

CAMBRIDGE SCHOLARS
PUBLISHING

Proceedings of the Second International Conference on Credit Analysis and Risk Management,
Edited by Pascal Gantenbein, Simone Westerfeld and Beatrix Wullschleger

This book first published 2014

Cambridge Scholars Publishing

12 Back Chapman Street, Newcastle upon Tyne, NE6 2XX, UK

British Library Cataloguing in Publication Data
A catalogue record for this book is available from the British Library

ISBN (10): 1-4438-6652-0, ISBN (13): 978-1-4438-6652-1

TABLE OF CONTENTS

PREFACE

Following the Second International Conference on Credit Analysis and Risk Management, which was organized in Basel in September 2013, we decided to publish a book with the respective conference proceedings. However, given the high relevance of this topic, we have invited several additional authors from the field to submit papers throughout the collection phase of the articles. We are now delighted to present the outcome of this process in the form of this book. The current volume comprises a spectrum of articles by both the keynote speakers and the academic presenters of the conference as well as additional inputs from academia and credit risk practice.

Credit risk is an important element in most financial transactions in some form and therefore plays a crucial role in different layers of economic activity. Three key elements can be distinguished, namely (1) the lender-borrower relationship which is at the core of the entire discussion, (2) the pricing of credit risk in financial markets, and (3) the relevance of financial stability and regulation related to the occurrence of credit risk. In this book, we strive to capture these areas in a comprehensive way although within these topics it will, of course, only be possible to highlight some of the current issues and questions related to them.

The first layer, the lender-borrower relationship and the intermediation function which banks assume in providing loans to the private and public sector is always dominated by two questions: First, which factors are important in determining credit volume, credit prices, and conditions to a client on an individual loan basis? In other words, how should credit-linked assets be rated, priced, monitored, and organized along their lives? And, second, how can a bank optimally structure its entire credit portfolio and which impact does the portfolio composition have on credit decisions and hedging?

Several features that are important in this respect will be discussed in the book, such as the ability to forecast distress (in the special case of SMEs), the relevance of soft information versus financial information about potential clients, the (eventually limited) role of the default history for enabling better credit decisions, and the effects of internal control in the credit assessment process. Regarding credit portfolio management, it is of utmost importance to understand the dominant risk factors for the entire portfolio, to be aware of potential contagion effects and correlated defaults across loan segments, and to control the optimal provision of economic capital. All these aspects will be addressed subsequently in the papers of tracks 1, 4, and 5.

A second layer which can be located in the pricing of credit risk in financial markets becomes important as soon as claims arising from bilateral lending get securitized and traded. First of all, it is apparent that pricing of credit risk is highly dependent on the economic environment. While in the wake of the subprime crisis, prices for assets of lower credit quality collapsed, hence leading to skyrocketing credit risk premiums in fall 2008, only a few years later, credit risk premiums dropped again to pre-crisis levels or even below. This shows that credit risk premiums obtained from financial markets, inter alia, are a function of both market fear and scarcity of investment alternatives.

However, especially in situations like the one described above, it is not trivial to keep credit risk and liquidity risk apart. Just remember that many investors buying so called toxic assets from banks and institutional investors during the financial crisis of 2008 meanwhile made a fortune with these positions. In other words, plenty of these assets were not as toxic as many investors thought in terms of credit risk, at least not in hindsight, but pricing undoubtedly was heavily influenced by illiquidity, as well. This again had to do with the forced sell-offs of these positions by many banks into a falling market. Hence, time constraints (due to economic, legal, or accounting related restrictions) may play an important role in explaining the pricing of credit risk in financial markets.

Some related topics covered in this book include the analysis of credit default swap (CDS) spread changes, the attribution of CDS spreads on both default premiums and liquidity premiums, the discussion of the often observed market segmentation in fixed-income securities, the changing risk perception for corporate bonds together with higher risk factor correlations throughout crises, and the ability to extract distance-to-default data for private firms from public markets. These issues will be mainly covered in papers of streams 1 and 3.

Probably the most relevant field in recent years, at least in public perception and measured by regulatory activity, has been the third layer mentioned above which is the discussion of systemic risk and financial market stability. In economies with a strong banking sector, credit crises may well have caused severe shocks in the banking industry, but these were traditionally contained within the respective national boundaries. However, both internationalization of banking activities and large-scale securitizations of loan and bond portfolios not only have contributed to better diversification opportunities for investors but likewise to an international dissemination of credit risk. Alongside this development, financial markets have seen a tremendous generation and distribution of credit derivatives such as CDS and index products. As a result, the risk of contagion has significantly increased given these multiple connections between international financial markets and institutions.

Obviously, several questions and objectives arise from this observation. First, given the sheer size of some banks as well as the interconnectedness in the sector, it is important to take a closer look into the prerequisites of financial stability. Key topics presented in papers of stream 2 include the analysis of default probabilities in the banking sector, the link between internal rating based (IRB) approaches and risk-weighted capital, and the relevance of liquidity risk in the financial system. Furthermore, the years since 2008 have advanced a new and highly interesting stream of research on the connection between credit crises and real estate crises which in turn typically have a strong impact on the entire economy.

All these topic areas will be reflected in papers of the streams Ratings (1), Regulation (2), CDS & Bond Pricing (3), Relationship Banking (4), and Credit Portfolio Models (5) as well as in the several further articles about the role and challenges of microfinance, recent considerations as to the capital structure decision, and the link between credit and real estate cycles.

With this book, we hope to provide you with many interesting and useful inputs for your academic and professional work in the field of credit risk. We are looking forward to an ongoing discussion of credit topics on the occasion of the 3rd International Conference on Credit Analysis and Risk Management to be held in Michigan (USA) on August 28/29th 2014 as well as the next Basel Conference in August 2015.

— Pascal Gantenbein, Simone Westerfeld and Beatrix Wullschleger
Basel 2014

Introduction[1]

A Summary of the Second International Conference on Credit Analysis and Risk Management: Basel Workshop on Credit Risk 2013

Simone Westerfeld[2]

In September 2013, the Second International Conference on Credit Analysis and Risk Management, the Basel Workshop on Credit Risk, was hosted in Basel, Switzerland. Jointly organized by the University of Applied Sciences Northwestern Switzerland and the Universities of Basel, Hohenheim, Oakland, Regensburg, and St. Gallen, the conference was the second in this set-up after the first event was organized in 2011 by the Oakland University, USA. The conference series is intended to establish a discussion platform on credit analysis and related topics for both academia and banking practice alike. In the course of the program, more than 70 international academics and practitioners gathered in Basel for two days to discuss keynotes and latest academic research categorized in the streams Ratings, Regulation, Credit Default Swap & Bond Pricing, Relationship Banking, and Credit Portfolio Models.

Various keynote speakers from different backgrounds started the conference and opened the floor for debate by providing hands-on insights from practitioner's and regulators perspectives: Armin Landerer, Head of Corporate Banking at Basel Cantonal Bank, opened the conference and elaborated on developments and trends in Credit Risk Management from a Commercial Bank's point of view in the Swiss banking environment.

---

[1] This article has been published with the title "Second International Conference on Credit Analysis and Risk Management 2013 in Basel - Challenging the Establishment" in 'Credit and Capital Markets', 2/2014, p. 367-375.

[2] Prof. Dr. Simone Westerfeld is from the Institute for Finance, School of Business, University of Applied Sciences Northwestern Switzerland in Basel.

Imène Rahmouni-Rousseau, representing the Financial Stability Board gave an overview on the FSB work agenda and its link to credit risk followed by a lively discussion with the audience. The speech of Markus Heusler, CEO of RSN Risk Solution Network AG, contributed to the topic by a presentation on rating model development for SME from an outsourcing company's perspective, including pitfalls and lessons learned over the last ten years.

Klaus Duellmann from European Central Bank (ECB) elaborated in his speech on the impact of Basel III on the International Banking System and perfectly rounded off the picture in adding a supervisor's perspective to the before stated FSB and banks' points of view. Finally, Jens Kuttig, Partner at zeb/rolfes.schierenbeck.associates, ended the keynote roundtable with the presentation of innovative trends in credit risk transfer and possible answers to the question where the secondary markets for credit risk might head to.

In the course of the academic program, 15 selected authors had the chance to present their latest research papers, each followed by a lively discussion with the audience. Based on the submitted abstracts of the presented academic papers, the subsequent section provides a brief overview on the topics covered during the two conference days:

The first stream covered predominantly rating-related topics and featured three contributions. In their paper "Forecasting Distress in European SME Portfolios" *Dimitra Michala, Theoharry Grammatikos* and *Sara Ferreira Filipe* (all from University of Luxembourg) develop distress prediction models for non-financial small and medium enterprises (SMEs) using a dataset from eight European countries over the period 2000-2009. The authors examine idiosyncratic and systematic covariates and find that macro conditions and bankruptcy codes add predictive power to their models. Moreover, industry effects usually demonstrate significance but provide only small improvements. The paper contributes to the literature in several ways: First, using a sample with many micro companies, it offers unique insights into European small businesses. Second, it explores distress in a multi-country setting, allowing for regional- and country-level comparisons. Third, the models can capture changes in overall distress rates and co-movements during economic cycles.

Sebastian Löhr (University of Hannover) and his co-authors *Arndt Claussen* (University of Hannover), *Daniel Rösch* (University of Regensburg) and *Harald Scheule* (University of Technology, Sydney) analyze in their paper "Valuation of Systematic Risk in the Cross-section of Credit Default Swap Spreads" the pricing of systematic risk factors in credit default swap contracts in a two-stage empirical framework. In the first pass, they estimate contract-specific sensitivities to several systematic risk factors by time-series regressions, using quoted credit default swap (CDS) spreads of 339 U.S. entities from 2004 to 2010. They find that the credit market climate, the cross-market correlation and the market volatility serve to explain CDS spread changes. In the second pass, they examine by cross-section regressions whether the contract-specific sensitivities to these systematic risk factors are priced in the cross-section of swap contracts, hereby controlling for individual risk factors such as credit ratings, liquidity and leverage. The authors find that their basic risk factors explain about 83% of the CDS spreads prior to the crisis and about 90% during the crisis.

In "An Empirical Analysis of Priced Systematic Risk on Bonds and Market Segmentation" *Terry Benzschawel* (Citi Bank), *Liang Fu* and *Austin Murphy* (both from Oakland University, Rochester) investigate the existence of segmentation in the market for fixed-income securities. Evidence is found of lower risk-adjusted returns being required for bonds making larger contributions to the risk of pure debt portfolios over the 2003-2011 interval. Significant abnormal returns existed for diversified investors taking short (long) positions on bonds with higher (lower) pure bond betas.

In the stream Regulation, three authors focused on regulatory aspects of credit risk. *Edward Altman* (New York University), *Francesca Campolongo* (European Commission), *Janko Cizel* (presenting author) and *Herbert Rijken* (both from University of Amsterdam) presented their article titled "Estimating the Probability of Default of the Western European Banks". In this paper the authors propose the novel methodology to produce long-term probabilities of default (PD) for the European listed and non-listed banks. The methodology relies on the observation that during times of financial turmoil, market valuation of banks to a large extent reflects the credit quality fundamentals. The authors estimate the distressed market-to-book model for the listed European banks, and apply the model to the non-listed banks to produce the implied distressed market-to-book ratios. Finally, they use the linking function constructed from about 1'500 bank failures in the U.S. to produce the expected default frequency for the entire spectrum of European banks.

Mike Mariathasan (University of Oxford) and *Ouarda Merrouche* (The Graduate Institute, Geneva, and CEPR) presented their paper "The manipulation of Basel Riskweights" as a contribution to the session on regulation. In their paper, the authors examine the relationship between banks' approval for the internal ratings-based (IRB) approaches of Basel II and the ratio of risk weighted assets over total assets. Analyzing a panel of 115 banks from 21 OECD countries that were eventually approved for applying the IRB to their credit portfolio, they find that the risk-weight density is lower once regulatory approval is granted. The effect persists when controlled for different loan categories, and the authors provide evidence showing that it cannot be explained by flawed modeling, or improved risk-measurement alone. Consistent with theories of risk-weight manipulation, they find the decline in risk-weights to be particularly prevalent among weakly capitalized banks, when the legal framework for supervision is weak, and in countries where supervisors are overseeing many IRB banks. The authors conclude that part of the decline in reported riskiness under IRB results from banks' strategic risk-modeling.

Ren-Raw Chen (Fordham University) and his co-authors *William Filonuk* (Bank of New York), *Dilip K. Patro* (Office of the Comptroller of the Currency) and *An Yan* (Fordham University) also analyze regulatory impacts in the credit context and presented their paper "Valuing Financial Assets with Liquidity Discount: An Implication to Basel III": The unprecedented financial crisis in 2007-8 and the largest bankruptcy in U.S. history prompted the expedited regulation in the financial industry. A new Basel Accord has been proposed to further regulate the main risk that caused the crisis – liquidity risk. In a recent paper, Chen (2012)[3] presents a liquidity discount model where financial securities can be evaluated with substantial discounts at the presence of a liquidity squeeze in the market place. In the presented paper, the authors adopt this model to evaluate a selection of 23 largest U.S. financial institutions (assets over $100 billion) to investigate the liquidity impact during the crisis period. The authors calibrate the model to market information such as market capitalization and volatility. They find that the model can provide significant predictive power of a firm's liquidity healthiness.

In the stream CDS & Bond Pricing, the following works caught participants' attention. "Liquidity premium in CDS market" is the title of the paper presented by *Kuate Kamga* (Goethe University Frankfurt) and his co-author *Christian Wilde* (Goethe University Frankfurt). The authors develop a state-space model to decompose bid and ask quotes of CDS into

[3] Chen, R.-R., 2012, "Valuing a Liquidity Discount," *Journal of Fixed Income*, 1 Winter 2012.

two components, fair default premium and liquidity premium. This approach gives a better estimate of the default premium than mid quotes, and it allows to disentangle and compare the liquidity premium earned by the protection buyer and the protection seller. In contrast to other studies, the model is sparse while still allowing for correlation between liquidity and default premia, which is supported by empirical evidence. The model is implemented and applied to a large data set of 118 CDS for a period ranging from 2004 to 2010. The authors find evidence that 1) the liquidity premium widens for the protection seller and the protection buyer in absolute terms during the crisis, 2) the protection buyer receives a larger liquidity premium than the protection seller, 3) during the crisis, the share of the liquidity premium earned by the protection seller increases, in particular for non-financials, 4) this is at the cost of the protection buyer, since the relative liquidity premium of the protection buyer decreases strongly after the beginning of the financial downturn, while that of the protection seller hardly changes, and 5) protection sellers generally require a lower liquidity premium for financial names than non-financial names. To the knowledge of the authors, this is the first paper that attempts to explain the liquidity premium of the protection seller relative to the liquidity premium of the bidder during the financial crisis.

In their paper "Default Probabilities and Interest Expenses of Privately Held Firms", *Jin-Chuan Duan* (National University of Singapore), *Baeho Kim* (Korea University Business School), *Changki Kim* (Korea University), *Woojin Kim* (Seoul National University) and *Donghwa Shin* (Princeton University) estimate term structures of default probabilities for private firms using Korean data comprising 1,440 default events from 29,894 firms between 1999 and 2011. They then study whether the reported interest expenses are reflective of the estimated default term structure. Each private firm's default likelihood is characterized by a forward intensity model employing both macro risk factors and firm-specific attributes derived from financial statements. Although private firms have no traded stock prices, the authors devise a way of obtaining a public-firm equivalent distance-to-default by projection, which references the distance-to-defaults of public firms with comparable firm attributes. Statistical tests indicate that the fitted model provides accurate multi-period forecasts of defaults for both financial and non-financial private firms. The used methodology can be directly applied by commercial lenders in charging appropriate interest rates upon lending decisions for different future periods.

The paper "The Correlation Puzzle: The Interaction of Bond and Risk Correlation" presented by *Sebastian Bethke* and co-authored by *Alexander Kempf* and *Monika Trapp* (all from University of Cologne) deals with diversification benefits, which depend on the correlation between assets, and the fact that asset correlation increases when it is most needed. The authors examine bond correlation using a broad sample of U.S. corporate bonds and find bond correlation to be higher during the financial crisis in 2008. Increased bond correlation results from higher correlation between corporate bond risk factors. Risk factor correlation in turn increases when investor sentiment worsens. This suggests that corporate bond investors change their perception of risk factors, which results in higher risk factor correlation and finally higher bond correlation.

The fourth stream displays latest research on Relationship Lending, exploring aspects of information asymmetries in the lending process. The paper "Hidden Gems and Borrowers with Dirty Little Secrets: Investment in Soft Information, Borrower Self-selection and Competition" was presented and written by *Reint Gropp* (Goethe University Frankfurt), *Christian Gruendl* (EBS Business School) and *Andre Guettler* (Ulm University). This paper empirically examines the role of soft information in the competitive interaction between relationship and transaction banks. Soft information can be interpreted as a private signal about the quality of a firm that is observable to a relationship bank, but not to a transaction bank. The authors show that borrowers self-select to relationship banks depending on whether their privately observed soft information is positive or negative. Competition affects the investment in learning the private signal from firms by relationship banks and transaction banks asymmetrically. Relationship banks invest more; transaction banks invest less in soft information, exacerbating the selection effect. Finally, the authors show that firms where soft information was important in the lending decision were no more likely to default compared to firms where only financial information was used.

The paper "Should Defaults Be Forgotten? Evidence from quasi-experimental variation in removal of negative consumer credit information" by *Marieke Bos* (Stockholm University) and *Leonard Nakamura* (Federal Reserve Bank of Philadelphia) deals with the fact that around the globe, credit bureaus restrict the length of time during which negative credit information can be retained. By exploiting a quasi-experimental variation in retention times of negative credit information, the authors find that a prolonged retention time increases the need for and access to credit and reduces the likelihood to default. In both regimes, less than 27 percent of individuals default again within two years after removal, suggesting that only a minority is inherently high risk or, alternatively, removal of credit arrears induce borrowers to exert greater effort. Either interpretation raises the possibility that forgetting defaults is welfare enhancing.

In "The Hidden Costs of Control – Evidence from Small Business Lending" the authors *Martin Brown* (University of St. Gallen), *Matthias Schaller* (University of St. Gallen), *Simone Westerfeld* (University of Applied Sciences FHNW) and *Markus Heusler* (RSN Risk Solution AG) use proprietary data on 3,360 credit assessments by 340 loan-officers at six banks and analyze how internal control affects the credit rating process. They document a positivity bias of control: Loan officers propose better ratings for their clients when they know that the rating is subject to internal approval. The evidence suggests that this positivity bias is driven by strategic behavior: Loan officers inflate proposed ratings in reaction to past downward corrections by their current approver. Moreover, experienced loan officers inflate those parameters of a credit rating which are least likely to be corrected by approvers. Overall, the authors find that internal control does not improve the informational efficiency of the credit assessment process.

Finally, the stream Credit Portfolio Models completes the academic program with a series of papers aiming to break new soil in modeling credit portfolio risk. *Xin Zhang* (VU University Amsterdam), *Bernd Schwaab* (European Central Bank) and *André Lucas* (Duisenberg School of Finance) presented a paper titled "Conditional Probabilities and Contagion Measures for Euro Area Sovereign Default Risk". The authors propose a novel empirical framework to assess the likelihood of joint and conditional failure for Euro area sovereigns. Their model is based on a dynamic skewed-t copula which captures all the salient features of the data, including skewed and heavy-tailed changes in the price of CDS protection against sovereign default, as well as dynamic volatilities and correlations to ensure that failure dependence can increase in times of stress. The authors apply the framework to Euro area sovereign CDS spreads from 2008 to mid-2011. The results reveal significant time-variation in risk dependence and considerable spill-over effects in the likelihood of sovereign failures. They also investigate distress dependence around a key policy announcement by Euro area heads of state on May 9, 2010, and demonstrate the importance of capturing higher-order time-varying moments during times of crisis for the correct assessment of interacting risks.

In the paper "Specification Risk and Calibration Effects of a Multifactor Credit Portfolio Model" by *Gregor Dorfleitner* (University of Regensburg), *Matthias Fischer* (University of Erlangen-Nürnberg) and *Marco Geidosch* (University of Regensburg) the authors point out a crucial source of specification risk when calibrating a typical industry-type, Merton-based credit portfolio model. In addition to equity prices and asset values, which are the classical choices, the authors consider credit default swap (CDS) spreads and Expected Default Frequencies (EDF, from Moody's KMV) as alternatives. Based on 40 large European companies from different industries, they calibrate a macroeconomic factor model with an OLS regression analysis for each specification and calculate the corresponding economic capital. The findings are: 1) on average 2 to 3 risk factors are needed to adequately model creditworthiness on the obligor level, 2) stock market variables are the most important risk factors, 3) model-implied credit correlation is extremely sensitive to the choice of the proxy for creditworthiness and 4) only the EDF specification leads to less economic capital as compared to regulatory capital according to Basel II while it is exceeded substantially by all other specifications. In particular, credit correlation in the CDS specification by far exceeds any estimate mentioned in the literature. Most importantly, the authors show that the economic capital of their sample portfolio can be reduced by 78%, depending on which variable to choose as proxy for creditworthiness.

The paper "Concentration risk in SME credit portfolios: the role of banks' portfolio composition policy and risk appetite" presented by *Michel Dietsch* (Université de Strasbourg) and co-authored by *Henri Fraisse* (Banque de France) and *Joël Petey* (Université de Strasbourg) focuses on particular aspects of SME financing in Europe and the appropriateness of current risk weights for SME lending. Knowing that risk weights depend strongly on asset correlations, the object of this paper is to estimate the potential for credit risk concentration arising from correlated defaults of small firms. The measurement of concentration risk needs to take into account borrowers' heterogeneity. One way to proceed is to extend the standard asymptotic single factor framework by introducing additional factors of systematic risk varying between groups of borrowers. Using a generalized linear mixed model, the paper extends the standard single-factor credit risk model to a multi-factor framework taking into account size and industry effects. The paper uses the French Credit Register and the rating histories of more than 400.000 French SMEs, covering the period from 2003 to 2011. Provided by the Banque de France ratings system, the sample allows considering the real portfolios of the five major banking groups in France. This paper shows that despite comparable portfolios in terms of size and industry distributions, there are sizeable differences in terms of economic capital across banking groups. The authors investigate whether such differences could be attributed to concentration of credit risk on specific size segments or industries or, on the contrary, are the result of different risk appetite levels across banks at the portfolio level.

Without exception, all of these recent works provide significant contributions to the understanding of credit analysis and risk management, and clearly demonstrate the need for ongoing research in this area. Given the fast-paced environment of today's global financial network, sophisticated but practicable models and effective regulation, alongside with well-wrought incentive schemes are more important than ever in order to address the currently imminent challenges. There was broad consent among all the participants that the recent and ongoing global financial crisis has exposed a weakness in credit analysis in the financial system. By encouraging the exchange of knowledge from multiple perspectives, the conference contributed to addressing these weaknesses and raising awareness for future challenges in the field of credit analysis and affiliated areas. We are looking forward to the next Basel Workshop on Credit Risk!

CHAPTER ONE

SETTING UP CREDIT RISK STRESS TESTS WITHIN A CANTONAL BANK

MICHAEL ACKERKNECHT AND STEFAN BENVEGNÙ[1]

I. Introduction

Within the last years, the mortgage sector in Switzerland experienced a strong dynamical development. A high immigration rate and continuously low interest rate levels led to an increased demand for residential property. Also firms used the favorable environment for refinancing and investments. As a consequence, retail banks strongly increased their loan volume – partially also to compensate the low interest margins. The Swiss National Bank and FINMA, the Swiss regulator, were both worried about this situation since they felt the banks could increase their risk exposure on their books. They started to take preventive measures such as the revision of the capital adequacy ordinance (Schweizerische Eidgenossenschaft 2013), the introduction of a self-regulation for mortgage lending by the Swiss bankers association (SwissBanking 2012) and the activation of the anti-cyclical capital buffer, which was increased again this year (SNB 2014b).

Facing the current market status, Thurgauer Kantonalbank (TKB) is well aware of its responsibility regarding both society and its owners. For a future-proof credit risk steering and controlling mechanism, it was decided to strengthen the credit risk control sector and to further broaden the already well seized toolset for analyzing credit risk. One of these measures is the introduction of credit risk stress testing.

---

[1] Michael Ackerknecht (michael.ackerknecht@tkb.ch) and Dr. Stefan Benvegnù (stefan.benvegnu@tkb.ch) are from Thurgauer Kantonalbank TKB.

In this article, we will show one way of setting up credit risk stress analytics for a mid-sized Cantonal bank. We will show in detail the applied methodology, the calculations and which effects the applied stress will have. As a proof of concept we built a tool prototype within a standard office toolset which we applied to the sub-portfolio of self-used residential mortgages.

II. Credit risk stress analytics at TKB

1. Description of the approach

The description and implementation of the stress scenarios focuses on the portfolio of self-used residential mortgages. Nevertheless, we try to keep the analyses and descriptions as general as possible to support the application also to other types of sub-portfolios.

The stress tests are specified by the following steps:

1. Definition of those portfolios to be subject to the particular stress test (Chapter II.2)
2. Definition of the key figures for measuring the results (Chapter II.3)
3. Derivation of the relevant risk factors – w.r.t the chosen portfolio (Chapter II.4)
4. Description of the used methodology and the applied assumptions (Chapter II.5)
5. Description of the effects of the risk factors using sensitivity analyses (Chapter II.6)
6. Derivation and description of a particular stress scenario (Chapter II.7)
7. Presentation of the stress testing results (Chapter II.8)
8. Challenges and improvements (Chapter II.9)
9. Conclusion (Chapter III.)

2. Selection of the portfolio

The TKB credit portfolio can be divided according to quite different criteria depending on requirement or usage of the portfolio. A partition that is frequently done is to separate credits to mortgages and to credits that are not mortgage backed.

For the purpose of stress analyses we can divide the portfolio according to the following criteria:

- Counterparty type: private household or company
- Collateral: mortgages and non-mortgage type
- Usage: if mortgage: type of usage (self-used, income-producing)

A generic subdivision of the mortgage portfolio is shown in the next figure.

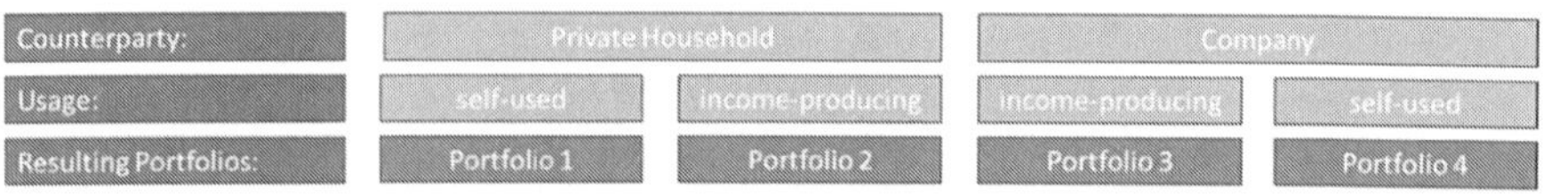

Figure 1-1: Subdivision of the mortgage portfolio (own representation).

The different counterparties belonging to the sub-portfolios can be represented according to the simplified object model shown in figure 1-2. The understanding of the model and the identification of the interdependencies within the model is one of the challenges to effectively calculate the stress tests.

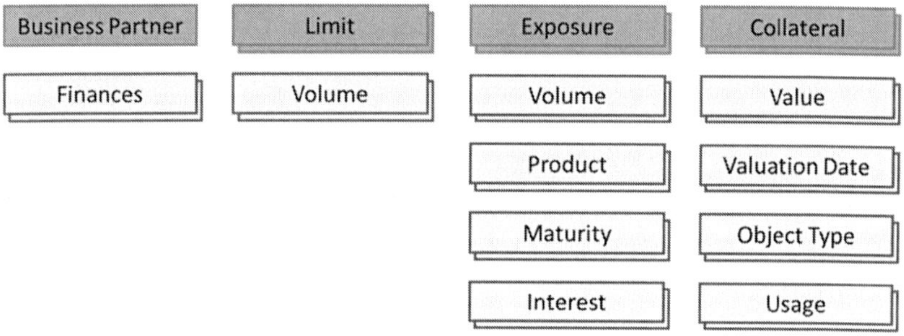

Figure 1-2: Object model (own representation)

3. Key figures for measuring the stress test results

Basically, every available credit risk measure can be used as a potential result figure for stress tests. The following criteria are important within the selection process: On the one hand the figure needs to be calculated in an effective and efficient manner by the financial institute. On the other hand, the cost/benefit ratio is essential, which may depend on seize and business model of the respective bank. Shown in figure 1-3, we give a generic overview about how such reasoning for a mid-sized Cantonal bank may look like.

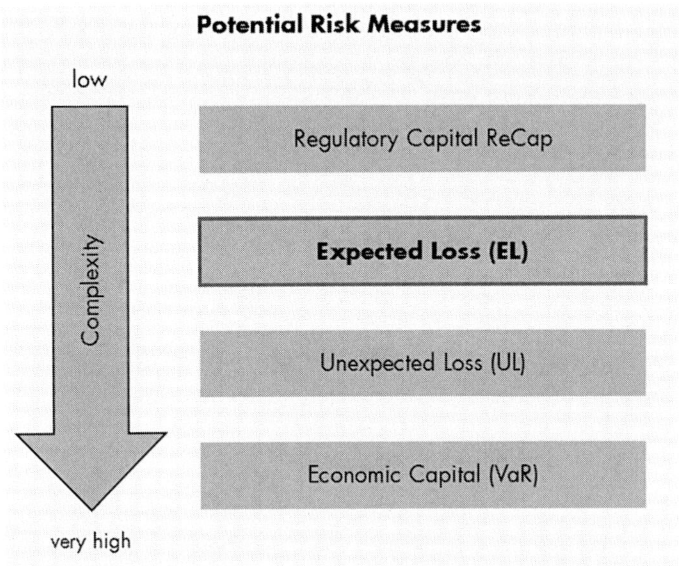

Figure 1-3: Possible Risk Measures (own representation)

TKB for example is not calculating Value-at-Risk (VaR) for the credit risk and costs for unexpected losses are charged according to regulatory requirements. As we believe that for stress testing purposes VaR figures are of limited value regarding the understanding of stress effects, those figures are not part of this study.

Furthermore, the regulatory requirement for TKB in form of regulatory capital according to the standard approach – without usage of ratings – makes Regulatory Capital a very insensitive stress testing quantity for meaningful and significant stress analyses.

Hence, the expected loss (EL) is the last remaining comprehensive risk figure that could be used as stress measure. In fact, this measure combines many important advantages without being too simple: it is a linear measure – it can be calculated on counterparty level and subsequently aggregated to portfolio level in any combination. And its inherent model uncertainty (model risk) is low compared to e.g. a VaR measure.

4. Risk factors

Basically every driver that leads to an economic effect can be regarded as a potential risk factor. Only few of them will have significant influence on the credit portfolio though. The identification of the relevant risk factors is therefore a central element in an economic stress calculation. One commonly used tool for this purpose is regression analysis in univariate or multivariate form. It will give an idea about how strong the effect of the chosen risk driver was on the portfolio given a certain historical time period of parameters – for example by looking at the effect on counterparty default rates. Yet, such a regression analysis is no proof for a cause-effect relation. It just shows dependencies between the analyzed parameters and can give a hint about a potential deterministic connection amongst them. Moreover, the realization of such a regression can only be made with an available respective loss database which is a veritable hurdle for many mid-sized banks even in these days.

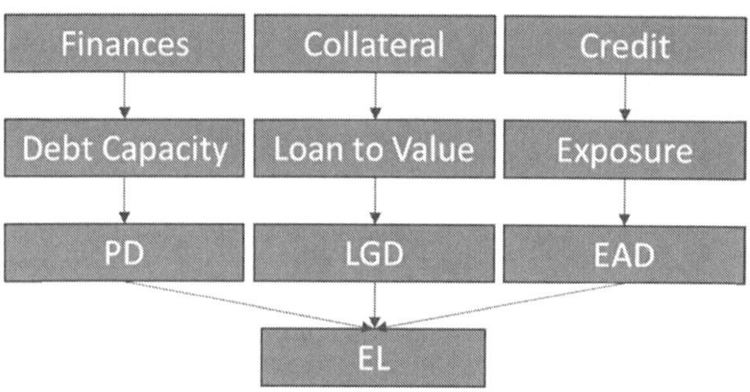

Figure 1-4: Calculation of the EL (own representation)

Leaving regression aside we are looking for macroeconomic drivers for which we can construct a direct functional chain using assumptions between these factors and our defined risk measure, the expected loss EL. For illustration purposes we will use an example portfolio of mortgages for self-used property throughout the article. As can be seen in figure 1-4, the expected loss is calculated via PD (probability of default), LGD (loss given default) and EAD (exposure at default) using the debt capacity (DC), the loan-to-value ratio (LTV) and the exposure (EXP). To find relevant risk factors we can start looking for drivers that potentially affect these figures. For this article we choose the following macroeconomic factors as risk drivers affecting the EL via PD: unemployment rate UR, gross domestic product GDP, and interest rates IR. Furthermore, we choose the real estate price as risk driver affecting the EL via the LGD and we assume the exposure to be constant – and hence the EAD.

5. Methodology and Assumptions

5.1 Approach

Generally, stress testing can be done either in a "top-down" or a "bottom-up" approach. We think of the top-down type as calculation of stress-effects to specific aggregated portfolio volumes such as e.g. the exposure of counterparties that have a certain financial capability. Under a stressed economic environment, let's say an increased interest rate, the financial capability to pay the mortgage will deteriorate and the exposure volume of counterparties corresponding to that financial capability will change. The bottom-up type instead will look at each single exposure in the portfolio and the stress will be applied to each counterparty and its associated exposure value. Lastly, there will be aggregations of figures to show the effect to the portfolio.

Yet, this effect is an aggregation of single effects whereas the top-down approach is the effect to aggregated volumes as was developed for example by RSN (RSN 2012). In the following we will describe a bottom-up stress analysis approach.

The effects of the stress scenarios are to be measured with the EL, in particular we are interested in its absolute level as well as the difference to the original value. The risk factors chosen in chapter II.4 are affecting PD and LGD in the following way:

- Increasing unemployment rate:
  Counterparty defaults as a consequence of the individual unemployment and therefore increasing PD
- Increasing interest rates:
  Increasing interest rate costs for the actual credit relation yields a worsened DC and hence an increasing PD
- Declining real estate prices:
  An unchanged credit exposure yields a higher LTV and thus a higher LGD for the respective credit relation

The stress effect will be calculated at counterparty level. Using the linearity of the EL the effect at the whole portfolio is easily obtained by summing the individual figures.

5.2 Stress factor effects

We assume that in the sensitivity analyses the chosen risk factors act in an isolated manner – i.e. all other factors are kept constant (ceteris-paribus approach). Though it will usually not happen in reality, the assumption has the advantage to show the pure impact without distortion.

5.3 Assumptions and models

For the determination of each of the three parameters PD, LGD and EAD constituting the EL, substantial model assumptions are necessary. For instance, the PD determination – which can be done in various ways – needs to be specified. Furthermore, we need to define how the spoken credit limits should be split up according to the underlying collateral types and how the segregation of the portfolio to private or commercial clients is made. These are in fact cumbersome but important details that need to be clarified thoroughly before a sound analysis of stress effects can be performed.

In this chapter we present the assumptions and model adjustments before we start with the details of the EL calculation in the subsequent chapter.

- Portfolio
  The portfolio is assumed to be static – i.e. positions will remain untouched even though the number of counterparties should decrease over time according to defaults. This is conservative on one hand and makes calculations easier on the other.

- Collateral value
  The valuation date of the residential property used as collateral could be several years old. Since the real estate price levels were constantly rising in the last years this has a substantial effect that needs to be corrected by a respective scaling, if desired.

- Spoken or contractual limits
  Since we are considering mortgages of private counterparties with self-used property we only take into consideration limits that relate to collateral that is self-used. Income-producing real estate is therefore not included and we leave out as well those limits that are collateralized simultaneously with both self-used and non-self-used property. In the example that is shown in figure 1-5 limit L1.1 for

counterparty 1 (BP 1) is included to the calculation whereas L1.2 will be discarded due to its underlying income-producing real estate. Looking at Counterparty 2 we discard it entirely since the respective limit isn't completely self-used.

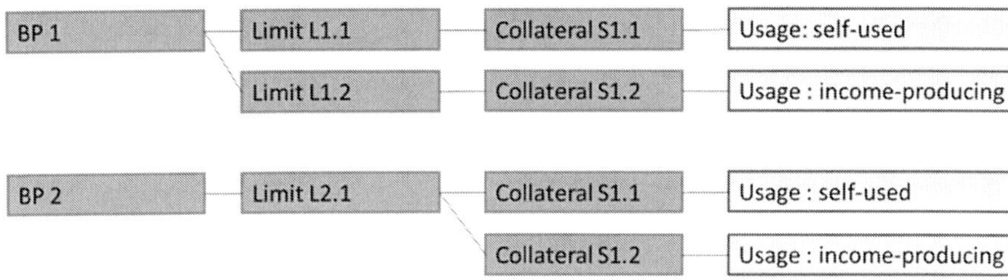

Figure 1-5: Limit example (own representation)

- LTV
  The LTV is calculated according to a gross figure in the following sense: as relation between the limit and the collateral value at counterparty level. A correction by potential pledges, other collateral types, liquidation priority or stakes of other lenders could be included but for the sake of simplicity is not considered for this article. We quote the LTV as a percentage value in the following way:

$$LTV = \frac{Limit_{BP}}{Value\ of\ the\ Collateral_{old} \times Change\ in\ Real\ Estate\ Prices_{since\ Valuation\ Date}}$$

- LGD mapping
  The LGD will be determined by a mapping according to the LTV – for details see next chapter II.5.4: calculation of the EL.

- Income
  For the stress scenarios in this article the income is essentially the salary of the private mortgage clients – we used the main salary plus potential additional income, if available. While technically not difficult, the salary is not stressed in our example. The reason is that for our risk drivers we chose mechanisms that are not connected to the salary component (see chapter II.6).

- Expenses regarding the residential real estate
  The maintenance costs for an owner of a residential real estate constitute of:

Interest expenses

Regarding interest costs we differentiate two types of expenses: effective and imputed. The imputed interest expense relates to the current interest level but with an additional security margin. Especially during the present lowest-level interest rate phase the imputed interest is of high importance. With most banks in Switzerland the imputed interest is around 5%. The imputed interest expense is therefore calculated with the imputed interest and the volume of the respective credit position.

Real estate maintenance

The expenses relating to the maintenance costs of the respective real estate property are approximated with 1% of the collateral value of the property. This is the usual long-term renovation cost assumption.

Amortizations

An LTV higher than 2/3 often implies amortization obligations. For example the self-regulation rules of the Swiss Bankers Association (SwissBanking 2014) that became mandatory (Schweizerische Eidgenossenschaft 2014) specifies that a new or increased mortgage has to be amortized to 2/3 of the collateral value within 15 years at most.

- Debt capacity

  The differentiation of effective and imputed interest expenses lead to analogously defined debt capacity (DC) values:

Imputed debt capacity

The imputed debt capacity (DC_{imp}) is calculated as the ratio of the imputed interest expenses (currently 5%) and the income:

$$DC_{imp} = \frac{Imputed\ Interest \times Limit + (1\% + x\%) \times Collateral\ Value}{Income}$$

Here, depending on the LTV, x will vary usually around a level of 1%.

Effective debt capacity

The effective debt capacity (DC_{eff}) is calculated as the ratio of the effective interest expense and the income:

$$DC_{eff} = \frac{Effective\ Interest \times Exposure + (1\% + x\%) \times Collateral\ Value}{Income}$$

Again, depending on the LTV, x will vary around a level of 1%.

➢ Mapping DC to PD

As described above the PD is a function of the DC – which will be realized via a mapping table. Generally, the imputed DC is used for the mapping, since this is the applied criteria for granting a loan. Should the effective DC exceed the imputed DC during the stress period, this will change and the effective DC will be used for the determination of the PD. Practically this corresponds to a PD flooring in times without strong interest rate stress.

➢ Time horizon

We calculate the stress scenarios over a period of 5 years. The current EL without stress is denominated by EL_{curr} , the current EL under stressed conditions is EL_1 (which is in other words the EL in the first year after a stress took place starting at time t = 0), the stressed EL in year 2 is called EL_2 and so on (see figure 1-6).

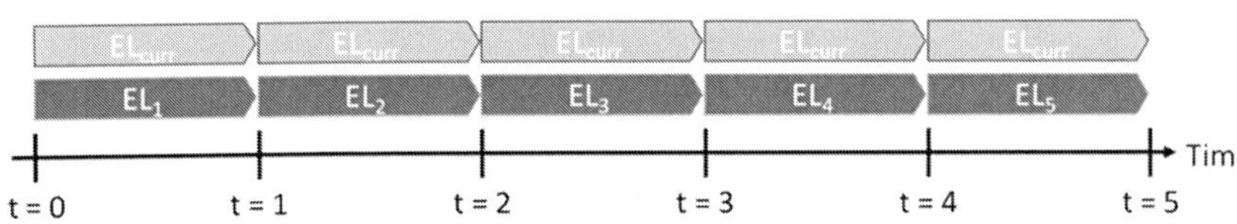

Figure 1-6: Time horizon (own representation)

➢ Extension assumptions of maturing mortgages

Since the stress period will last for several years, we need to make assumptions regarding the pricing conditions of (tranches of) mortgages reaching their maturity. For example:

- The mortgage will be extended.
- The new loan interest rate corresponds to the assumed stressed interest rate.
- The new maturity will be placed beyond the stress horizon – i.e. only one adjustment will be made for each loan.
- There will be no amortization made by the client.

These are all conservative assumptions – the client will not improve its conditions regarding product, term and interest rate.

➢ EAD

The EAD is identified with the Limit mainly to avoid the usage of the drawdown factor. For private mortgages this is feasible since the usage is usually identical with the limit anyway.

In the following we use exemplary values for illustration and for calculation purposes.

5.4 Calculation of the EL

The calculation of the EL as a product of PD, LGD and EAD is shown again as a schematic in figure 1-7:

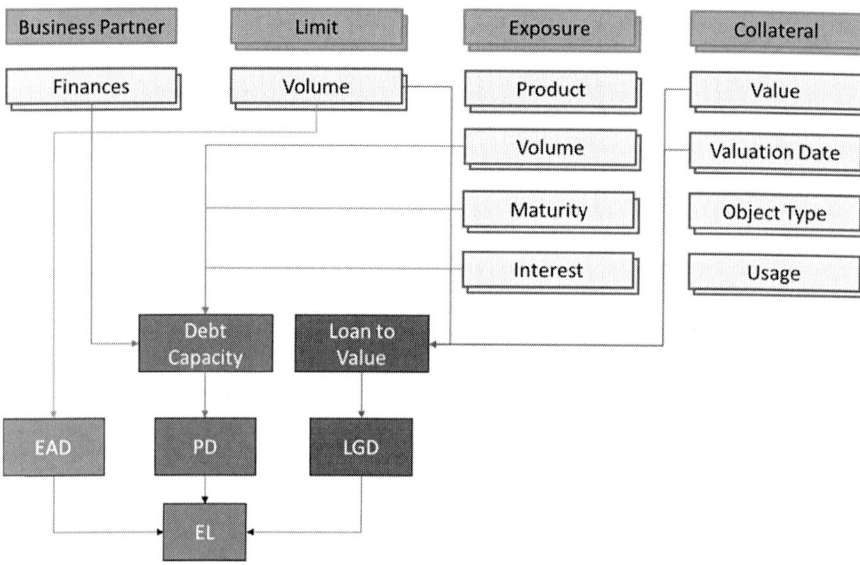

Figure 1-7: EL calculation overview (own representation)

In the stress scenarios the EL is calculated as follows:

PD

With the PD calculated as a function of the DC of the client, this represents basically a stylized rating model. As such, the relationship will be supplied by an external or internal rating provider. Since we use a mapping table we need to put the clients to DC classes with associated PDs. For simplicity, our model doesn't include rating migrations during the quite long stress period.

DC interval (%)	0 - 25	25 - 35	35 - 45	45 - 60	> 60
Associated PD (%)	0.10	0.15	0.25	2.0	50.0

Table 1-1: PD mapping (example values). Example: The PD of a client with 23% DC will be 0.1%.

LGD

The LGD will be determined by the LTV according to the collateral value of the real estate property. Again, we construct different LTV intervals which are then mapped to the respective LGDs. As in the previous case this mapping is usually supplied by the rating provider and therefore is considered to be given for this article. In contrast to the previous case we calculate the LGD as a volume weighted sum of the LGDs – due to a difference in the construction of the LTV-LGD-mapping, the below given table is a marginal mapping instead of a cumulative one. The LGD values are illustrative.

LTV interval (%)	0 – 65	65 – 70	70 – 75	75 – 80	80 – 85	85 – 90	90 – 95	95 - 100	> 100
Associated LGD (%)	0	20	25	30	35	40	45	50	100

Table 1-2: LGD mapping (example values). Example: A client with an LTV of 72.5% gets an LGD of (13*0% +1*20% + 0.5* 25%)/14.5 ≈ 2.24%.

EAD

As stated in chapter II.4 we identify the EAD using the respective Limit.

Chapter II.4 and II.5 together constitute the basis on which the stress analysis can be set up. The respective results will be shown in the next chapters.

6. Sensitivity analysis

6.1 Real estate stress

The real estate stress assumes a change of the real estate prices and hence a change of the respective collateral values. A decline of the property price negatively affects the LTV and therefore leads to a worsened LGD (see figure 1-8 for the functional chain).

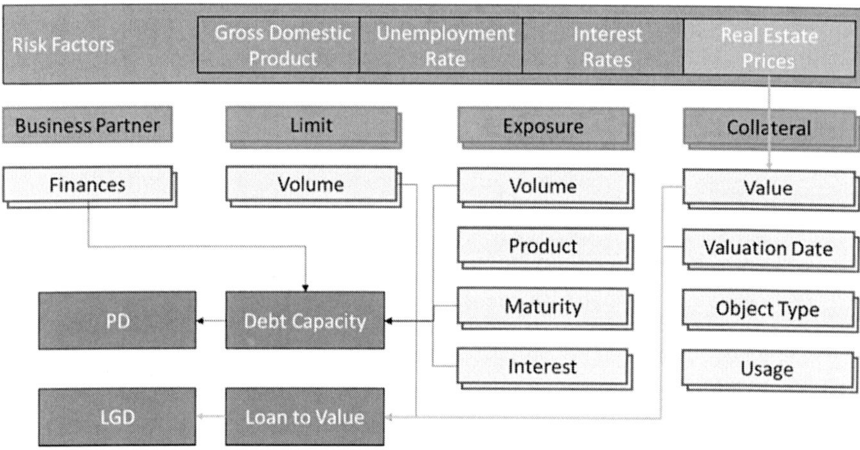

Figure 1-8: Real estate stress (own representation)

The change in LTV can be calculated as follows assuming the ceteris paribus approach:

$$LTV_{new} = \frac{Limit_{BP}}{Collateral\ Value_{curr} \times (1 + Stress\ Factor)}$$

Where:

- The current collateral value is obtained by scaling the potentially several years old assigned collateral value of the object using its estimation date and a corresponding real estate index (see chapter II.5.3). For Switzerland the commonly used index is the Wüest & Partner index that can be downloaded at the Swiss National Bank's statistical website (SNB 2014).
- The stress factor is given as a percentage change of the real estate price.
- The LTV increase moves the loan volume to higher LTV intervals having higher LGD values (see Table 1-2) which then lead eventually to a higher EL.
- To display the realized stress effect as a whole, the LTV is calculated for each yearly interval during the stress period.

Example

Assume the limit to be 700 and the collateral value to be 1‘000. The pre-stress LTV amounts then to 70% which – distributed to the 5% wide LTV intervals – means that we need 14 intervals with 50 units of limit volume in each (see figure 1-9).

Figure 1-9: Example real estate stress (own representation)

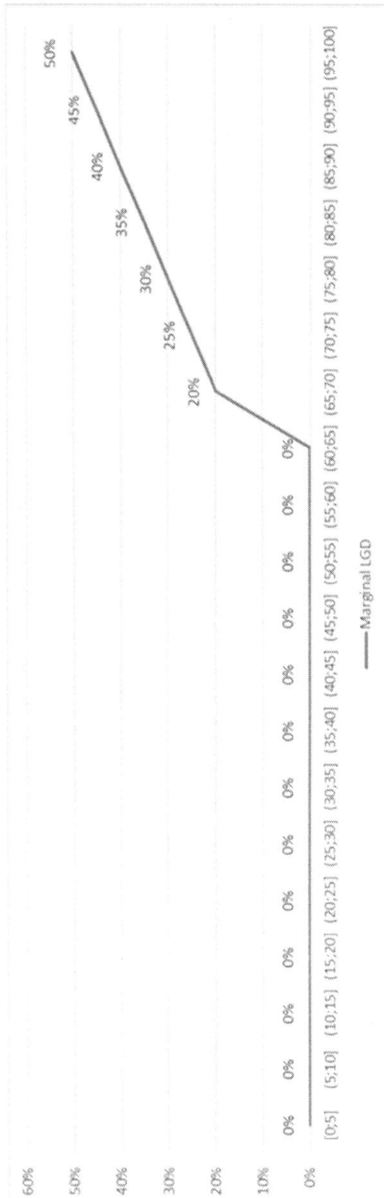

Figure 1 10: Marginal LGDs (own representation)

With the marginal LGDs from table 1-2 that are displayed graphically in figure 1-10, the nominal or $LGD calculates to 0%*650 + 20%*50 = 10 which, expressed in relative terms, amounts to an LGD of ca. 1.43%.

Let the collateral value drop by 20% from 1‘000 to 800. Then the new LTV rises to 87.5% since the limit remains unchanged at 700. Then we get 17 intervals filled with 40 units of volume each and interval 18 contains 20 units. We clearly see how the exposure volume moves to intervals with higher LGDs. The $LGD calculates then to 0% * 520 + 20% * 40 + 25% * 40 + 30% * 40 + 35% * 40 + 40% * 20 = 52 which also in relative terms is substantially higher than before, namely around 7.43%. The EL increases accordingly – and linearly.

6.2 Interest rate stress

A stressed interest rate level affects the clients DC and hence also it’s PD. Since many mortgages in Switzerland have fixed interest rate conditions the stress will show up according to the term structure of the credit portfolio.

As a side condition we need to include the imputed DC the client had to comply with at the date the contract was made. As long as the effective DC does not exceed the imputed DC the PD will remain unaffected (see also chapter II.5.3).

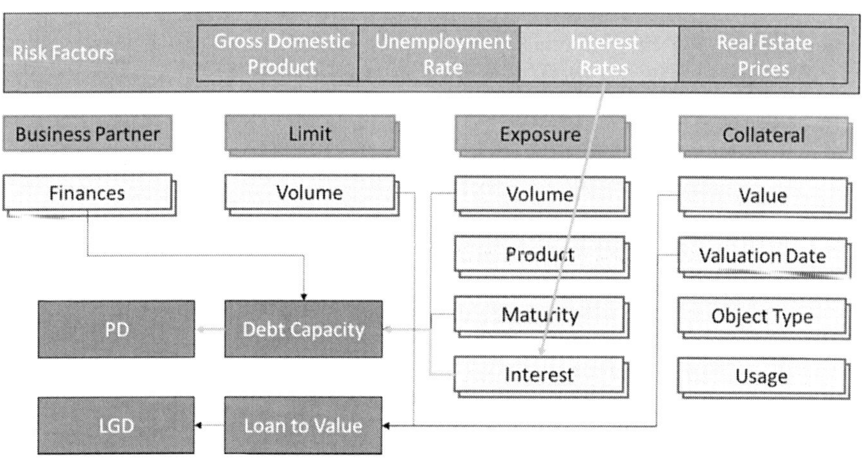

Figure 1-11: Interest rate stress (own representation)

	Year 1	Year 2	Year 3
Limit	500	500	500
Income	100	100	100
Imputed interest	5%	5%	5%
Real estate maintenance	1%	1%	1%
Effective interest rate	3%	5%	7%
Imputed DC	30%	30%	30%
Effective DC	20%	30%	40%
PD	0.1%	0.1%	0.2%

Table 1-3: Interest rate stress example.

The example in table 1-3 shows that the interest rate level continuously increases and the effective DC exceeds the imputed DC at year 3. The PD is then calculated by using the effective DC and increases.

6.3 Stress of the unemployment rate

The effect of a stressed unemployment rate works via the income of the counterparty which changes the DC and eventually the PD. This is shown as a schematic in figure 1-12. Yet, to set up a functional chain between the changed unemployment rate and the income of a counterparty within our credit portfolio is not as straight-forward as with the two previous stress types. We need to take quite substantial assumptions – but we think that they are chosen rather conservatively in the following way:

- An increased unemployment rate signifies a proportionally equal rise of unemployment of private customers present as counterparties within our credit portfolio. If, for example, the UR rises from 2% to 4%, we assume that the portion of newly unemployed persons, namely 2%, will equally show up in our portfolio.
- An unemployment doesn't mean that the respective counterparty immediately defaults on its debt. There are different possibilities how the effect of unemployment could be mitigated. For example there could be a second domestic income or additional financial capacity that has not been taken into account in the mortgage documentation. As a simplified assumption we shortcut the DC-PD chain and postulate that 50% of the unemployed counterparties will be subject to a default.

- As next assumption we have to specify the timing of the defaults. The social security measures in Switzerland prevent an immediate income loss of the insured private person (AHV Taggeldversicherung). We thus assume a delayed effect that is equally distributed to two years. Altogether we have increasing defaults of 25% of the original UR increase in the first year and 25% in the second year.

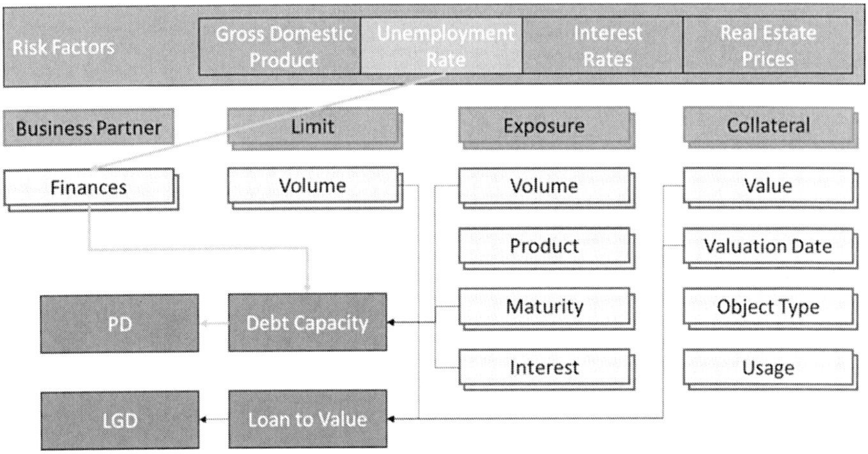

Figure 1-12: Stress of the unemployment rate (own representation)

After we specified the amount and timing of the defaults that are caused by the unemployment in our credit portfolio we have to clarify the default mechanism. This is implicitly done by interpreting the two yearly default rates of 25% times the percentage unemployment rate rise in the last point above as a rise in the portfolio PD. For a homogeneous portfolio this is a plausible approach, otherwise we would need to separate the portfolio to homogeneous sub-portfolios and to specify for each sub-portfolio the relative PD increase by the UR stress. The functional chain is displayed in figure 1-13.

Example

Suppose the portfolio PD in year 1 is 1% and 1.25% in year 2 and let the unemployment rate rise from 2% to 4%. Then the PD for the first year after the rise will increase by a nominal value of 0.5% to 1.5% and in the second year by again 0.5% to 1.75%.

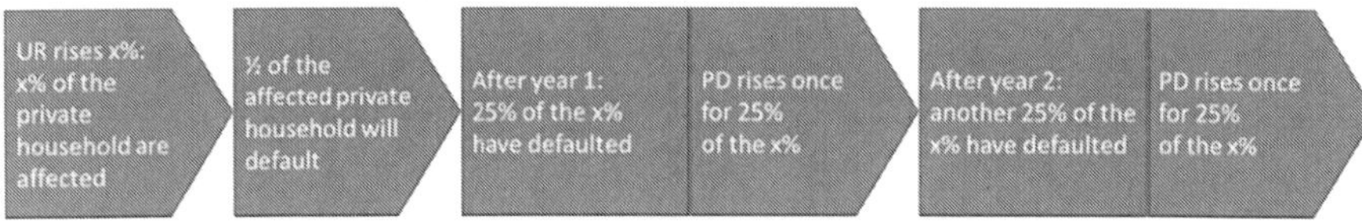

Figure 1-13: Assumptions of the stress of the unemployment rate (own representation)

6.4 GDP stress

With the GDP stress we are even farther away from a direct effect on the credit risk parameters LTV and DC as we were with the unemployment rate. But the UR can help us in the way that we can assume an interdependency between the two macroeconomic indicators since in economically difficult times (GDP doesn't grow or even decreases) the UR will often raise. To give an indication how GDP varies according to a change in UR one can e.g. perform a regression analysis which usually yields exploitable results. In such a way the GDP stress is reduced to the UR stress and is not further discussed in this article.

7. Derivation and description of a stress scenario

In this chapter we like to derive a consistent stress scenario that we want to use and discuss later on. The stress parameters will be the same as in the previously shown sensitivity analyses. The difference to the sensitivity analysis (ceteris paribus) is yet the simultaneous moving of the various stress parameters – which we will illustrate at an example below.

7.1 Description of a showcase stress scenario

The economical recovery with positive GDP growth rates during the years 2010 until 2013 abruptly comes to an end in mid 2014. Political tension between Russia and the West are paralyzing the economy and uncertainty rises. As a consequence also the Swiss economy stagnates with almost no GDP growth which then results in a 0.5% raise of the UR. The demand for residential property shrinks – fewer and fewer people can afford themselves to own home and don't want to increase their leverage. Because of the new immigration restrictions in Switzerland and better working conditions in other countries people hesitate to move to Switzerland or even leave the country. The housing bubble bursts with a decline of the real estate prices by 15% in the first year and 5% in the second. This restates the price level of 2007 and prices remain constant in subsequent years.

The Swiss National Bank adheres to the current interest rate and foreign exchange policy. The key interest rate remains historically low to support the industry and economy. The flooring of the Swiss franc needs to be defended since Switzerland – even though not performing well – is seen a secure heaven for foreign money.

7.2 Stress scenario parameters

Parameter	Today	Year 1	Year 2	Year 3	Year 4
GDP-growth	Not relevant	0%	0%	0%	0%
Unemployment rate	3.3%	3.8%	4.3%	4.8%	5.3%
Interest rate level	2.45%	2.45%	2.45%	2.45%	2.45%
Real estate price level	100%	85%	80%	80%	80%

Table 1-4: Parameters of the stress scenarios. The table above summarizes the parameters of the above stress scenario.

Using the sensitivity analyses derived in chapter II.6 the effects of this scenario can be easily calculated.

8. Stress test results

The results of the sensitivity analyses and the stress scenario will be presented in this chapter. We use an illustrative example portfolio (self-used residential property) reflecting a mid-sized Cantonal bank. The used parameters from chapter II.5.4 are as well equipped with example values. The results show the stressed EL level in comparison to the original one – which itself is therefore set to 100%.

8.1 Sensitivity analysis results

Real estate stress

Since we assume the portfolio as being static and since the real estate stress has a direct effect to the portfolio EL, there is no timing structure regarding the results and we can simply start with the shock at t=0 and immediately decline the real estate prices.

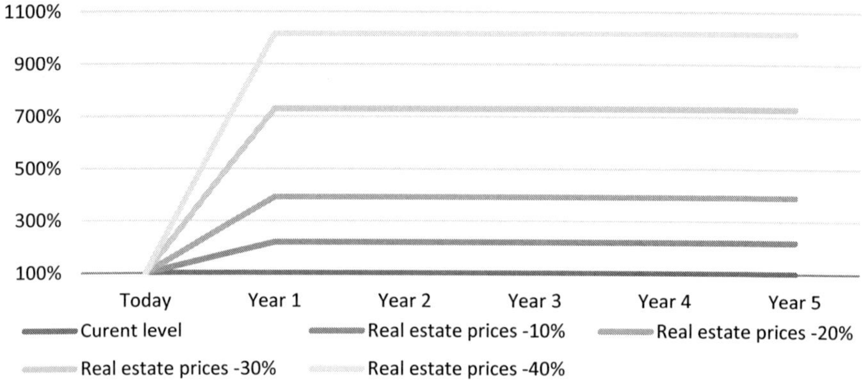

Figure 1-14: Real estate price stress: Change of the stressed EL compared to the current EL (own representation).

We observe that the real estate stress has strong and direct effect to the portfolio EL. At the largest stress of -40% the EL rises to more than the tenfold current value. During the Swiss real estate crisis in the 90s the prices declined between 1993 and 1999 on average by 37% with the largest price drop of -9% in the year 1993 (SNB 2014).

Interest rate stress

The interest rate stress doesn't affect the portfolio as a whole. The maturity term structure of the credit positions does play a key role. The counterparty's DC that has a mortgage with a maturity of ten years will change in ten years at the earliest. This means that the EL for this counterparty doesn't change for at least ten years even in an interest rate stress period. The stress will affect only the maturing loans and those that are subject to a repricing. Because of this term structure dependence we will examine below two types of interest rate changes:

- An immediate and constant interest rate change to a high value right from the beginning at t = 0.
- A linear interest rate increase for the entire stress period using a constant yearly amount.

The differences between these two stress types is shown in figure 1-15.

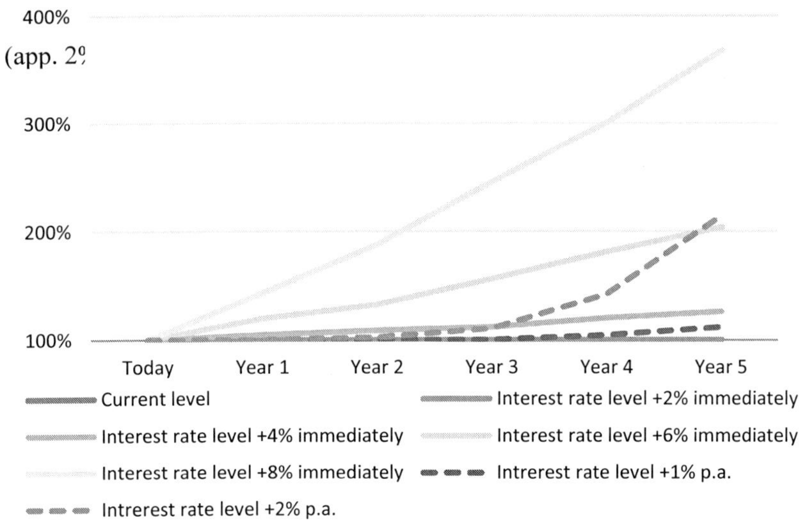

Figure 1-15: Interest rate stress: Change of the stressed EL compared to the current EL (own representation).

We observe that the interest rate stress reacts relatively slow and for interest rate increases up to 2% there is no effect at all. The reason for the latter is the current low interest rate market level of below 3%. Even with an increase of 2% the effective rate lies below the imputed interest rate of 5% which yields no change - and therefore no worsening - of the DC.

The effect of an immediate interest rate rise has instead disproportionate effects: an 8% shock increases the EL after 4 years by almost a factor of 4. Yearly constant interest rate increments affect the portfolio less strongly at the beginning, then pick up quite fast but the EL increase clearly remains weaker compared to an immediate stress.

Since 1977 the Swiss mortgage interest rate level never exceeded 8% (SNB 2014). An immediate shock of 6% or a linear increase of 1% per year would thus roughly reach the historical peak with the current level taken as basis. The two higher stress assumptions of +8% immediate and +2% per year would exceed the historical extreme quite strongly instead.

Stress of the unemployment rate

The stress of the unemployment rate (UR) impacts the EL via higher default rates as described above. Again, we need to differentiate between a one-off increase of the UR or a steady longer lasting increase. With the latter, the EL reaches a constantly higher level since the continuously increasing unemployment steadily pushes counterparties to default. With a singular UL increase the EL will rise too but then come back to its original level. Only in a limited time period more defaults will show up but thereafter the defaults will be as they were before. For the first year there are no additional defaults because one of our assumptions was that the effects will be delayed because of the national unemployment insurance. The following picture shows the results:

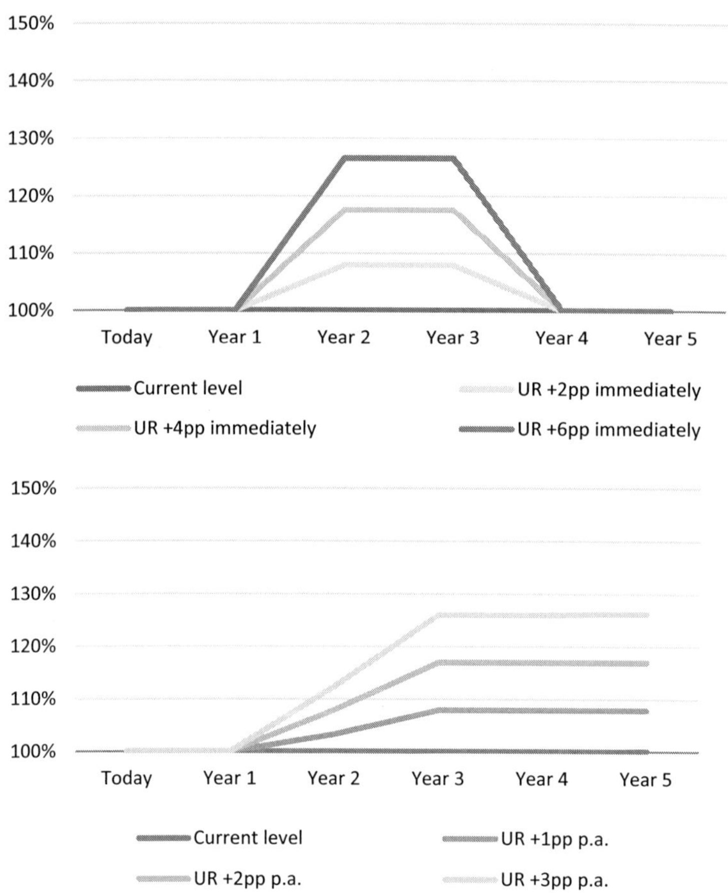

Figure 1-16: Stress of the unemployment rate: Change of the stressed EL compared to the current EL (own representation)

Historically, the yearly increase of the unemployment rate in Switzerland has shown its peak of nominal +2.1 percent in the year 1993 compared to the previous years. Even over a period of 2 years (+3.7%), 3 years (+4.4%) and 4 years (+4.5%) year 1993 had the highest increases. Sustainably, there has never been a nominal unemployment rate increase of more than 2% (SNB 2014). The performed sensitivity analyses thus are covering well the historically observable circumstances.

8.2 Summary

The previous chapters showed that the different sensitivity and stress analyses have varying effects to the EL. In all our stress assumptions the specific parameter settings exceeded the historically observed circumstances at least for around 30 years in the past. In comparing the analyses we noticed that:

- The real estate stress has by far the largest effects to the EL - with a potential increase up to the 10th of the original level.
- The immediate interest rate stress affects the EL with a relatively large delay, yet the effects are increasing in time and would rise even more in a longer stress period. The linear stress with constant yearly rates has less strong effects to the EL as the immediate one. Generally, compared to the real estate stress the interest rates stress doesn't reach the high EL levels even with the strongest interest values.
- The direct effects of the UR and GDP stresses are relatively modest. But we have to bear in mind that especially with the GDP stress in reality there would be collateral events that have the potential to increase the EL in addition, e.g. the GDP stress is likely to be accompanied with a decline of the real estate prices.

8.3 Results of the stress scenarios

In contrast to the sensitivity analysis the stress scenario is a combination of several risk factors. Below we show again the applied assumptions:

Parameter	Today	Year 1	Year 2	Year 3	Year 4
GDP growth	Current level	0%	0%	0%	0%
Unemployment rate	3.3%	3.8%	4.3%	4.8%	5.3%
Interest rate level	2.45%	2.45%	2.45%	2.45%	2.45%
Real estate price level	100%	85%	80%	80%	80%

Table 1-5: Parameter settings of the used stress scenario.

For a better transparency we show the effects of each of the different risk factors. As already observed the real estate stress dominates, the GDP and the triggered increase in the UR only have marginal effects. The EL rises up to the fourfold of the original level.

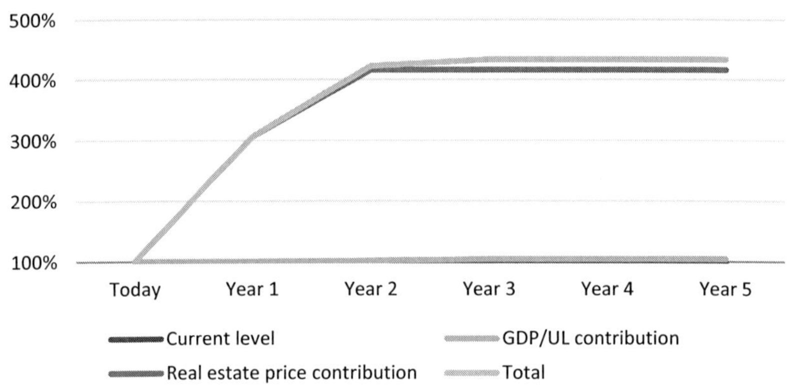

Figure 1-17: Stress scenario: Change of the stressed EL compared to the current EL (own representation)

9. Challenges and improvements

9.1 Challenges

➢ Data requirements

One of the biggest challenges was the receiving of the suitable data in an acceptable quality for the analyses. An understanding of the respective object- and data model has to be gained and several data queries had to be performed before the desired data was extracted from the system. For example, in almost every financial institute there have been changes in the data systems and therefore breaks in the history of the required data that one needs to handle. Here, additional measures and assumptions are necessary.

➢ Defining the portfolio

The exact definition of the portfolio cut - e.g. the privately used real estate - requires a thorough analysis if the client structure. In our analysis, for a counterparty having a mortgage for a self-used residential house and another for a small trade building we only took the residential house into account. The detailed extraction of the data structure from all available data usually needs the support of database specialists.

9.2 Potential improvements

➢ More detailed analysis

The obtained results and analyses need to be put to a next level of detail. Not all weaknesses and pitfalls have been detected yet. Especially the concordance with the already existing credit risk reports has to be established.

➢ Extension to further collateral types

The presented analysis contained mortgage type collateral only. We call this the gross view. In a next step one could include other types of collateral, e.g. special purpose accounts, security papers, etc. to mitigate the risk further in a net view.

➢ Object type differentiation

Another possibility is the differentiation according to the object type. In the analysis the collateral was specified by being self-used real estate. To be more specific in the distinction of the object type yields a better understanding of the materiality and thus a better risk classification.

➢ Effects to other financial figures

The results of the stress tests can be used for analyses of other financial figures, such as the effect of the stress to the financial return of the bank or to the equity ratio.

III. Conclusion

The article showed a specific stress analysis and stress testing approach to a sub-portfolio of the mortgage portfolio of a mid-sized cantonal bank. Various sensitivity and stress analyses have been performed and the effects quantified and described. The definition of the functional chain and the application to the defined portfolio are the central points of the analysis. The results show that even with an ostensibly simple portfolio the results can be quite intricate. We observe that the portfolio reacts rather different to various risk factors such as interest rates, real estate prices, GDP and unemployment rates. We note especially:

- The used time period for which the stress will be applied plays an important role. We used a time horizon of five years for this study. For interest rate stresses where the maturity term structure is key, higher interest rates have a delayed effect and the usage of a shorter time horizon could lead to an underestimation of the stress effect.
- The largest and most direct effect can be observed with the stress of the real estate prices. Declining prices have an immediate impact to the collateral which leads to higher losses.
- The rise of the unemployment rate or a stagnating GDP will only moderately affect the portfolio instead.

The results presented in this article are the starting point of a comprehensive stress analysis. The next steps comprise the sustainable implementation of the used prototype, the extension to the remaining portfolios and the detailing of the results as well as the alignment to the existing risk and financial analyses. The extension of the analysis to the corporate portfolio will be the next challenge to be solved.

References

Risk Solution Network AG, 2012, "Internal documentation Schweizerische Eidgenossenschaft 2013"

Schweizerische Eidgenossenschaft. 2013. "Verordnung über die Liquidität der Banken: Liquiditätsverordnung (LiqV)" [online]. URL: http://www.admin.ch/opc/de/official-compilation/2012/7251.pdf [Stand 20.02.2014]

Schweizerische Nationalbank SNB. 2014. "Statistisches Monatsheft März 2014" [online]. URL: http://www.snb.ch/de/iabout/stat/id/statdata [Stand 12.04.2014]

Schweizerische Nationalbank SNB. 2014. "Antrag der Schweizerischen Nationalbank auf Erhöhung des antizyklischen Kapitalpuffers"[online]. URL: http://www.snb.ch/de/mmr/reference/pre_20140123/source/pre_20140123.de.pdf [Stand 06.05.2014]

SwissBanking. 2012. "Schweizerische Bankiervereinigung SwissBanking: Richtlinien betreffend Mindestanforderungen bei Hypothekarfinanzierungen" [online]. URL: http://www.swissbanking.org/20120601-3300-veb-sr_mindestanf_hypofinanzierungen_final-akn.pdf [Stand: 29.03.14]

CHAPTER TWO

VALUING FINANCIAL ASSETS WITH LIQUIDITY DISCOUNT: AN IMPLICATION TO BASEL III

REN-RAW CHEN, WILLIAM FILONUK, DILIP K. PATRO AND AN YAN[1]

Abstract

The unprecedented financial crisis in 2007 and 2008 and the largest bankruptcy in U.S. history prompted expedited regulation in the financial industry. A new Basel Accord has been proposed to further regulate the main risk that caused the crisis: liquidity risk. In a recent article, Chen (2012) presents a liquidity discount model in which financial securities can be evaluated with substantial discounts at the presence of a liquidity squeeze in the market place. In this article, we adopt this model to evaluate a selection of the 23 largest U.S. financial institutions (assets over $100 billion) to investigate the liquidity impact during the crisis period. We calibrate the model to market information such as market capitalization and volatility. We find that the model can provide significant predictive power of a bank's liquidity health.

---

[1] Ren-Raw Chen, Ph.D. is from Graduate School of Business Administration Fordham University. William Filonuk, MBA worked for Bank of New York and passed away in 2013. Dilip K. Patro, Ph.D. is from Office of the Comptroller of the Currency. An Yan, PhD. is from Graduate School of Business Administration Fordham University. We thank Siliang Zhang for the outstanding research assistance. The views expressed here are authors' own and do not reflect those of the institutions for which they work. The full version of the paper has been published in the Journal of Fixed Income (Vol. 22, No. 3, p. 45-63, December 2013).

Summary of the Paper

The unprecedented financial crisis in 2007 and 2008 and the largest bankruptcy in U.S. history prompted quick passage of financial industry regulation. At the international level, a new Basel Accord has been proposed to further regulate the main risk that caused the crisis—liquidity risk. The consultative documents entitled "Strengthening the Resilience of the Banking Sector" (Basel Committee on Banking Supervision, 2009) and "International Framework for Liquidity Risk Measurement, Standards, and Monitoring" (Basel Committee on Banking Supervision, 2010) are a part of the Basel Committee's ongoing work in response to the crisis. These two documents mention liquidity risk specifically as part of the Basel III regulation.

In looking at banks' liquidity health, it is important to understand the definition of default because of the impact defaults can have on financial liquidity. Financial economists and accountants have different concerns regarding a firm's default risk. Financial economists are concerned with no-arbitrage pricing and hence define a firm's default by whether a firm has sufficient assets to pay for all of its debts. In other words, a firm must have a positive liquidation value to survive, or it must be in default. Accountants, on the other hand, are concerned only with whether a firm has enough liquid assets to pay for its short-term (within one year) liabilities. The former is "economic default," and the latter is "liquidity default."

By definition, the total value of all debts must exceed the value of the next-period debt. As a result, in usual situations (in which a firm can easily liquidate any portion of its assets), the firm should face an economic default before it faces a liquidity default. In other words, if a firm is under the threat of liquidity default, then it could have already defaulted under economic terms. In a "squeezed" environment (such as the recent financial crisis), however, assets cannot be liquidated easily and therefore suffer from huge liquidity discounts, which deviate substantially from the fundamental values of those assets. As a result, valuable assets are sold at large discounts because firms are forced to liquidate such assets quickly in order to pay for short-term liabilities, and the liquidity default may come before the economic default.[2]

[2] Many of the assets recovered handsomely after the crisis. The Fed Reserve Bank announced its large profits in its holding of mortgage-backed securities. The decision to purchase large volumes of assets through March 2010 came in two steps. In November 2008, the Federal Reserve announced purchases of housing agency debt and agency mortgage-backed securities (MBS) of up to $600 billion.

We use the Geske (1977) model to describe the capital structure of a firm. The economic and liquidity defaults defined earlier are formalized under the Geske model. Economic default in the Geske model is when the total value of assets (assumed perfectly liquid) falls below the total value of debts. Liquidity default in the Geske model is when the compressed (by liquidity discounts) value of assets falls below the immediate cash obligation. In order to compute the compressed value of assets, we employ the liquidity model by Chen (2012).

Combining the Geske (1977) and Chen (2012) models, this article provides empirical analysis of financial institutions' asset values. By adopting both models and using market information to calibrate the model, this study can evaluate the liquidity impact on the banks during the crisis period. We find that the model can provide significant explanatory power of a bank's liquidity health. As a result, regulators can use the model developed in this article to monitor the liquidity condition for the entire banking industry once all the banks in the industry are included. Furthermore, each bank can also adopt this model to understand its own liquidity risk and adopt necessary steps to enhance its liquidity (in compliance with the Basel regulation) before it is too late.[3]

Let the asset (only one class to begin with) of a financial company follow the Black–Scholes model:

$$\frac{dA}{A} = \mu_A dt + \sigma_A dz \,, \tag{1}$$

In March 2009, the Federal Open Market Committee (FOMC) decided to substantially expand its purchases of agency-related securities and to purchase longer-term Treasury securities as well. With total asset purchases of up to \$1.75 trillion, total Federal Reserve assets doubled compared to total assets prior to 2008. The FOMC stated that the increased purchases of agency-related securities should "provide greater support to mortgage lending and housing markets" and that purchases of longer-term Treasury securities should "help improve conditions in private credit markets" [Federal Reserve Bank of New York, 2011]. The Treasury Department also established a program to purchase agency MBS beginning in September 2008. By the program's termination at year-end 2009, it had purchased \$220 billion of such securities. This program was much smaller than the Federal Reserve's Large-Scale Asset Purchases (LSAPs), and no specific purchase amount targets were announced, so our analysis does not include this program.

[3] To facilitate implementation of the combined model, this study adopts the assumptions made separately by the two models. This approach, however, does create minor consistency issues (to be addressed in more detail later), but the empirical results should be robust nonetheless.

where z is Brownian motion and μ_A and σ_A are drift and diffusion, respectively. For simplicity, we assume that the firm has two debts (to be extended to multiple-coupon debts)[4], both zero coupon, with face values K_1 and K_2 and maturities T_1 and T_2, respectively.

When the economy is "normal" and the market is perfectly liquid,[5] it must be the case that defaults can occur only as the result of economic reasons. In the Merton [1974] and Geske (1977) models, "economic default" is defined as $A_{T_1} < \overline{A}_{T_1}$, where $\overline{A}_{T_1}$ represents the total value of debts (see Geske for details). The equity value under this case, presented by Geske, is given by

(2)

$$E_t = A_t N_2\left(d_1^+, d_2^+; \sqrt{\tfrac{T_1-t}{T_2-t}}\right) - e^{-r(T_1-t)} K_1 N_1(d_1^-) - e^{-r(T_2-t)} K_2 N_2\left(d_1^-, d_2^-; \sqrt{\tfrac{T_1-t}{T_2-t}}\right),$$

where $N_2(x_1, x_2; \rho)$ is the bivariate normal probability function with limits x_1 and x_2, correlation ρ, and

$$d_i^\pm = \frac{\ln A_t - \ln X_i + (r \pm \sigma_A^2)(T_i - t)}{\sigma_A \sqrt{T_i - t}}$$

$$X_1 = \overline{A}_{T_1}$$

$$X_2 = K_2$$

When the economy is under liquidity stress, the asset value is compressed. For this scenario, we represent the liquidity-compressed price as $a \times A = A^*$, where $0 < a < 1$. As a result, the liquidity default is defined (going concern) as $A_{T_1}^* < K_1$. The equity value then is given by

$$(2^*) \qquad E_t^* = e^{-r(T_1-t)} \mathbb{E}_t\left[E_{T_1}\left(\max\{A_{T_1}^* - K_1, 0\}, K_2\right)\right]$$

[4] But under a specific seniority order, as Geske and Johnson [1984] assume.

[5] The day-to-day usual and minor liquidity discounts are assumed away here.

where $E_{T_1}\left(\max\{A^*_{T_1} - K_1, 0\}, K_2\right)$—that is, the equity value at time T_1—is a call valuation with $\max\{A^*_{T_1} - K_1, 0\}$ as the underlying asset value and K_2 as the strike price.

Equation (2*) indicates that in a state where the firm survives, it must be that the firm has enough assets $A^*_{T_1}$ to pay for its current debt K_1. If so, the debt is paid for by the assets, and the firm's assets reduce to $A^*_{T_1} - K_1$. As a result, the Geske model will price the equity using $A^*_{T_1} - K_1$.[6]

Equation (2*) can be implemented only numerically. In the empirical work, $A^*_{T_1}$ is approximated as follows:

$$(3) \qquad A^*_{T_1} = A^*_t \exp\left(-\tfrac{1}{2}\sigma^2_A + \sigma_A \int_t^{T_1} dz\right)$$

which is equivalent to the lognormal process without drift. Note that A^*_t is computed using Equation (44). The equity value at time T_1, E_{T_1}, is carried out using the Black–Scholes model by substituting $\max\{A^*_{T_1} - K_1, 0\}$ for the underlying asset value. To carry the call values at T_1 back to t to arrive at E^*_t, the standard binomial model with 100 steps is used.[7]

Now, we introduce the Chen model for liquidity discounts. To evaluate the discount (or premium) caused by illiquidity, one needs a convex (or concave) relationship between the asset value (A) of the firm and the fundamental economy (proxied by wealth, W). The liquid asset value is computed by the binomial model of Cox, Ross, and Rubinstein (CRR): At a given future date (T), the asset value is convex in wealth. In this article, we specify a call payoff to capture such convexity.[8] That is, we specify that $A_T = \max\{W_T - K, 0\}$, where K, the strike price of the call,

[6] Given that this is only a one-period calculation, the Geske model is identical to the Merton model.

[7] Note that in the empirical work, the illiquid asset value is assumed to follow the same lognormal distribution as the liquid asset value.

[8] We also tried put payoff, and the result is similar. As Chen [2012] points out, any convex function is good enough to generate a liquidity discount.

represents the convexity of the payoff. In Chen, the underlying wealth variable, W_T, is assumed to follow a lognormal distribution with mean μ_W and variance σ_W^2.

Chen argues that the larger the convexity, the larger the discount. As a result, the "liquidity health" of the assets (A) is determined by K. When $K = 0$, illiquidity has no impact on the asset value A. Later on, we calibrate this parameter to the firm's spreads.

According to Chen, when no trading is permitted for the asset,[9] the illiquid price is computed by the following equation:

$$(4) \qquad A_t^* = \frac{1}{R(t,T)}(\mathbb{E}[A_T] - \beta^{\$}\{\mathbb{E}[W_T] - R(t,T)W_t\}),$$

where $R(t,T) = e^{r(T-t)}$ is the risk-free money market account and $\beta^{\$} = \frac{\text{cov}[A_T, W_T]}{\text{var}[W_T]}$ is known as the dollar beta. This solution must be computed numerically.

Figure 1 is generated using the following parameters:

K	r	μ	σ	$T-t$	No. of Steps
80, 100, 120	5%	0.6	0.8	1	100

where the liquid price (plotted vertically) is computed using the CRR binomial model and the illiquid price is computed using Equation (4) (plotted horizontally).

[9] The "k" parameter is set to 0.

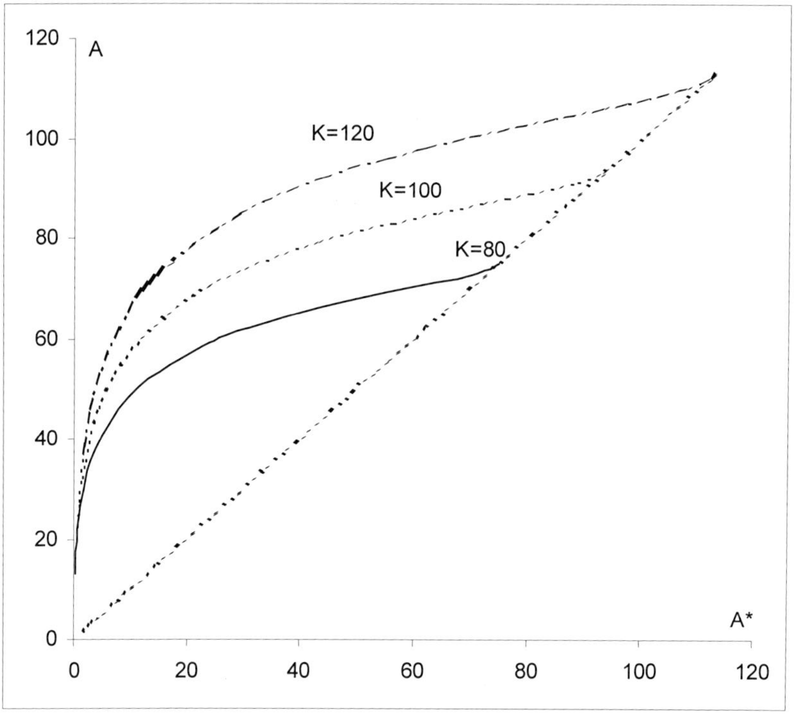

Figure 1: Relationship between Liquid Price (A) and Illiquid Price (A*) under Various Convexity Levels.

Note: The plot depicts the relationship between liquid asset value (A) and illiquid asset value (A^*). The state variable is assumed to be lognormally distributed with $\mu_W = 0.6$, $\sigma_W = 0.3$. The liquid price is computed by the CRR binomial model with $r = 5\%$, $T - 1 = 1$, and $N = 100$. The illiquid price is computed by Equation (4).

In Figure 1, the horizontal axis represents the illiquid value of the asset (symbolized by A^*), and the vertical represents the liquid value (symbolized by A). The 45-degree line represents perfect liquidity, in which there is no difference between the liquid and the illiquid values. The solid curve, dotted curve, and the dash-dotted curve represent different magnitudes of the convexity parameter, K. As Figure 2-1 illustrates, the greater the convexity, the greater the discount.

With the liquidity discount model and the capital structure model established, it is possible to now value a bank's assets. We continue to use the parameters with a choice of $K = 80$ in the previous subsection for the Chen model to compute the illiquid asset value A_t^*. For the capital structure model, we assume the following:

K_1	K_2	σ_A	r	T_1	T_2
50	50	0.3	0.05	1	2

Note that for every given A_t, we use the economic default model—Equation (2)—to compute the liquid equity value E_t. At the same time, we use the liquidity discount model (demonstrated in Figure 1) to compute the illiquid asset value A_t^*.[10] Then Equation (2*) is used to compute the illiquid equity value E_t^*.

We apply the model to examine the 23 largest banks in the United States to investigate how their assets are affected if the market faces a liquidity squeeze. We use market information—that is, market capitalization and its volatility—to infer the implied liquid and illiquid asset values. These values differ from the book value of assets in that they reflect the evaluations of equity investors. In other words, we assume that equity investors correctly evaluate the firm's assets and credit risk (via its capital structure) and assign a value to the equity. When the market is free from a liquidity squeeze, then the equity value should reflect the perfectly liquid asset value. Similarly, when the market is under a liquidity squeeze, the asset value is compressed and the equity value is also lowered to reflect the liquidity-discounted asset value.

The data we use in this study contain Lehman Brothers and a set of the 23 largest banks in the United States during the period from January 2004 to December 2009. This period covers the peak of the real estate bubble and the financial crisis trigged by the Lehman default. The debt data, obtained from FactSet, include all the liabilities issued by the banks. Using the coupon, maturity, and other specific information (e.g., floating/fixed, call/put provision, amortization, and other miscellaneous items), we estimate the cash flows and bucket them into monthly amounts (month-end). In the empirical work, however, we further group these numerous

[10] One needs to infer the wealth value W from the CRR binomial model and then compute the illiquid asset value using Equation (4).

cash flows into two cash flows K_1 and K_2. In the empirical work, we sum up all the first-year cash flows as K_1. To calculate K_2, we sum up all the second-year cash flows and then add half of all the remaining cash flows.

The equity data are obtained monthly (month-end) from Yahoo.com and used to compute the equity volatility and market capitalization. The outstanding shares are obtained from the annual reports (to compute market capitalization). The risk-free rate used in the corporate finance model (Equations 2) and (2^*)) is the three-month Treasury rate taken from Bloomberg.

The findings can be broken into three different groups. The first group consists of liquidity-healthy banks: BBT, STT, BK, TRV, BRK.A, and PNC.[11] The second group consists of banks that were healthy until the crisis occurred (month 58): PRU, USB, STI, COF, FITB, ALL, PFG, and AIG. This group of banks was deeply affected (spillover) by the Lehman bankruptcy. The third group of banks demonstrated early signs of liquidity weakness: WAMUQ, C, BAC (not so early), SLM, GS, FRE, FNM, GNW, and AXP. These banks were similar to Lehman in their liquidity vulnerability.

Out of the 23 banks in the sample, FNM (Fannie Mae) and FRE (Freddie Mac) are the two poorest performers. Throughout the sample period, they never demonstrated enough liquidity, even during the peak of the bubble. This result is striking in the sense that they were more highly rated by rating agencies than all the other banks in the sample, likely because of implicit guarantees by the government.

Another point deserving special mention is that GS (Goldman Sachs) was the only bank (except for FNM and FRE) that demonstrated liquidity weakness at the time (month 42, or July, 2007) when Bear Stearns' two troubled hedge funds unfolded. Because GS is the largest investment bank, its liquidity weakness at the beginning of the crisis signals that the whole investment banking industry may be vulnerable to liquidity risk.

In this article, we combine Chen's (2012) liquidity discount model and Geske's (1977) corporate finance model to estimate the asset value of the 23 largest U.S. banks. We discover that in almost no circumstance between 2004 and 2009 were these banks dominated by economic default. Rather, they were affected by liquidity default.

Furthermore, in hindsight (in-sample test), our model is quite predictive in the liquidity discounted value of the assets. As a result, the model we propose in this article is a reasonable tool for banks and

---

[11] The appendix lists the banks' full names.

regulators to use in monitoring the liquidity health of either individual financial institutions or the entire economy.

A natural extension of our model can be used to study liquidity discounted value for various asset classes. In this article, we calculate only one asset value—the aggregated value of all of a firm's assets. To provide better risk management, it is conceivable to provide valuation for each of the distinctive asset classes (e.g., Treasuries versus mortgage-backed securities).

References

Basel Committee on Banking Supervision. 2009. "Strengthening the Resilience of the Banking Sector." http://www.bis.org/publ.bcbs164.pdf.

Basel Committee on Banking Supervision. 2010. "Basel III: International Framework for Liquidity Risk Measurement, Standards and Monitoring." http://www.bis.org/publ/bcbs188.pdf.

Chen, R-R. 2012. "Valuing a Liquidity Discount." *The Journal of Fixed Income* 21 (3): 59-73.

Federal Reserve Bank of New York. 2011. *Economic Policy Review*.

Geske, R. 1977. "The Valuation of Corporate Liabilities as Compound Options." *Journal of Financial and Quantitative Analysis* 12 (4): 541-552.

Geske, R., and H. Johnson. 1984. "The Valuation of Corporate Liabilities as Compound Options: A Correction." *Journal of Financial and Quantitative Analysis* 19 (2): 231-232.

Imbierowicz, B., and C. Rauch. 2012. "The Relationship between Liquidity Risk and Credit Risk in Banks." Working PaperGoethe University Frankfurt.

Merton, R.C. 1974. "On the Pricing of Corporate Debt: The Risk Structure of Interest Rates." *Journal of Finance* 29 (2): 449-470.

CHAPTER THREE

DO BASEL III CAPITAL AND LIQUIDITY RATIOS PREDICT BANK DISTRESS? EVIDENCE FROM EUROPE

JANKO CIZEL, EDWARD ALTMAN, FRANCESCA CAMPOLONGO AND HERBERT RIJKEN[1]

Abstract

This paper develops a novel early-warning signal model for European listed and non-listed banks to study the ability of the measures introduced or improved by Basel III (Basel Committee on Banking Supervision, 2008, 2010 and 2011)to predict bank distress. Basel III framework has introduced a number of important changes in the sphere of bank regulation. Among others, it updated the existing capital regulation, both in terms of capital and risk coverage, and introduced two new funding liquidity ratios. One of the main assumptions underlying these changes is that the levels of the capital and liquidity ratios positively correlate with the level of bank financial health. This paper empirically investigates the validity of this assumption by testing the additive ability of the new Basel III ratios to predict distress events of European banks during the 2007-2012 period. We find that Basel III measures as a whole have only a small incremental out-of-sample contribution in discriminating between distressed and non-distressed banks, once we control for other traditionally

[1] Janko Cizel is a PhD candidate at the VU University Amsterdam and Tinbergen Institute. Edward Altman is the Max L. Heine Professor of Finance at the Stern School of Business, New York University. Francesca Campolongo is from European Commission, Joint Research Centre/Ispra, Italy. Herbert Rijken is the Professor of Finance at the VU University Amsterdam.

used CAMEL[2] and macroeconomic variables. We do find, however, that liquidity coverage ratio and risk weighted assets display marginally significant association with bank distress.

We also find that a high fraction of intangibles in bank capital corresponds with higher vulnerability to distress. Finally, we propose a novel accounting-based distance-to-default measure, constructed via the application of Bayesian Model Averaging, which outperforms all existing CAMELS and Basel measures in predicting bank distress, both in-sample and out-of-sample.

Summary of the Paper

This paper develops a novel early warning signal model for European banks and studies the extent to which the capital and liquidity measures proposed by Basel III regulation were predictive of distress events of Western European banks during the 2008-2012 financial crisis.

Basel III directives (Basel Committee on Banking Supervision, 2008, 2010 and2011) were designed to address the inadequacies of the existing Basel II framework, exposed by the widespread financial turmoil following the financial meltdown in 2008. The prevailing view underlying the changes in Basel regulation is that the recent financial disruptions in the Western banking systems stem from the interplay of the following major factors: (1) insufficient capitalization, both in terms of quantity and quality of capital, that failed to capture the build-up of on-and-off-balance sheet risks, (2) excessive maturity mismatch, driven by bank funding structures biased towards short-term funding sources, and (3) insufficient holding of high quality liquid assets that would allow financial institutions to independently cope with short-term funding squeezes.

Basel III attempts to address these shortcomings by updating the existing capital regulation, as well as by introducing a new liquidity regulation, a hitherto uncharted territory in the previous Basel accords. With respect to the former, it aims to increase the quantity and quality of bank capital buffers by: (1) raising the minimum level of core Tier 1 equity capital to 4.5% of risk-weighted assets, (2) introducing an additional capital conversion buffer of 2.5%, and a countercyclical buffer of 0-2.5%, (3) increasing the quality of the capital base by requiring intangible assets such as goodwill and deferred taxes to be deducted from regulatory capital, and (4) improving risk coverage by insisting on

[2] CAMEL is an acronym that relates to the following dimensions of bank performance: Capital adequacy, Asset quality, Management quality, Earnings, and Liquidity.

stronger capital treatment of securitization and trading book exposures, as well as by stipulating more stringent requirements pertaining to counterparty credit risk.

With regard to liquidity regulation, Basel III introduces two new liquidity ratios: (1) the liquidity coverage ratio and (2) the net stable funding ratio. The former focuses at the ability of banks to meet short-term cash outflows in stressed funding conditions, and the latter is a longer term structural ratio that measures the liquidity mismatches of the entire bank balance sheet. The proposed liquidity regulation stipulates that banks hold a minimum level of both ratios, and hence gives banks an incentive to mobilize more stable funding sources.

While the motivations behind the changes in Basel III are widely accepted, there is surprisingly little empirical evidence in support of the view that the improvement in the updated capital and liquidity measures would ameliorate banks' financial health and reduce financial distress amongst global banks. This paper tests these premises by studying the extent to which the updated capital and liquidity measures predicted bank distress events in a cross-section of Western European banks during the period 2008-2012.

To this end, we develop an early warning signal model of bank distress, that builds on the insights of the large literature on bank failures in the U.S. (examples of the most recent studies include Cole and White (2012) and DeYoung and Torna (2013)). We estimate the model on a large sample of Western European banks. Since outright bank bankruptcies in Europe are rare, we construct an alternative distress indicator, which relies on bank-specific state interventions. Specifically, we define distress events as the first time a given bank in a sample experiences one of the following: (a) bankruptcy/liquidation, (b) equity injection by the state (including nationalization), or (c) a bridge loan by the state. Our sample contains a total of 134 bank distress events over the period of the recent crisis.

Our early-warning model of bank distress features four groups of variables. The first group pertains to the so called CAMELS rating system, which is the acronym that stands for Capital adequacy, Asset quality, Management quality, Earnings quality, Liquidity, and Sensitivity to systemic risk. The system is widely used by the regulators in the U.S. in order to assess the health of financial institutions, and has received relatively large empirical support in the U.S.-based studies of bank distress (e.g. Cole and White, 2012).

The second group of variables used in our model are macroeconomics measures, such as the real GDP growth, and inflation. In line with Betz et al. (2014), we find that inclusion of macroeconomic indicators improves the out-of-sample predictive power relative to models, based exclusively on accounting-based variables.

Third, we include a number of measures that directly or indirectly relate to the changes in regulation implemented in Basel III. Specifically, we analyze the discriminative power of the equity ratios (quantity of capital), the level of intangibles in the capital base (quality of capital), risk weighted assets, off-balance sheet assets (asset quality), and two Basel liquidity ratios. We find that the quality of capital base, risk weighted assets, and off-balance sheet assets serve as relatively strong predictors of future distress. With regard to liquidity, we find a limited evidence of predictive power for the liquidity coverage ratio, and no evidence for the stable funding ratio. While most of the above Basel-based variables are statistically significant, they display only a modest improvement in the quality of the out-of-sample model predictions relative to the CAMELS and macroeconomic variables.

Finally, we include the Merton (1974)-based distance-to-default (DD) measure. Despite its strong theoretical foundation, one of the main problems of the measure is that it can be directly computed only for listed banks. Since listed banks constitute only a small fraction of the European banking universe, the raw DD measure cannot be used as an early warning signal for most of the banks. We circumvent this problem by proposing a novel implied Distance-to-Default measure. The implied DD measure is constructed by modelling the raw DD for listed banks via accounting-based measures and applying the model estimates to the non-listed banks. Since there is very little theoretical guidance on an optimal model of DD (based on the accounting information), we follow the Bayesian Model Averaging approach, which considers a multitude of accounting-based DD models and selects the ones with the highest evidence in the data. We show that the implied DD measure exhibits a strong out-of-sample distress forecasting performance, even after controlling for CAMELS variables, BASEL variables, and macroeconomic measures.

The paper contributes to the existing literature on bank distress in a number of important ways. First, it is the first to empirically assess the justifications that underlie Basel III changes in capital and liquidity standards. Second, we extend the market-based distance-to- default measure to non-listed banks, and show that the resulting measure significantly outperforms (both in- and out-of sample) other early warning measures suggested by the past literature. Third, we contribute to the small but growing literature on the distress risk of European banks, which has significantly lagged the U.S.-based bank-distress research, primarily due to the relative lack of clean credit events. Similar to Betz et al. (2014), our definition of distress event circumvents the problem of missing bank bankruptcies, yet credibly captures the events that point to significantly weak banks.

References

Basel Committee on Banking Supervision .2008. "Principles for sound liquidity risk management and supervision." http://www.bis.org/publ/bcbs144.htm

Basel Committee on Banking Supervision. 2010. "Basel III: international framework for liquidity risk measurement, standards and monitoring." http://www.bis.org/publ/bcbs188.pdf

Basel Committee on Banking Supervision. 2011. "Basel III: a global regulatory framework for more resilient banks and banking systems." http://www.bis.org/publ/bcbs189_dec2010.pdf

Betz, F., S. Oprica, T.A. Peltonen, and P. Sarlin. 2014. "Predicting distress in European banks." *Journal of Banking & Finance* 45: 225–241.

Cole, R. A., and L. J. White. 2012. "Deja-vu all over again: The causes of U.S. commercial bank failures this time around." *Journal of Financial Services Research* 42 (1-2): 5–29.

DeYoung, R., and G. Torna. 2013. "Nontraditional banking activities and bank failures during the financial crisis." *Journal of Financial Intermediation* 22 (3): 397–421.

Merton, R. C. 1974. "On the pricing of corporate debt: The risk structure of interest rates." *The Journal of Finance* 29 (2): 449–470.

CHAPTER FOUR

THE CAPITAL IMPACT ON LARGE EUROPEAN BANKS LESSONS FROM THE BASEL III MONITORING

KLAUS DUELLMANN[1,2]

I. Introduction

When the global financial crisis reached its peak after the collapse of Lehman Brothers, regulators, encouraged by the G20, initiated a series of wide-ranging changes to the then current international regulatory framework of Basel II. The reforms augmented the Basel II framework, which had still not been fully implemented by all member states of the Basel Committee on Banking Supervision (BCBS), with minimum liquidity standards as well as macroprudential additions to the regulatory minimum capital requirements. The short time-frame of about one year for agreement on the new Basel III framework (see BCBS, 2010a and b) by all member states of the BCBS can only be explained by the immense pressure on decision-makers to do their utmost to prevent any repetition of the financial crisis that had brought the global financial system to the brink of the abyss.

As the regulatory community had to act swiftly, it was not possible to anticipate all the effects that the new rules would have on the banking system. Nevertheless, several projects were launched to measure not only the immediate impact of higher capital requirements (see BCBS, 2010d) but also their impact on the real sector (see BCBS, 2010c). Since this work was undertaken on a best effort basis and based partly on hitherto untested

[1] This publication should not be reported as representing the views of the European Central Bank (ECB). The views expressed are those of the author and do not necessarily reflect those of the ECB.

[2] Dr. Klaus Duellmann is from European Central Bank (ECB).

models, the BCBS initiated the semi-annual Basel III monitoring exercise on the impact of the reforms as a flanking measure. This ongoing exercise is designed to accompany the gradual "phasing in" of Basel III up to its full implementation (see, for example, BCBS, 2014b). The European Banking Authority (EBA) in London simultaneously began a parallel exercise focused on EU member countries.

This paper summarizes key results from this European exercise, which are published semi-annually on the EBA website (see, for example, EBA (2014) as the most recent report). Its focus is on the process of how European banks have adapted to the new regulatory requirements. The European implementation of the Basel III framework entered into force at the beginning of 2014. The results presented in this note, which are based on an earlier period, therefore refer to the original Basel III framework and do not reflect European specificities.

Furthermore, this note does not capture the two new liquidity measures, namely the short-term Liquidity Coverage Ratio, the methodology of which was substantially amended in September 2012 and January 2013, and the Net Stable Funding Ratio, the methodology of which is still under review. This means that it would be difficult to undertake a more in-depth analysis of the dynamics of the adaptation process. Instead, the focus is on the capital ratios and the leverage ratio, which was introduced as a supplementary measure for the (risk-sensitive) capital ratios.

To ensure a smooth transition without forcing banks to restrict the supply of credit in their home economy, a transition period of six years was agreed, starting in 2013. The following results always refer to the "fully loaded" definitions, i.e., after all transition reliefs, including those which extend beyond 2019, have run out (see section 94ff BCBS, 2010a). These transition reliefs pertain to the regulatory capital figures, but also affect capital thresholds and capital buffers, such as the capital conservation buffer, which are reported in this note at their final (maximum) levels. It should be noted that this approach applies a regulatory standard which first becomes effective for the current balance sheet of banks only after a number of years. In contrast to some industry studies, it disregards any mitigating management action, for example, adjustments to portfolios or even the business model, planned by the banks for the transition period until the fully loaded rules become effective.

If not stated otherwise, the reference date is 30 June 2013. At that time, 174 banks were participating in the EU monitoring exercise. These are commonly divided into Group 1, which comprises 43 large, internationally active banks with a minimum Tier 1 capital of €3 billion, and the remaining 131 banks, which comprise Group 2. In many countries, this sample covers all banks eligible for Group 1 and, on average, about 30% of Group 2 banks (measured by their total risk-weighted assets in their member state). Figures may vary for specific analyses since not all participating banks submitted data on all aspects, and a slightly smaller sample is used for the time series analysis in order to ensure the stability of the sample over time. Banks report their figures at group level, and only stand-alone institutions report on a stand-alone basis.

The heterogeneity of the results in Group 2 poses a significant obstacle to their interpretation. In some countries, this group includes fairly large banks which are not included in Group 1 solely because they focus on domestic business. This group can also include highly specialized banks,such as a Pfandbriefbank in Germany, as well as savings banks and mutuals. For this reason, results are often analysed and reported on a more granular basis that distinguishes between different types of Group 2 banks (see, for example, the German Basel III report (Deutsche Bundesbank, 2014). Since such a breakdown is not available at the European level, this note focuses on Group 1 banks.

In order to compare regulatory ratios on an aggregated level in a meaningful way, the figures of individual banks need to be weighted. In the Basel III monitoring exercise, this is done by considering a "composite" bank: A capital ratio, for example, is computed by first adding the individual banks' amount of capital (i.e., the numerator) and dividing the outcome by the sum of their risk-weighted assets (i.e. the denominator).

1. Capital ratios and their drivers

One of the major objectives of Basel III was to enhance the quantity and quality of regulatory capital that acts as a safety buffer if a bank gets into trouble. One experience of the crisis was that substantial parts of regulatory capital, in particular hybrid instruments, were ineffective at absorbing losses. Two courses of action were adopted to solve this issue. First, the regulatory minimum levels of capital will be increased and, second, only capital of the highest quality will be eligible as Common Equity Tier 1 (CET1) capital in the future.

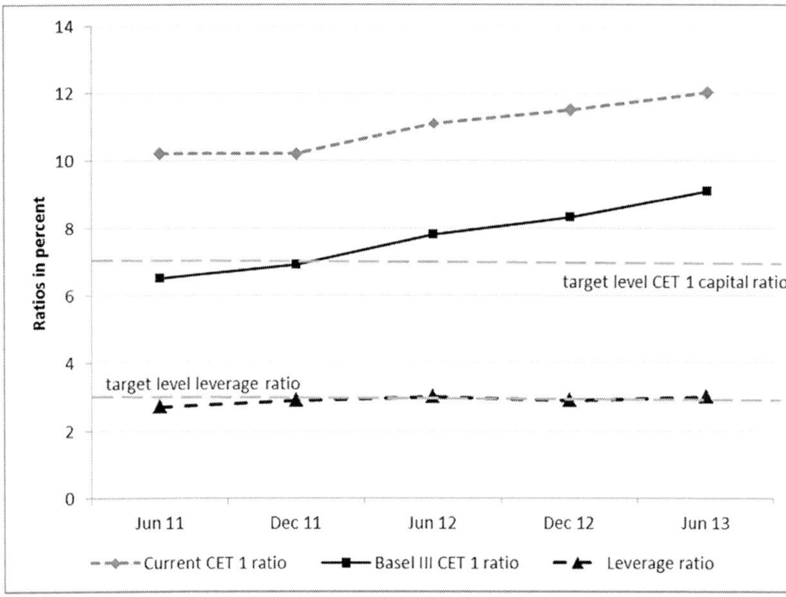

Figure 4-1: CET1 capital ratios (according to current and "fully loaded" Basel III standards) and the leverage ratio in Group 1 (with target ratios of 7% for the CET1 capital ratio (which includes the 2.5 pp capital conservation buffer) and 3% for the leverage ratio).

Figure 4-1 shows the CET1 capital ratios for Group 1 banks from June 2011 until June 2013, also including a capital surcharge of up to 2 pp for those Group 1 banks which are Globally Significant Institutions (GSIBs, see BCBS, 2011). Two findings are obvious: First, the Basel III CET1 capital ratio is well (about 3-4 pp) below the respective capital ratio under current (i.e., Basel II/CRD III) definitions. Second, European Group 1 banks have been successful in gradually increasing CET1 capital ratios over the observation period. Whereas they were always, on average, well above the 4.5% minimum ratio, in June 2012 they also surpassed, on average, the 7% target ratio that includes additionally a 2.5 pp capital conservation buffer. Although banks are not strictly required to hold this buffer, they face automatic restrictions in paying out dividends when the capital conservation buffer becomes depleted. Therefore, it is a common view that this 7% threshold has effectively become the new "minimum".

The improvements in banks' capital ratios on average cannot mask the existence of a shortfall in the case of a number of banks that were still below the 7% threshold in June 2013. The aggregate shortfall of those banks, however, showed a remarkable decline from €228 billion in June 2011 to €36.3 billion in June 2013, even including the capital surcharge for GSIBs.

In June 2013, 95% of the participating Group 1 banks are above this threshold compared to only 46% in June 2011 when the monitoring results were first made public. A significant part of this improvement was almost certainly due to the recapitalization exercise that the EBA started in late 2011. About 60, often the largest banks, which are also part of Group 1, were requested to raise their level of capital so that they would still be able to meet a specific capital threshold if all their sovereign exposures were marked-to-market. The deadline for reaching this threshold was the end of June 2012, well within the observation period in Figure 4-1.

The progress achieved by banks over the observation period can be attributed both to improvements in the numerator of the capital ratio and to changes in the denominator. At the same time, the minimum CET1 capital threshold increased from originally 2% under Basel II to 4.5%. How the overall impact of these different factors can be broken down into contributions by single factors is a natural question which is addressed in the following section.

2. Measuring the total impact of Basel II and its factor contributions

The Basel III framework contains mainly five drivers that impact the capital buffer of a bank, namely

- A new definition of capital that is mainly restricted to common shares and retained earnings for joint stock companies.
- Regulatory adjustments, mainly a new set of deductions from capital, for example, for goodwill and other intangibles or for deferred tax assets.
- Adjustments to risk-weighted assets in order to ensure that all material risks are captured in the capital framework.
- New minimum capital thresholds, for example, 4.5% instead of 2% for CET1 capital.
- A GSIB capital surcharge of 0 – 2.5 pp depending on whether a bank has been classified as GSIB and, if so, to which bucket of systemic importance it has been assigned.

In order to assess the impact of the first three of these drivers, the Basel III monitoring looks at the repective relative changes either over time or compared to the current capital standard. A change in the numerator, however, affects the capital ratio to a different extent than the same change in the denominator. Furthermore, the increase in the minimum threshold would not be captured at all if only one-dimensional relative changes, such as the relative change of capital or risk-weighted assets, were considered.

The "Total Impact Measure" (TIM) has been developed to compare the contributions of all five drivers on a common basis. Since the capital ratio is the focal point of measuring the solvency of a bank, the TIM essentially focuses on the actual capital buffer that a bank holds above its minimum. More precisely, the TIM measures the decrease in the actual buffer due to the five drivers listed above. Its workings are shown in Figure 4-2.

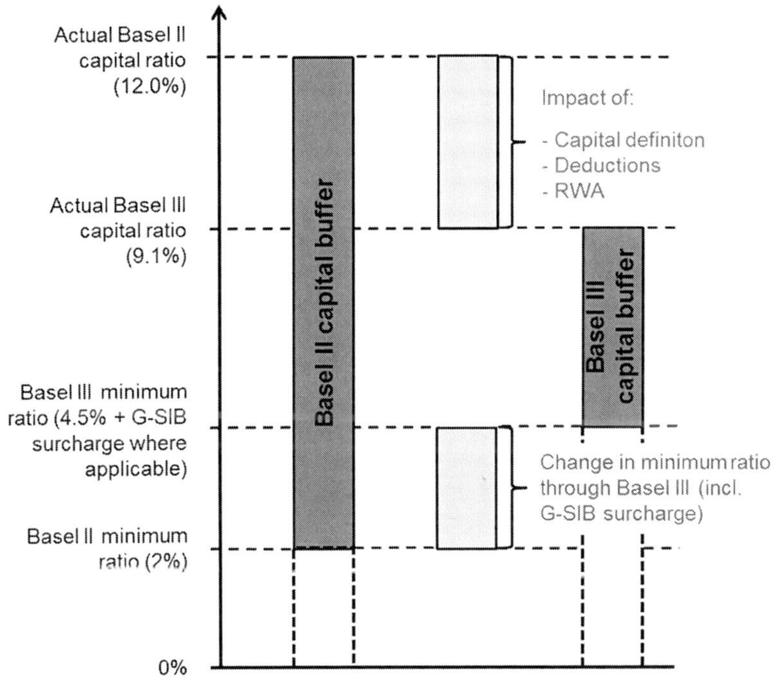

Figure 4-2: Total impact measure of the effect of the Basel III framework on the capital buffer that a bank holds above the regulatory minimum capital ratio

Assume a bank has an actual capital ratio of 12% under the previous Basel II framework. Considering a minimum CET1 capital ratio of 2%, the resulting actual capital buffer amounts to 10%. Let the capital ratio decrease to 9.1%, while the minimum threshold increases to 4.5% under the Basel III framework. Then, the buffer falls to 4.6% as a consequence of these two effects. The reduction in the buffer by 10 pp – 4.6 pp = 5.4 pp is defined as the total impact. This total impact, of which 2.5 pp are due simply to the higher minimum threshold for the capital ratio, can be further decomposed as follows.

Let r denote the capital ratio, C the amount of capital, D the amount of new deductions from capital under Basel III, R the amount of risk-weighted assets and m the minimum ratio. Then, the actual capital buffer b is defined by

$$b = \frac{C - D}{R} - m = r - m$$

Let Δb_i be the TIM of the i-th bank, i.e., the change in the capital buffer due to the application of the Basel III framework, ΔC_i its change in capital and so forth. The GSIB surcharge g_i is multiplied by the indicator function which is one if the i-th bank is a GSIB and zero in all other cases. Then, a little bit of algebra gives

$$\Delta b_i = \frac{\Delta C_i}{R_i + \Delta R_i} - \frac{\Delta D_i}{R_i + \Delta R_i} - \frac{\Delta R_i}{R_i + \Delta R_i} \cdot r_i - \Delta m - g_i \cdot 1_{\{i \in GSIB\}}.$$

This last equation reveals the additive effect of the five drivers of the TIM. Loosely speaking, the changes in capital, deductions, and risk-weighted assets need to be scaled by a multiplier in order to become percentage point changes of the capital buffer.

If this formula for the TIM is applied to the actual figures of the CET1 capital ratio in June 2013, the following breakdown of the total impact is obtained: The most important driver of the total impact is the elevated minimum ratio (39%), followed by the new deductions (21%) and higher risk-weighted assets (17%). The stricter definition of the capital instead plays a minor role (6%). The remaining 16% is due to the GSIB surcharge.

Although the GSIB surcharge works in a similar way to an increase in the minimum ratio, it differs in that it does not affect all banks. This has an effect on the aggregation of the TIM for the total sample of banks. Without the GSIB surcharge, the composite bank approach would be the straight forward solution. Including the GSIB surcharge in the aggregation for the total sample of banks, however, requires weighting the banks, which is done by the amount of their risk-weighted assets.

The Basel III monitoring allows a more granular assessment of the main drivers. For Group 1 banks, goodwill, for example, is by far the most important factor in driving the impact of deductions. More than one-third, i.e., 13.3% out of the 29.8% capital reduction due to deductions (measured relative to the gross CET1 capital), is due to goodwill.

The change in risk-weighted assets of 9.9% is mainly driven by three factors. First, there are credit value adjustments for counterparty credit risk, which are the most important factor as they contribute an increase by 4.2%. The second most important driver (3.5%) are the new requirements for risk-weighted assets which fall below the 10% and 15% limits for CET1 capital deductions. These 10% and 15% limits refer to the "threshold deductions". In Europe, these consist of significant investments in the common shares of unconsolidated financial institutions and deferred tax assets. They need not be deducted in full, but only if they exceed 10% of a bank's CET1 capital. They also have to be deducted if the sum of both exceeds 15% of a bank's CET1 capital. The amount of both items that is not deducted in the calculation of CET1 capital needs to be risk-weighted at 250% (see sections 87-89 of BCBS, 2010a). The third most important driver of changes in risk-weighted assets (2.3%) are securitization and other exposures, which were previously deducted at 50% from Tier 1 capital and 50% from Tier 2 capital (see section 90 of BCBS, 2010a).

3. The Leverage Ratio: a non risk-sensitive fall-back measure

The leverage ratio is a new, non-risk sensitive measure that was introduced into Basel III with a view to migrating to a Pillar 1 treatment (i.e., to become a mandatory minimum standard) based on appropriate review and calibration (see section 17 of BCBS, 2010a). It should serve two purposes: first, to constrain the build-up of leverage in the banking sector in order to mitigate pro-cyclical effects of time-variant risk-sensitive capital ratios and, second, to act as an additional safeguard against model risk and measurement error (see section 16 of BCBS, 2010a).

The leverage ratio is defined by Tier 1 capital minus deductions in the numerator and an exposure measure in the denominator that generally follows the accounting measure of exposure.

The mean leverage ratios from 2011 until June 2013 are shown in Figure 4-1. In contrast to the capital ratios, improvement in the leverage ratios is slow at best. One explanation for this is undoubtedly the expectation that the leverage ratio will remain a standard under ongoing review, whereas the risk-sensitive capital requirements were already agreed in 2010. Although it needs to be disclosed from 2015 onwards, it will not become a binding standard until after it has been finally reviewed by the Basel Committee in 2017. Furthermore, the leverage ratio indeed underwent a number of significant changes in January 2013, which will result in relief for banks overall when these changes are also adopted in the European implementation of Basel III (see BCBS, 2014a). The differences in the capital ratios and the leverage ratios in Figure 4-1 give some information as to the kind of measures banks have taken: The much stronger increase in the CET1 capital ratio relative to the leverage ratio signals that banks have achieved this improvement not only by strengthening their capital basis but also by de-risking, since de-risking contrary to an increase in capital improves only the capital ratio but not the leverage ratio. It should be noted, though, that this inference refers to the total sample, i.e., the composite European bank, and may differ across banks and countries.

In June 2013, the average leverage ratio of 41 Group 1 banks was 3.0%, and 66% of those banks would have met the calibration target, which is also 3%. At first sight, these leverage ratio numbers may appear to be low considering that the leverage ratio should serve only as a safeguard, while the risk-sensitive capital ratios should still be the main solvency measures. Banks improving their risk-sensitive capital ratios, which they have to do in order to fill the shortfall that still exists, should generally have a positive impact on the leverage ratio. Therefore, we also consider the leverage ratio and the corresponding capital shortfall that can be expected conditional on the assumption that all banks at least meet a minimum Tier 1 capital ratio of 8.5%, i.e., 6% minimum and in addition a 2.5 pp capital conservation buffer.

Considering leverage ratio results conditional on banks having attained at least the 8.5% target level of their Tier 1 capital is, however, not always conservative with respect to the implications for the leverage ratio. It implicitly assumes that banks reach the 8.5% threshold by increasing their capital or decreasing the amount of their deductions. If banks, for example, replace credit exposures to small and medium-sized firms by sovereign bonds of their home country, which generally have a zero risk weight, they can improve their risk-sensitive capital ratios through lower risk-weighted assets in order to reach the 8.5% threshold, but without any positive impact on the leverage ratio.

Conditional on the assumption that banks with a capital shortfall from their Tier 1 capital ratio have increased their capital to meet the 8.5% threshold, 24% of Group 1 banks would still not meet the leverage ratio target of 3%. The shortfall from the 3% target would decrease, however, from €101 billion to €50 billion. It is the view of the author that these are still relatively high figures considering the intended "safeguard nature" of the leverage ratio. Furthermore, in June 2013 Europe was certainly not at the peak of an economic cycle, which should be the time when the leverage ratio would be expected to kick in as a binding standard to restrain excessive leveraging.

The wrong incentives would be set, however, if the leverage ratio were to become the primary limiting standard for a substantial number of banks even in normal times: banks would be encouraged to increase their profits through higher margin income from more risky investments, since higher risks are not picked up by the risk-insensitive leverage ratio. This reasoning is not new, but it was already a key argument for replacing the Basel I framework by the more risk-sensitive approach of Basel II.

In order to avoid this — from a prudential perspective — undesirable outcome, both measures need to be calibrated appropriately relative to each other. The extent to which both measures are binding is a reason for considering this "relative calibration" in more detail. Both measures require the same amount of Tier 1 capital if the leverage exposure (LE), i.e., the denominator of the leverage ratio, times 3% equals the amount of risk-weighted assets (RWA) times 8.5% (including a 2.5 pp capital conservation buffer). In other words, the capital ratio — and not the leverage ratio — is the binding measure as long as

$$\frac{\text{RWA}}{\text{LE}} > \frac{3}{8.5}.$$

Figure 4-3 shows the RWA/LE ratios from June 2011 to June 2013. In December 2012, this ratio fell below 35.3% and since then the leverage ratio has, on average, become the more binding constraint.

II. Summary and conclusions

The Basel III monitoring exercise reveals that European banks have generally made good progress in meeting the "fully-loaded" new regulatory requirements, although considerable efforts still have to be made by a significant number of banks. The EBA recapitalization exercise in 2011-2012 was a positive contributory factor in this process.

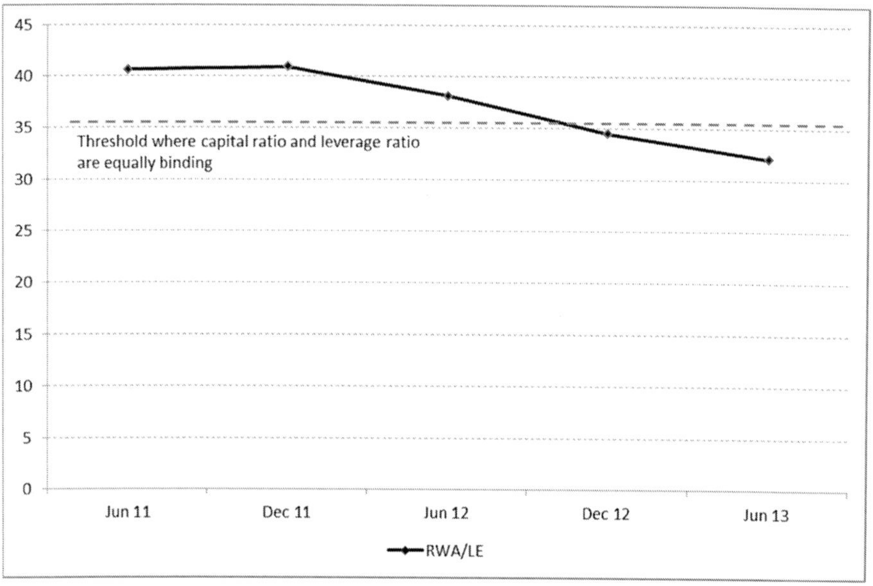

Figure 4-3: Risk-weighted assets (RWA) divided by leverage exposure (LE) on average for Group 1 banks in percent.

The capital shortfall of 39 large (Group 1) banks measured relative to a 7% CET1 minimum capital ratio and also including the capital surcharge for GSIBs declined sharply from €228 billion in June 2011 to €36 billion in June 2013. Given that the shortfall amount assuming the full implementation of Basel III was only 4.4% of their CET1 capital in June 2013, these challenges should be manageable without causing — from a macroeconomic perspective, undesirable — deleveraging effects. Furthermore, banks have various options for meeting the new standards. Besides increasing their capital, they will most likely adjust their portfolios in order to economize on the amount of risk-weighted assets. A comparison of capital ratios and leverage ratios over time indicates that banks have indeed made ample use of such mitigating actions.

It should be noted, however, that results are often quite heterogeneous, both within and across different countries, which means that conclusions in this note will not hold for every bank and, possibly, not even for every participating country individually.

Fulfilling the leverage ratio target of 3% remains a challenge for many banks in the sample, even when the risk-sentive capital ratios are assumed to be already met. Care needs to be taken in its final calibration in order to ensure that this measure does not supersede the risk-sensitive capital ratios in normal times.

References

Basel Committee on Banking Supervision. 2010. "Basel III: A global regulatory framework for more resilient banks and banking systems." http://www.bis.org/publ/bcbs189.pdf.

Basel Committee on Banking Supervision. 2010. "Basel III: International framework for liquidity risk measurement, standards and monitoring." http://www.bis.org/publ/bcbs188.pdf.

Basel Committee on Banking Supervision. 2010. "An assessment of the long-term economic impact of stronger capital and liquidity requirements." http://www.bis.org/publ/bcbs173.pdf.

Basel Committee on Banking Supervision. 2010. "Results of the comprehensive quantitative impact study." http://www.bis.org/publ/bcbs186.pdf.

Basel Committee on Banking Supervision. 2011. "Global systemically important banks: Assessment methodology and the additional loss absorbency requirement — final document." http://www.bis.org/publ/bcbs207.htm.

Basel Committee on Banking Supervision. 2014. "Basel III leverage ratio framework and disclosure requirements." http://www.bis.org/publ/bcbs270.pdf.

Basel Committee on Banking Supervision. 2014b. "Basel III Monitoring Report." http://www.bis.org/publ/bcbs278.pdf.

Deutsche Bundesbank. 2014. "Ergebnisse des Basel III-Monitoring für deutsche Institute Stichtag 30. Juni 2013.", available only in German language http://www.bundesbank.de/Navigation/EN/Core_business_areas/Banking_supervision/Basel3/Basel3_Monitoring/basel3_monitoring.html.

EBA. 2014. "Basel III monitoring exercise — Results based on data as of 31 December 2012." https://www.eba.europa.eu/-/eba-publishes-results-of-the-basel-iii-monitoring-exercise-as-of-30-june-2013.

CHAPTER FIVE

CREDIT CYCLES AND REAL ESTATE CYCLES

PASCAL GANTENBEIN AND SIMON ZABY[1]

Abstract

We analyze the relationship between credit cycles and real estate cycles. Until recently, there has been quite little research on this topic. However, the subprime crisis of 2007-2009 has fostered an academic literature dealing with both real estate valuation driving credit markets and vice versa. Our categorization of the respective literature shows that expected collateral values and probabilities of real estate crises may be distorted, this way leading to more lending and hence to a higher demand for real estate and higher property prices. There is evidence for a mutual relationship of these two markets rather than for one market leading the other. However, turning points and structural breaks tend to occur when valuation divergences become increasingly apparent to investors and lenders.

I. Introduction

In most economies, housing wealth assumes a substantial proportion of national asset volume and very often even exceeds investments held in stocks or bonds. Also the production of real estate as well as goods and services around it represent an important part of national production. As a result, variations and especially collapses of real estate prices do have severe and multiple impacts on the economy. Since real estate is often largely debt-financed, real estate cycles and credit cycles are seen to be closely linked together. For instance, when fearing the emergence of a real estate bubble, regulators and central banks very often take measures making bank lending less attractive, such as increasing interest rates or

[1] Prof. Dr. Pascal Gantenbein and Dr. Simon Zaby are from University of Basel.

regulatory capital buffers. But in fact, very little is actually known about the mutual relationship of these two markets.

There are multiple links between real estate markets and credit markets. Conceptually, these two markets influence each other in both ways. First, real estate markets affect credit markets directly and indirectly. Properties very often serve as collateral for debt financing and hence support lending activity. However, if asset values deteriorate in a real estate bust, lending institutions face higher credit risk. Indirect links have the same origin, but the transmission takes place through the securities markets. In this case, investors, institutions or individuals other than the initial lending bank may be negatively affected. Such transmission became the key problem for many international banks and asset managers in the course of the financial crisis of 2007-2009.

Conversely, credit market activities and expected credit risk also impact real estate prices. Again, there are several ways for this to happen, but the main transmission occurs through lending volumes. Low prices for credit risk supposedly lead to higher credit demand and supply, while high credit risk premiums exhibit the opposite effect and potentially lead to credit rationing. Apart from changes in the market environment, regulation directed towards reducing credit exposure (such as, e.g., some elements of Basel III) may lead to a lower propensity of banks to engage in certain lending and, as a result, to a lower credit volume which again may impact real estate prices.

The objective of this article is to categorize and analyze these multiple influences between credit markets and real estate markets that are often hypothesized. We first provide a theoretical foundation of the various linkages from a valuation perspective. In the following parts, we then highlight some recent empirical findings on these relationships. Especially since 2008, there has been a growing field of empirical research on real estate related risk in conjunction with credit risk. Finally, we conclude and summarize the results.

II. Theoretical foundation of credit risk and real estate markets

To capture the links between credit risk and real estate, we establish a valuation framework based on the theoretical foundations of price determinants in the real estate market. In the present analysis, we focus on determinants that are connected to credit risk.

Prices of properties first of all are driven by local demand and supply. While the latter is mainly determined by price elasticity and zoning regulations, the demand side is, among other things, closely linked to credit markets and the cost of capital. Specifically, *capitalization rates* mirror the overall interest rate level in an economy as well as systematic risks in real estate markets. Although both of these risks are perceived as market risks, aggregate demand and hence the implied cap rates also reflect the overall credit risk level of the average real estate investor in the market. Furthermore, unlike in the classical framework of perfect capital markets, diversification of real estate portfolios is costly and difficult to achieve in reality. Also, some properties or investors bear a high degree of specificity. For these reasons, the prices and the implied rates may, as well, reflect unsystematic risks of specific properties or investors. Hence, also specific investor or real estate investment situations may be priced regarding credit risk. Obviously, if lenders assume lower credit risk levels on average, this has a positive impact on lending activity and, as a result, on real estate price levels.

At the same time, real estate very often serves as collateral for mortgage loans, hereby expected to increase the safety level for the lender and allowing either for a reduction of the credit cost or an increase in lending volume. In some market periods, this mutual influence leads to parallel growth of credit volumes and real estate prices. For example, the Swiss domestic mortgage volume between 2003 and 2013 has grown from roughly 542 to 877 billion Swiss Francs, i.e., by approximately 62 percent. Interestingly, residential real estate prices in the same period on average have risen by a very similar percentage number, precisely by 37-82 percent, depending on the index type and segment. On average, both markets have grown by about 5.5 to 6 percent every year over the past decade.

The key underlying driver of both the credit market and real estate market is the *business cycle*. Although this is particularly true for real estate activity in the commercial sector, also rental income in the residential market may suffer in severe market downturns. This market risk again can have a negative impact on investor liquidity and solvency, potentially resulting in a credit risk for the lender. For instance, such situations often occurred in the aftermath of the real estate downturn in the early 1990s in several European countries. This is just one example for the strong link between the business cycle and the credit cycle. Another transmission mechanism between the business cycle and real estate markets are *demographic changes* in terms of migration. Obviously, the relative economic attractiveness of a country or an economic zone is a major driver of migration behavior, i.e., in- and outflows that impact demand for real estate in the space or asset market (or both), depending on the structure of the demand.

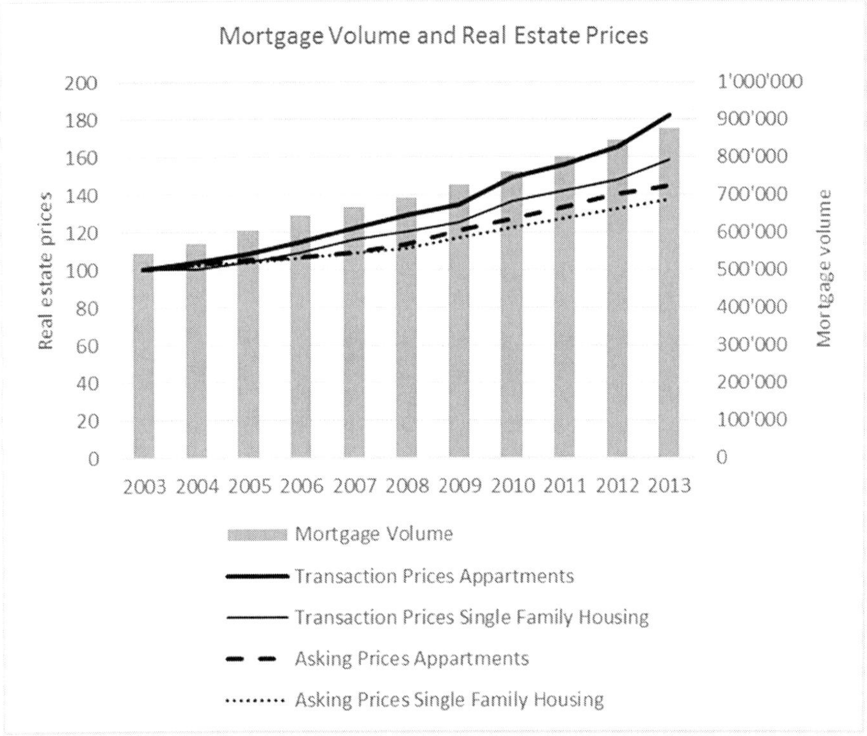

Figure 5-1: Mortgage Volume and Real Estate Prices in Switzerland 2003-2013. Transaction price series are based on indices provided by Fahrlaender und Partner, while asking price series are based on Wueest und Partner. Mortgage volumes are based on statistical data obtained from the Swiss National Bank (Monthly Statistical Bulletin January 2014).

A further very important driver that draws a link to our initial point of implied cap rates is the *availability of capital*. The abundance (or the scarcity) of investment capital directly influences the price of capital and of credit risk. It is itself driven by the investors' attitudes about risk and their needs to allocate resources. In real estate booms, investors and very often also lending institutions tend to underestimate risks and to believe in a continuation of the positive price trend. But even if the risk assessment is appropriate, there might still be the simple need to allocate capital. This is, e.g., the case for the growing segment of institutional investors. In Switzerland, for instance, pension funds currently manage assets of over 600 billion Swiss Francs, while both the insurance sector and institutions of collective capital investments (CIC) cover almost 500 billion Swiss Francs each that need to be invested. Part of that volume goes into real estate.

Hence, there are diverse channels through which real estate markets can influence credit markets and vice versa. In the subsequent parts of our analysis, we give an overview of some of the empirical research that has been brought forward in the context of the above developed hypotheses.

III. The impact of real estate markets on lending activity

Already before the financial crisis of 2007-2009, Pavlov and Wachter (2006) have argued that there is a potential for market wide underpricing of mortgage default risk. They provide evidence that underpricing becomes more probable with increasing time since the last real estate crash on the one hand and with higher volatility of the underlying asset on the other hand. Both elements contribute to the difficulty of assessing the true value of the underlying real estate market.

Most literature on this issue, however, has been published only after the crisis. Goetzman et al. (2012) show that the appreciation of home-loan collateral value has affected both the demand and the supply side of mortgage market. They find that past home price increases lead to low estimated probabilities of a real estate crash. Interestingly, not only the application rate but also the approval rate of subprime mortgages has risen over their sample period. Likewise, Nneji et al. (2013) argue that after year 2000, bubbles were driven to a larger extent than before by the expectation of future asset price growth and less by fundamental factors. The authors call this phenomenon a "rational bubble". Clearly, the existence of such a bubble again has an effect on collateral value.

Furthermore, LaCour-Little and Yang (2010) show that expected price appreciation not only leads to higher mortgage volumes but also to a higher proportion of mortgage contracts with deferred amortization that, as well, contributes to higher credit risk. This is consistent with the observation of Shan (2011), that there has been a volume increase in reverse mortgages along with the house price growth before 2007. Likewise, Borgersen and Greibrokk (2012) analyze the relationship between expected excess gains on housing and the incentives to increase housing leverage, leading to a risk both for the mortgagees and the mortgagor.

Altogether, there seems to be rather strong evidence for the hypothesis that asset values in real estate markets deliver a strong impact on credit market activity and credit risk.

IV. The impact of credit markets on real estate markets

Regarding the influences in the opposite direction, there has been substantial research documenting a positive link between lending and the development of real estate prices. Specifically, a considerable field of research has focused on Alt-A and subprime lending and the growth of a real estate bubble in the United States. Pavlov and Wachter (2011), for example, provide empirical evidence for the hypothesis that more aggressive mortgage lending leads to an appreciation of the underlying real estate asset prices. In particular, their findings show that such lending activity magnifies the real estate cycle, i.e., contributes to stronger price increases in the boom, followed by sharper price declines in the crisis.

In a similar line of argumentation, Pennington-Cross and Ho (2010) show that the specific features of hybrid mortgage loans led to higher default probabilities due to the stronger exposure to payment shocks and high leverage in 2007, this way contributing to the crisis in the mortgage and real estate markets. Panagopoulos and Vlamis 2009 analyze the link between bank lending and real estate crises and document a strong relationship between over-borrowing, real estate bubbles, and subsequent banking crises. Interestingly, Berkovec et al. (2012) also highlight the importance of non-bank lending as an often neglected but considerable factor explaining the U.S. housing bubble.

On a positive note and regarding REITs, Ooi et al. (2012) as well as Hardin III et al. 2011 show that lines of credit may be beneficial for the stability of the real estate sector as they provide some type of insurance for REITs against credit rationing in times of crisis. Furthermore, MacKinnon (2011) gives evidence that REITs on average have better access to capital even when credit markets are tight. And Harrison et al. (2011) argue that liquidity through higher credit lines is associated with a better performance of REITs. Regarding the importance of macroeconomic factors, Yunus (2012) shows for securitized real estate markets that changes in GDP as well as in stock markets, the monetary base, inflation, and long-term interest rates exhibit a significant, however, only short-term impact on international real estate returns.

Overall, also the hypothesis of credit markets driving real estate markets cannot be rejected based on recent research. In fact, there is a rather new but significant real estate literature documenting that credit markets strongly impact real estate activity.

The question, however, remains why and how turning points can occur, i.e., whether there is a leading market or whether there are exogenous events triggering a change in this self-enforcing mutual relationship between the two markets. Most of the above mentioned papers explicitly or implicitly give a clear answer on this; namely, that the likelihood of such events increases when market participants (both real estate investors and lending institutions) become aware of divergences between actual and fundamentally justifiable real estate prices, including the awareness about other market players' needs to invest.

V. Conclusions

Both the theoretical approach and empirical evidence support an overall positive relationship between real estate markets and credit markets during stable times.

Precisely, there is evidence for underestimating real estate related risks and overestimating long-term collateral values in times of real estate booms. In such situations, a "rational bubble" may emerge, when real estate prices turn out to be increasingly determined by price expectations rather than by fundamental economic factors. In the credit markets, both demand and supply grow as the application and approval rates of loans rise. As a result, amortization schemes tend to be prolonged, and mortgage volumes grow. At the same time, lending itself turns out to be a key driver of real estate demand and positively impacts real estate prices. Consequently, there is a strong link between borrowing from banks and non-banks and real estate cycles.

However, it is unclear at first sight whether real estate prices drive credit volumes on the basis of expected collateral values or whether the mechanism just works in the opposite direction, namely that more lending contributes to a higher demand for properties. As the proportion of reverse mortgages in most economies is relatively small compared to the proportion of new mortgages, there is strong evidence for more lending leading to higher real estate prices. As a matter of course, higher real estate prices also require buyers to obtain more financing. While for some investors, the better availability of credit contributes to a higher demand for real estate, the resulting price growth of real estate as a backlash impacts their suitability as collateral. This again impacts credit availability for buyers in the next round and thus has a self-enforcing effect. Both the theoretical and the empirical discussion show that real estate markets are directly linked to the business cycle, which again is a determinant for the credit cycle.

Altogether, there is more evidence for a mutual relationship than for one market leading the other. However, turning points seem to occur when it becomes apparent for a larger number of market participants, that the level of expected real estate values cannot be sustained either because the economic environment has changed or because information about real estate markets has improved.

References

Berkovec, J., Y. Chang, and D. McManus. 2012. "Alternative Lending Channels and the Crisis in the U.S. Housing Markets." *Real Estate Economics* 40 (1): 8-31.

Borgersen, T.A., and J. Greibrokk. 2012. "Reflections on LTV, risk and incentives in mortgage markets." *Journal of European Real Estate Research* 5 (3): 199-210.

Goetzmann, W.N., L. Peng, and J. Yen. 2012. "The Subprime Crisis and House Price Appreciation." *Journal of Real Estate Finance and Economics* 44: 36-66.

Hardin III, W.G., and M.D. Hill. 2011. "Credit Line Availability and Utilization in REITs." *Journal of Real Estate Research* 33(4): 507-530.

Harrison, D.M., K.L. Luchtenberg, and M.J. Seiler. 2011. "REIT Performance and Lines of Credit." *Journal of Real Estate Portfolio Management* 17(1): 1-14.

LaCour-Little, and M., J. Yang. 2010. "Pay me now or pay me later: Alternative Mortgage Products and the Mortgage Crisis." *Real Estate Economics* 38 (4): 687-732.

MacKinnon, G. 2011. "Do REITs have an Advantage When Credit is Tight?" *Journal of Real Estate Portfolio Management* 17(1): 15-25.

Nneji, O., C. Brooks, and C. Ward. 2013. "Intrinsic and Rational Speculative Bubbles in the U.S. Housing Market: 1960-2011." *Journal of Real Estate Research* 35 (2): 121-151.

Ooi, J.T.L., W. Wong, and S. Ong. 2012. "Can Bank Lines of Credit Protect REITs against a Credit Crisis?" *Real Estate Economics* 40 (2): 285-316.

Panagopoulos, Y., and P. Vlamis. 2009. "Bank Lending, Real Estate Bubbles, and Basel II." *Journal of Real Estate Literature* 17 (2): 295-310.

Pavlov, A., and S. Wachter. 2006. "The Inevitability of Marketwide Underpricing of Mortgage Default Risk." *Real Estate Economics* 34 (4): 479-496.

Pavlov, A., and S. Wachter. 2011. "Subprime Lending and Real Estate Prices." *Real Estate Economics* 39 (1): 1-17.

Pennington-Cross, A., and G. Ho. 2010. "The Termination of Subprime Hybrid and Fixed-Rate Mortgages." *Real Estate Economics* 38 (3): 399-426.

Shan, H. 2011. "Reversing the Trend: The Recent Expansion of the Reverse Mortgage Market." *Real Estate Economics* 39(4): 743-768.

Yunus, N. 2012. "Modeling Relationships among Securitized Property Markets, Stock Markets, and Macroeconomic Variables." *Journal of Real Estate Research* 34 (2): 127-156.

CHAPTER SIX

TRADE CREDIT AND BANKRUPTCY: AN EMPIRICAL INVESTIGATION

EMILIA GARCIA-APPENDINI AND JUDIT MONTORIOL-GARRIGA[1]

Abstract

Using a sample of firms matched with their suppliers, we study the use of debt in trade credit and in bank lines of credit as the firm approaches bankruptcy. We find that during the periods leading to bankruptcy firms in financial distress draw down heavily on lines of credit and increase significantly their debt in accounts payable. However, creditor support to distressed firms differs significantly depending on the type of contract with the borrower. On average, secured debtholders (banks) withdraw their support later than unsecured suppliers. However, among the latter, a hold-up problem emerges whenever creditors are dependent on the distressed firm. In this case, dependent suppliers support distressed clients for longer periods and with larger credit commitments.

I. Introduction

In this paper we analyze the evolution of the two major sources of working capital financing as firms approach bankruptcy: supplier's trade

---

[1] Prof. Emilia Garcia-Appendini, Ph.D. is from the University of St Gallen, E-mail: emilia.garcia@unisg.ch. Judit Montoriol-Garriga, Ph.D. is from "la Caixa" Research Department, E-mail: montoriol@gmail.com.
Many thanks to Mike Jacobs, Jr. for providing the data on lines of credit and to Marco Forletta for research assistance. We also thank seminar participants of the University of St. Gallen and Université de Neuchâtel for useful comments. We are grateful to CAREFIN for providing financial support.

credit and the use of bank lines of credit (LOC).[2] Consistently with a strong increase in demand for credit, we find that during the periods leading to bankruptcy firms in financial distress draw down heavily on lines of credit and increase significantly their debt in accounts payable. On the other hand, creditor support to the failed firms differs significantly depending on borrower characteristics. Banks initially increase their limits in their lines of credit, and subsequently reduce them around one and a half years previous to default. On the other hand, suppliers withdraw their support to their clients as early as five years previous to default. However, a hold-up problem emerges whenever creditors are dependent on the distressed firm. In this case, dependent suppliers support distressed clients for longer periods and with larger credit commitments.

When firms enter financial distress, their ability to raise external financing is severely curtailed, and their cash flow is scarce. Their limited ability to raise new funds makes distressed firms more likely to use existing sources of external financing. Previous literature has shown that firms significantly increase their use of bank lines of credit as they approach default (see for example Jimenez et al, 2009). Regarding the use of trade credit, Molina and Preve (2012) find that firms in financial distress use a significantly larger amount of trade credit to substitute alternative sources of financing. Evans and Koch (2007) and Jorion and Zhang (2009) show that the largest exposures of defaulted firms correspond to supplier credit. However, to the best of our knowledge there is no evidence of how the use of trade credit evolves as the firms approach default. Our first contribution of this paper is therefore to show that the use of trade credit in defaulted firms follows a hump-shaped pattern, with the peak occurring two years before default.

We next analyze the supply side of credit as firms approach default. For bank credit, we look at how the limits on lines of credit change as the firms approach bankruptcy. For trade credit, we use a matched sample of firms with their suppliers and analyze how the proportion of sales to the defaulted firms and the accounts receivable of the suppliers of defaulted firms change over time. We find striking differences between bank and trade credit. Limits on lines of credit initially increase for defaulted firms, consistently with previous evidence that finds that banks renegotiate — rather than accelerate — corporate loans at the first signs of distress (see,

[2] Accounts payable are, on average, 11 to 17% of total assets throughout different types of firms and different economies (See cross-country comparisons of the use of trade credit in Rajan and Zingales (1995) and Giannetti (2003)). On the other hand, recent literature for the US quantifies the undrawn amount in bank lines of credit to be around 10-13% of a firm's assets (see e.g. Sufi, 2009).

e.g., Roberts and Sufi (2009) and the references therein). Significant reductions in limits to lines of credit are only observed on average one and a half years before default. Suppliers on the other hand reduce their proportion of sales to clients that eventually go bankrupt earlier than banks, on average four to three years before default. We observe a similarly decreasing but less pronounced trend for the accounts receivable of suppliers of defaulted firms, suggesting that suppliers pull out of distressed firms on average one and a half years before banks.

From the creditors' point of view, it would be optimal to accelerate the loans or end the credit relationship with the client as soon as they discover that the firm has fundamental solvency problems (as opposed to temporary financial difficulties). Two non-mutually exclusive explanations could drive the observed heterogeneity in exit times across different creditors. One, which we cannot rule out due to data limitations, is that suppliers have better or timelier information about the underlying credit quality of firms (Biais and Gollier, 1997; Burkart and Ellingsen, 2004). The other explanation is that the contracts (implicit or explicit) between the borrower and the creditors give different incentives to support firms in financial difficulties. We focus the remainder of the paper on examining the incentives of different types of creditors to support the eventually failed firms.

Banks' contracts, on the one hand, have several features that reduce their losses given default, for example seniority (Longhofer and Santos, 2000) and collateral (see e.g. Rajan and Winton, 1995). In addition, banks have access to a more diversified portfolio of borrowers relative to suppliers, as they are not limited by industry or market concentration constraints. These mechanisms increase the probability of lending to or renegotiating with distressed firms relative to other unsecured, junior and less diversified creditors such as suppliers, because they reduce the banks' losses given default. In addition, seniority also increases the benefits from helping firms in times of bad performance (Longhofer and Santos, 2000).

Contracts with the suppliers, on the other hand, are much less formal than bank contracts and hence lack a contractual seniority and a formal collateral (Cuñat and Garcia-Appendini, 2012).[3,4] In line with these issues, some theories claim that suppliers that start losing confidence progressively withdraw their support to distressed clients (Baxter, 1967;

[3] In fact, the short-term nature of trade credit can be explained as a form of gaining effective seniority relative to other claimants (Longhofer and Santos, 2003).

[4] Some theories claim that one advantage of suppliers is that the good they supply can serve as collateral. In the US, however, the legal period over which a supplier may seize the supplied good is only 10 days after delivery (Garvin, 1996).

Titman and Wessels, 1988; Andrade and Kaplan, 1998). However, when the client-supplier relationship is valuable, suppliers may benefit from helping their clients in bad times. For example, Wilner (2000) shows that dependent trade creditors grant more concessions to customers in financial distress than what would be granted by lenders in a competitive credit market. Similarly, Cuñat (2007) finds that when clients are hard to substitute suppliers increase trade credit provision to clients that are experiencing temporary liquidity shocks. Empirical evidence is roughly consistent with the latter theories. For example, Hertzel et al (2008) and Jorion and Zhang (2009) show that the bankruptcy of a client has a negative impact on the value of the supplier, suggesting that client relationships are valuable for the suppliers. [5,6] Garcia-Appendini and Montoriol-Garriga (2012) find that the most liquid suppliers increased their provision of trade credit to constrained firms during the 2007-2008 credit crunch; however, the ability of suppliers to support their clients is limited to temporary liquidity shocks. Consistently with the idea that relationships are valuable, Franks and Nyborg (1996) and Evans and Koch (2007) find that suppliers with private benefits can force inefficient liquidations. Our paper reconciles the literature by showing that supplier support to their debtors depends on the characteristics of the relationship and the market structure of the distressed client.

This paper is related to the corporate finance literature that looks into whether trade credit is used by firms to complement or substitute bank credit. Empirical evidence about these relationships is mixed. For example, Petersen and Rajan (1997) find that small private businesses without access to bank credit lines use the more expensive trade credit as a substitute. Similarly, trade credit has been shown to be critical to finance investment for constrained firms (Carbó-Valverde, Rodríguez-Fernández and Udell (2008)). On the other hand, Cook (1999) and Garcia-Appendini (2010) find evidence that banks are more likely to lend to firms financed by their suppliers, implying that these are complementary sources of financing. Both views have yet not been reconciled convincingly due to lack of data. This paper will shed light on the substitution view of trade credit by analyzing the behaviour of distressed firms.

This paper is also related to the financial distress literature, by analyzing the effect of financial distress on the use of trade credit as a

[5] Bankruptcies can also affect the value of lender banks. See for example Dahiya et al (2003).

[6] Relationships are also valuable from the client's perspective: In fact, McMillan and Woodruff (1999) find that suppliers in Vietnam offer more credit when it is difficult for the customer to find alternative suppliers.

substitute of alternative sources of financing. Our findings also contribute to the exposure at default (EAD) quantification literature by showing the importance of the availability and use of other substitute sources of short term financing, like credit from suppliers, to determine the extent to which distressed firms increase their use of bank lines of credit prior to default.

The remainder of the paper is organized as follows: In Section 2 we describe the data. In Section 3 we present our basic results with the main differences between the average supplier and the average bank. In Section 4 we further explore the heterogeneity within suppliers regarding support to clients in financial distress. Finally, we conclude in Section 5.

II. Data

Our data results from merging information from five different data sets: Quarterly balance sheet information comes from Compustat for the universe of US-incorporated, non-financial firms, with non-missing asset information between 1976 and 2007. We identify bankrupt firms in this dataset if either (1) the given firm is included in the Center for Research in Securities Prices (CRSP) dataset as "delisted", with delist codes corresponding to bankruptcy (i.e., codes 572 or 574), or (2) the firm is listed in Moody's Ultimate Recovery Database (MURD). From MURD we obtain detailed information on the use of LOC (LOC limit; used and unused LOC balances) for bankrupt firms up to five years prior to their bankruptcy date. We complement information on the use of lines of credit for non-bankrupt firms from Capital IQ (CIQ).[7]

For a sub-sample of our firms we obtain information about their key customers using the Customer Segment File in Compustat. In accordance with SFAS Nos. 14 and 131, public firms have to disclose the identity and total amount of sales to customers whose purchases represent more than ten percent of the firm's total annual sales. We search the customers' names within Compustat to obtain balance sheet information for the clients. The main advantage of using this data is that the analysis is based on actual supplier-customer relationships, so we can control for supply and demand factors. However, the matched sample has some limitations. For example, data on key clients contain information only for clients representing at least 10% of supplier sales, so suppliers with diversified sales portfolios do not disclose some of their most important clients. Further, some suppliers report generic client names which cannot be matched with Compustat

[7] Information on lines of credit starts in year 1996. For all other variables our sample starts in year 1976.

Panel A: Unmatched sample

Variable	All Firms N. Obs	Mean	Median	St. Dev.	Non-bankrupt firms N. Obs	Mean	Median	St. Dev.	Bankrupt firms N. Obs	Mean	Median	St. Dev.
Log of total assets	477'684	4.98	5.07	2.76	459'925	4.94	5.02	2.78	17'759	5.82	5.91	2.06
Accounts Payable / LT Assets	332'094	0.16	0.06	0.27	325'431	0.16	0.06	0.27	6'663	0.13	0.08	0.17
LOC limit / LT Assets	15'159	0.20	0.13	0.22	13'858	0.18	0.13	0.19	1'301	0.36	0.21	0.37
LOC balance / LT Assets	35'201	0.09	0.03	0.13	33'367	0.08	0.03	0.13	1'834	0.15	0.07	0.20
Tangible assets / Total Assets	462'554	0.26	0.16	0.26	444'935	0.26	0.16	0.26	17'619	0.31	0.25	0.25
Quarterly sales growth	423'437	-0.03	0.03	0.46	406'878	-0.03	0.03	0.46	16'559	-0.02	0.02	0.39
Net profit margin	441'735	-0.12	0.35	3.01	424'784	-0.12	0.36	3.04	16'951	0.06	0.26	2.06
Cash flows / Total Assets	421'513	-0.03	0.02	0.21	405'458	-0.03	0.02	0.21	16'055	0.00	0.02	0.10
Market to book value of equity	358'278	3.76	1.52	9.21	344'702	3.83	1.53	9.35	13'576	1.97	1.21	4.36
Debt / Total Assets	447'336	0.30	0.18	0.51	430'744	0.30	0.18	0.51	16'592	0.44	0.38	0.41
Capital expenditures / Total Assets	406'524	0.02	0.01	0.03	390'141	0.02	0.01	0.03	16'383	0.02	0.01	0.03
Covenant violations	259'928	0.06	0.00	0.24	248'134	0.06	0.00	0.24	11'794	0.14	0.00	0.35

Panel B: Matched supplier-client sample

Variable	All Suppliers N	mean	p50	sd	Supp. of non-bankr. clients N	mean	p50	sd	Suppliers of bankrupt clients N	mean	p50	sd
I. Supplier variables												
Log of total assets	210'707	4.69	4.62	2.44	63'596	4.88	4.79	2.22	5'203	5.38	5.38	2.13
Accounts Receivable / LT Assets	168'578	0.16	0.08	0.24	51'403	0.16	0.10	0.23	4'283	0.18	0.10	0.26
Accounts Payable / LT Assets	170'401	0.09	0.04	0.17	51'845	0.09	0.04	0.15	4'275	0.10	0.05	0.18
LOC limit / LT Assets	7'911	0.19	0.13	0.23	2'835	0.20	0.16	0.21	134	0.29	0.21	0.34
LOC balance / LT Assets	17'864	0.09	0.03	0.13	6'742	0.08	0.03	0.12	368	0.12	0.07	0.14
Tangible assets / Total Assets	207'739	0.28	0.20	0.24	62'816	0.27	0.20	0.24	5'093	0.32	0.27	0.23
Quarterly sales growth	197'642	-0.02	0.03	0.40	61'041	-0.02	0.03	0.38	5'026	-0.02	0.02	0.34
Net profit margin	203'082	-0.04	0.33	2.33	62'827	0.06	0.33	1.93	5'138	0.18	0.26	1.12
Cash flows / Total Assets	181'203	0.00	0.03	0.10	55'947	0.01	0.03	0.08	4'368	0.02	0.03	0.06
Market to book value of equity	178'783	2.65	1.50	3.73	53'901	2.44	1.54	3.03	4'208	1.92	1.31	2.36
Debt / Total Assets	200'246	0.26	0.19	0.30	60'998	0.24	0.18	0.28	4'941	0.29	0.25	0.26
Capital expenditures / Total Assets	179'134	0.01	0.01	0.02	56'710	0.01	0.01	0.02	4'415	0.02	0.01	0.02
Covenant violations	104'072	0.06	0.00	0.24	34'923	0.06	0.00	0.24	2'168	0.09	0.00	0.28
II. Client Variables												
Weight	170'424	0.58	0.51	0.36	117'528	0.59	0.52	0.36	10'006	0.58	0.50	0.35
Client log of total assets	127'516	9.41	9.68	2.05	117'515	9.34	9.64	2.04	10'001	10.15	10.09	2.11
Client net profit margin	116'279	0.32	0.28	0.24	107'025	0.33	0.29	0.24	9'254	0.22	0.21	0.18
Client accounts payable / LT Assets	87'711	0.13	0.09	0.13	84'786	0.130	0.089	0.130	2'925	0.09	0.08	0.06

This table contains selected summary statistics for the firms in our data. Panel A describes variables for the firms in the unmatched sample. In Panel B, section I, we describe the suppliers while in section II we describe the clients. For a description of data sources please refer to the text.

Table 1: Descriptive Statistics.

data. For the remaining firms that do list names of actual clients, we use data mining techniques, like algorithms that match the number of common characters across names, to match these names to companies whose data are available in Compustat. There are few perfect string matches for the client names. We manually match the remaining names to complement our database. We are unable to find matches for many clients, for example small unlisted firms, foreign firms, or firms for which balance sheet information is not available in Compustat for the period in which they were reported to be clients. Table 1 contains key descriptive statistics for our baseline unmatched sample (Panel A) and the supplier-customer matched sample (Panel B).

III. The evolution of credit as the firm approaches default

We start our empirical analysis by analyzing the within-firm evolution of the ratios of trade and bank credit to firm assets as the firms approach default, and comparing this with non-defaulted firms. Because the value of assets is likely to fall as firms approach default (for example due to fire sales), we scale debt items with respect to a fixed level of long term assets, i.e., the average value of assets of the firm 17 or more quarters before default.[8] To assign bankruptcy dates to our control sample of non-defaulted firms, we randomly associate non-defaulted firms that were active around the time of bankruptcy to one defaulted firm within the same 2-digit SIC code. On each subsample of bankrupt and non-bankrupt firms we estimate the following firm fixed-effects specification:

$$\frac{Debt_{it}}{LTAssets_i} = \alpha_i + \sum_{s=0}^{16} \beta_s Default_{it+s} + \Gamma * \mathrm{X}_{\mathrm{it}} + \eta_{it} \, . \quad (1)$$

In the above equation, debt numerators of the dependent variables are accounts payable and the used portion of all existing lines of credit, respectively; $Default_{t+s}, s = 0,1,..,16$ are 17 dummy variables taking a one if default occurred s periods after t, or zero otherwise; and X_{it} is a matrix of firm-specific time-varying characteristics which include: log of assets, total debt to total assets, sales growth, tangible assets to total assets, net profit margin, market to book value of equity, cash flows to total assets, and capital expenditures to total assets.

Table 2 contains the results of estimating equation (1) on the subsamples of non-bankrupt firms (odd columns) and bankrupt firms (even columns). For the ease of interpretation of the results, in Figure 1 we plot the within-firm evolution of the debt ratios of bankrupt and non-

[8] Scaling by these values restricts our sample to firms that were active 17 or more periods before default. Our results do not change if we choose other denominators for long term assets, such as average assets 12 or more periods before bankruptcy, or the maximum value of assets previous to bankruptcy.

	Panel A: Accounts Payable / Long-Term Assets				Panel B: LOC balance / Long-term Assets			
	(1)	(2)	(3)	(4)	(5)	(6)	(7)	(8)
	Non bankrupt	Bankrupt	Non bankrupt	Bankrupt	Non bankrupt	Bankrupt	Non bankrupt	Bankrupt
Default	-0.00244	0.0239*	0.00413*	-0.0140	0.00570	0.153***	-0.00763**	0.278***
	[0.00258]	[0.0134]	[0.00235]	[0.0101]	[0.00462]	[0.0177]	[0.00319]	[0.0257]
Default +1	-0.000848	0.0519***	0.00653***	0.0114	0.000895	0.107***	-0.00638**	0.495***
	[0.00262]	[0.0131]	[0.00239]	[0.0103]	[0.00470]	[0.0176]	[0.00323]	[0.0251]
Default + 2	0.00117	0.0576***	0.00890***	0.0175*	-0.000324	0.101***	-0.00668**	0.303***
	[0.00266]	[0.0129]	[0.00244]	[0.00998]	[0.00491]	[0.0174]	[0.00329]	[0.0246]
Default +3	0.00335	0.0686***	0.0118***	0.0315***	0.00238	0.0856***	0.000511	0.193***
	[0.00269]	[0.0128]	[0.00251]	[0.00989]	[0.00518]	[0.0171]	[0.00334]	[0.0244]
Default +4	0.00387	0.0792***	0.0153***	0.0350***	0.000305	0.0815***	-0.00506	0.0836***
	[0.00273]	[0.0128]	[0.00253]	[0.0103]	[0.00565]	[0.0176]	[0.00338]	[0.0246]
Default +5	0.00305	0.0747***	0.0128***	0.0365***	0.00524	0.0746***	-0.00266	0.0670***
	[0.00275]	[0.0130]	[0.00256]	[0.0104]	[0.00603]	[0.0179]	[0.00340]	[0.0250]
Default +6	0.00151	0.0882***	0.0147***	0.0362***	0.00761	0.0928***	-0.00503	0.0567**
	[0.00277]	[0.0131]	[0.00261]	[0.0105]	[0.00639]	[0.0183]	[0.00343]	[0.0252]
Default +7	0.00427	0.0959***	0.0159***	0.0410***	0.00420	0.105***	-0.00564	0.0563**
	[0.00283]	[0.0131]	[0.00269]	[0.0107]	[0.00678]	[0.0189]	[0.00352]	[0.0258]
Default +8	0.00163	0.0842***	0.0172***	0.0293***	0.00140	0.0977***	-0.00911**	0.0139
	[0.00287]	[0.0131]	[0.00274]	[0.0101]	[0.00723]	[0.0197]	[0.00356]	[0.0258]
Default +9	0.00126	0.0743***	0.0195***	0.0258**	0.00406	0.0895***	-0.00884**	0.0518**
	[0.00295]	[0.0130]	[0.00281]	[0.0105]	[0.00803]	[0.0206]	[0.00365]	[0.0256]
Default +10	-0.000205	0.0719***	0.0196***	0.0276***	0.00261	0.0774***	-0.00997***	0.0301
	[0.00298]	[0.0132]	[0.00284]	[0.0104]	[0.00895]	[0.0229]	[0.00370]	[0.0258]
Default +11	0.00140	0.0576***	0.0197***	0.0145	0.0139	0.0654***	-0.00567	0.0399
	[0.00307]	[0.0135]	[0.00294]	[0.0109]	[0.00969]	[0.0246]	[0.00382]	[0.0266]
Default +12	-0.000940	0.0609***	0.0190***	0.00971	0.0139	0.0639**	-0.00892**	0.0301
	[0.00314]	[0.0137]	[0.00301]	[0.0107]	[0.00962]	[0.0257]	[0.00390]	[0.0270]
Default +13	-0.00386	0.0488***	0.0135***	0.00804	0.0224**	0.0329	-0.0106***	0.0375
	[0.00319]	[0.0140]	[0.00306]	[0.0113]	[0.00969]	[0.0274]	[0.00395]	[0.0277]
Default +14	-0.00298	0.0402***	0.0203***	0.0132	0.0154	-0.00623	-0.00816**	0.0290
	[0.00330]	[0.0144]	[0.00314]	[0.0113]	[0.00995]	[0.0297]	[0.00409]	[0.0282]
Default +15	0.00263	0.0418***	0.0242***	0.0118	0.0101	0.000541	-0.00930**	0.0199
	[0.00343]	[0.0149]	[0.00327]	[0.0118]	[0.0101]	[0.0310]	[0.00428]	[0.0295]
Default +16	0.00266	0.0365**	0.0206***	0.00480	0.0148	0.00162	-0.00378	-0.000443
	[0.00349]	[0.0151]	[0.00336]	[0.0117]	[0.0102]	[0.0318]	[0.00436]	[0.0298]
Firm controls	No	No	Yes	Yes	No	No	Yes	Yes
Constant	0.163***	0.123***	-0.213***	-0.433***	0.0818***	0.103***	0.0903***	0.106***
	[0.000262]	[0.00179]	[0.00240]	[0.0175]	[0.000491]	[0.00561]	[0.000324]	[0.00347]
Observations	309,060	6,108	172,341	3,726	31,981	1,661	296,579	5,726
R-squared	0.000	0.045	0.146	0.297	0.001	0.082	0.000	0.108
Number of firms	11,372	176	7,952	152	1,884	92	11,366	175

The dependent variable is the ratio of accounts payable to long-term assets (col 1-4) and drawn balances in lines of credit to long-term assets (col 5-8). Default + s is a dummy variable containing a 1 if the firm went into bankruptcy s periods after the period, 0 otherwise. Estimation period is from the first quarter of 1996 to the fourth quarter of 2007.Estimations are done over a sample of non-bankrupt firms in odd-numbered columns, and bankrupt firms in even columns. Non-bankrupt firms were randomly assigned to a bankrupt firm in the same 2-digit SIC code industry to associate them with a bankruptcy dates. Specifications in columns 3, 4, 7, and 8 contain the following firm time-varying controls: log of total assets, sales growth, tangible assets to total assets, net profit margin, market to book value of equity, cash flows to total assets, and capital expenditures to total assets. All estimations contain firm fixed effects

Table 2: Evolution of debt in trade credit and bank lines of credit.

bankrupt firms, corresponding to the sum of the estimated constant term plus the estimated coefficients of the 17 default dummies $Default_{t+s}$ of the specifications in columns 1, 2, 5, and 6. From Panel A in Table 2 and Figure 1 we observe that the long-term ratio of accounts payable to assets is around 16% and stays constant for non-defaulted firms. In contrast, defaulted firms initially increase their accounts payable to assets ratio until seven quarters previous to bankruptcy, when the ratio starts decreasing again until it reaches the minimum levels of 15%. From Panel B of Table 2 and Figure 1, we find that the behavior of bank debt in lines of credit, as measured by the drawn balances in lines of credit, is strikingly different. In this case, non-bankrupt firms keep their bank debt constant at around

8% of assets. In contrast, and consistent with the findings of Jimenez et al (2009) on a sample of Spanish firms, we find that bankrupt firms increase their debt in lines of credit significantly as they approach bankruptcy, and do not revert to their initial debt levels. In columns 3, 4, 7, and 8 of Table 2, we find that these basic patterns (i.e., bank debt increasing steadily as firms approach bankruptcy, hump-shaped evolution of accounts payable) are maintained even after conditioning on time-varying firm characteristics and year fixed effects that could affect the use of these two types of debts.[9]

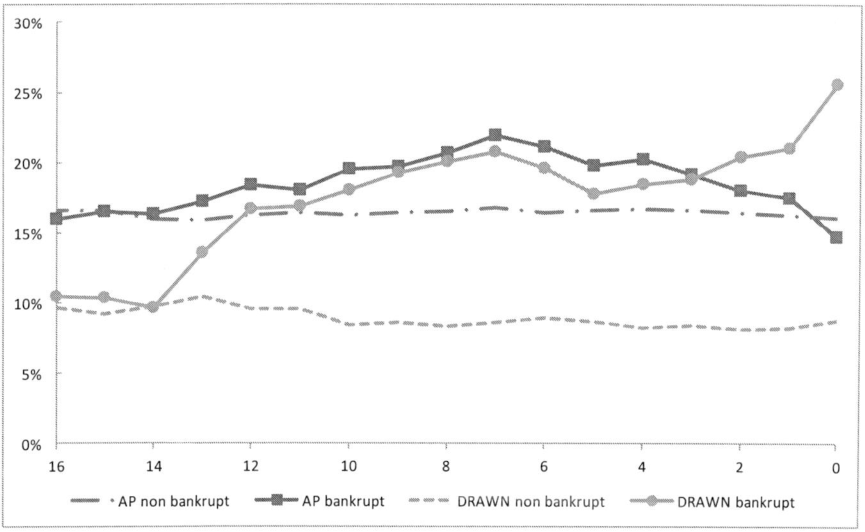

Each line in this figure plots the constant term plus the estimated coefficients of the default coefficients in Table 2 (columns 1, 2, 5, and 6, respectively). The horizontal axis is the time to bankruptcy. AP is accounts payable, DRAWN is the drawn balance in lines of credit. Debt variables are measured as percentage of long-term assets (i.e. assets 17 periods or more before bankruptcy).

Figure 1: Evolution of trade credit and drawn balances in LOC in the periods leading to bankruptcy.

With the findings in Table 2, we are not able to identify whether the observed effects are demand or supply driven. We are not able to identify whether the observed effects are demand or supply driven. We nevertheless expect most of the observed increases in the use of credit to be demand-driven, as we expect struggling firms with low levels of cash

[9] Similar results also hold when we do the estimations on the subsample of firms for which we have supplier information.

flow to have high needs of external financing. However, with likely low z-scores and distressed financial ratios, their ability to raise external financing is limited. Therefore, their only possibility would be to use their pre-committed lines of credit, or to extend the periods of payment to their suppliers.

To partially overcome this identification problem, we examine what happens from the supply side of credit. For banks, we observe the limits in lines of credit for each firm. To the extent that through the use of covenants banks are able to adjust the limits in the lines of credit for distressed firms, the limits in lines of credit will be a good proxy for the amount of credit that banks desire to supply to a given firm each period. For trade credit, on the other hand, we use our matched customer-supplier sample and center our attention on the suppliers of the distressed firms. In particular, we focus on two variables: (i) the proportion of sales to the failed customer as a fraction of the total sales of the supplier, and (ii) the total amount of accounts receivable of suppliers of failed firms.[10] We follow a similar estimation strategy as in equation (1) but running the regressions on these supply-side variables instead of the demand-side debt ratios as dependent variables. Results of these estimations are contained in Table 3 for banks, and Table 4 for suppliers.

The estimations in Tables 3 and 4 show significant differences between the behavior of credit providers for bankrupt versus non-bankrupt firms. For the ease of interpretation of the results, as before we summarize the estimated coefficients of Tables 3 and 4 in Figure 2, Panel A and B (respectively). Results show that banks initially *increase* the limits on lines of credit to bankrupt firms from 30% to a maximum of 43% of long-term assets. Limits on lines of credit only start decreasing around the sixth quarter before default, by 1 to 1.5%, and then again two quarters before bankruptcy by an additional 2%. Non-bankrupt firms have on average much lower debt capacities even 16 quarters before the default of industry peers, and the evolution of their limits on lines of credit is more stable, although on average we do observe a slight reduction in their limits in lines of credit.[11] These patterns are observed also after conditioning on firm characteristics.

---

[10] The supplier-customer matched sample does not contain information about which proportion of the total accounts receivable of the supplier corresponds to each client.

[11] This result is somewhat unexpected and warrants future research. By construction of our sample, the non bankrupt firms are firms that did never go into any bankruptcy procedures as of 2012 (i.e., even 5 years after the observation period). Why banks reduce their limits on lines of credit while increasing the limits

	Panel A: Line of credit limits / Long term assets				Panel B: Covenant Violations			
	(1)	(2)	(3)	(4)	(5)	(6)	(7)	(8)
	Non bankrupt	Bankrupt	Non bankrupt	Bankrupt	Non bankrupt	Bankrupt	Non bankrupt	Bankrupt
Default	-0.0123*	0.0917***	-0.00457	0.127***	0.0136***	0.269***	0.00531	0.209***
	[0.00718]	[0.0209]	[0.00763]	[0.0300]	[0.00402]	[0.0242]	[0.00473]	[0.0279]
Default +1	-0.0118	0.172***	-0.00860	0.209***	0.0212***	0.329***	0.0149***	0.240***
	[0.00721]	[0.0205]	[0.00778]	[0.0313]	[0.00403]	[0.0218]	[0.00478]	[0.0258]
Default + 2	-0.0164**	0.190***	-0.0135*	0.198***	0.00766*	0.269***	0.00111	0.179***
	[0.00750]	[0.0203]	[0.00810]	[0.0297]	[0.00401]	[0.0187]	[0.00477]	[0.0221]
Default +3	-0.0156**	0.195***	-0.0183**	0.200***	0.00620	0.191***	-0.000790	0.140***
	[0.00775]	[0.0203]	[0.00845]	[0.0293]	[0.00396]	[0.0181]	[0.00474]	[0.0214]
Default +4	-0.0171**	0.199***	-0.0261***	0.198***	0.00595	0.148***	-0.000151	0.0860***
	[0.00833]	[0.0206]	[0.00917]	[0.0298]	[0.00392]	[0.0179]	[0.00466]	[0.0210]
Default +5	-0.0207**	0.192***	-0.0340***	0.191***	0.00145	0.0775***	-0.00221	0.0127
	[0.00861]	[0.0211]	[0.00940]	[0.0299]	[0.00386]	[0.0177]	[0.00459]	[0.0208]
Default +6	-0.0239***	0.193***	-0.0355***	0.188***	-0.00275	0.0319*	-0.00375	-0.0206
	[0.00907]	[0.0213]	[0.00961]	[0.0293]	[0.00378]	[0.0176]	[0.00450]	[0.0205]
Default +7	-0.0193**	0.211***	-0.0291***	0.217***	-0.00281	0.00915	-0.00828*	-0.0215
	[0.00935]	[0.0217]	[0.00996]	[0.0307]	[0.00378]	[0.0176]	[0.00454]	[0.0205]
Default +8	-0.0204**	0.213***	-0.0307***	0.206***	0.000389	0.0132	-0.00401	-0.0285
	[0.00955]	[0.0221]	[0.0104]	[0.0303]	[0.00377]	[0.0176]	[0.00452]	[0.0206]
Default +9	-0.0128	0.177***	-0.0206*	0.181***	-0.00455	-0.0119	-0.00400	-0.0528**
	[0.0101]	[0.0229]	[0.0112]	[0.0312]	[0.00377]	[0.0177]	[0.00453]	[0.0205]
Default +10	-0.00734	0.158***	-0.0109	0.147***	-0.0101***	0.0205	-0.00629	0.00841
	[0.0104]	[0.0251]	[0.0116]	[0.0309]	[0.00378]	[0.0180]	[0.00453]	[0.0208]
Default +11	-0.00120	0.132***	-0.00715	0.144***	-0.00712*	-0.0185	-0.00422	-0.0151
	[0.0109]	[0.0268]	[0.0122]	[0.0342]	[0.00381]	[0.0184]	[0.00459]	[0.0215]
Default +12	-0.00235	0.120***	-0.0128	0.102***	-0.000840	-0.0171	0.00506	-0.0264
	[0.0108]	[0.0279]	[0.0129]	[0.0350]	[0.00384]	[0.0186]	[0.00461]	[0.0216]
Default +13	0.0133	0.131***	0.00747	0.111***	-0.00305	-0.0327*	0.00431	-0.0437*
	[0.0109]	[0.0296]	[0.0126]	[0.0372]	[0.00388]	[0.0191]	[0.00466]	[0.0225]
Default +14	0.0163	0.108***	0.00907	0.0574	-0.00883**	-0.0444**	-0.00268	-0.0354
	[0.0112]	[0.0317]	[0.0128]	[0.0366]	[0.00392]	[0.0195]	[0.00472]	[0.0229]
Default +15	0.0181	0.0984***	0.0288**	0.0820**	-0.0116***	-0.0336*	-0.00626	-0.0406*
	[0.0114]	[0.0332]	[0.0129]	[0.0389]	[0.00395]	[0.0199]	[0.00475]	[0.0232]
Default +16	0.0338***	0.0904***	0.0254**	0.0732*	-0.0116***	-0.0514**	-0.00509	-0.0406*
	[0.0115]	[0.0339]	[0.0126]	[0.0386]	[0.00399]	[0.0203]	[0.00480]	[0.0230]
Firm controls	No	No	Yes	Yes	No	No	Yes	Yes
Constant	0.177***	0.221***	-0.166***	-0.240*	0.0591***	0.111***	-0.0638***	-0.0387
	[0.000903]	[0.00995]	[0.0185]	[0.139]	[0.000509]	[0.00428]	[0.00534]	[0.0464]
Observations	13,399	1,153	10,229	722	246,928	11,794	188,840	8,977
R-squared	0.004	0.182	0.137	0.284	0.000	0.057	0.011	0.075
Number of firms	1,071	85	892	66	9,932	499	9,242	476

The dependent variable is the ratio of limit on lines of credit to long-term assets (col 1-4) and covenant violation dummy (col 5-8). Default + s is a dummy variable containing a 1 if the firm w ent into bankruptcy s periods after the period, 0 otherw ise. Estimation period is from the first quarter of 1996 to the fourth quarter of 2007.Estimations are done over a sample of non-bankrupt firms in odd-numbered columns, and bankrupt firms in even columns. Non-bankrupt firms w ere randomly assigned to a bankrupt firm in the same 2-digit SIC code industry to associate them w ith a bankruptcy dates. Specifications in columns 3, 4, 7, and 8 contain the follow ing firm time-varying controls: log of total assets, sales grow th, tangible assets to total assets, net profit margin, market to book value of equity, cash flow s to total assets, and capital expenditures to total assets. All estimations contain firm fixed effects

Table 3: Evolution of bank support to clients: Limits in lines of credit, covenant violations.

---

to firms that eventually went bust, and whether this is endogenous to bankruptcy, remains an open question.

	Panel A: Sales as % of total supplier sales				Panel B: Total accounts receivables to LT Assets			
	(1)	(2)	(3)	(4)	(5)	(6)	(7)	(8)
	Non bankrupt	Bankrupt	Non bankrupt	Bankrupt	Non bankrupt	Bankrupt	Non bankrupt	Bankrupt
Default	-0.00996	-0.0538**	-0.00238	-0.0704**	0.000380	-0.00567	0.00134	0.00682
	[0.00781]	[0.0256]	[0.00926]	[0.0325]	[0.00392]	[0.0146]	[0.00391]	[0.0155]
Default +1	-0.00331	-0.0801***	0.00358	-0.121***	0.00247	0.0134	0.00481	0.00406
	[0.00788]	[0.0237]	[0.00911]	[0.0282]	[0.00394]	[0.0133]	[0.00385]	[0.0133]
Default + 2	-0.00827	-0.0631***	0.000898	-0.0962***	0.00958**	0.0360***	0.00668*	0.0175
	[0.00798]	[0.0213]	[0.00934]	[0.0253]	[0.00399]	[0.0120]	[0.00394]	[0.0120]
Default +3	-0.00463	-0.0579***	0.00168	-0.0962***	0.00835**	0.0405***	0.00703*	0.0287**
	[0.00791]	[0.0207]	[0.00928]	[0.0241]	[0.00398]	[0.0118]	[0.00394]	[0.0118]
Default +4	-0.00486	-0.0635***	0.00170	-0.0902***	0.00406	0.0342***	0.00213	0.0227*
	[0.00787]	[0.0198]	[0.00938]	[0.0237]	[0.00397]	[0.0113]	[0.00398]	[0.0116]
Default +5	-0.000715	-0.0508**	0.0136	-0.0575**	0.00760*	0.0265**	0.000596	0.0269**
	[0.00799]	[0.0202]	[0.00933]	[0.0236]	[0.00403]	[0.0114]	[0.00393]	[0.0114]
Default +6	0.0110	-0.0480**	0.0233**	-0.0408*	0.00996**	0.0424***	-0.000758	0.0226**
	[0.00794]	[0.0190]	[0.00933]	[0.0219]	[0.00400]	[0.0107]	[0.00397]	[0.0106]
Default +7	0.00277	-0.0402**	0.0150	-0.0190	0.00870**	0.0348***	0.000745	0.0253**
	[0.00788]	[0.0191]	[0.00944]	[0.0225]	[0.00398]	[0.0109]	[0.00401]	[0.0112]
Default +8	0.00146	-0.0351*	0.0143	-0.0190	0.0115***	0.0276**	0.00813**	0.0198*
	[0.00791]	[0.0193]	[0.00928]	[0.0234]	[0.00400]	[0.0109]	[0.00396]	[0.0116]
Default +9	-0.00205	-0.0360*	0.00118	-0.0256	0.0177***	0.0318***	0.00774*	0.0179
	[0.00792]	[0.0198]	[0.00938]	[0.0235]	[0.00401]	[0.0112]	[0.00397]	[0.0116]
Default +10	-0.000462	-0.0508***	0.0123	-0.0186	0.0197***	0.0190*	0.00559	0.0131
	[0.00812]	[0.0197]	[0.00964]	[0.0231]	[0.00407]	[0.0112]	[0.00406]	[0.0116]
Default +11	0.00478	-0.0497**	0.0188*	-0.0250	0.0140***	0.0142	0.00767*	0.00922
	[0.00818]	[0.0198]	[0.00974]	[0.0244]	[0.00412]	[0.0111]	[0.00413]	[0.0117]
Default +12	0.0134	-0.0489**	0.0262***	-0.0203	0.00608	0.0255**	0.00546	0.0249**
	[0.00830]	[0.0208]	[0.00970]	[0.0251]	[0.00414]	[0.0116]	[0.00408]	[0.0120]
Default +13	0.0167**	-0.0280	0.0229**	-0.00252	0.00805*	0.0226**	0.00753*	0.00873
	[0.00843]	[0.0203]	[0.00986]	[0.0245]	[0.00421]	[0.0113]	[0.00412]	[0.0118]
Default +14	0.0277***	-0.0272	0.0269***	0.0150	0.0116***	0.0244**	0.00884**	0.00189
	[0.00851]	[0.0201]	[0.0100]	[0.0227]	[0.00423]	[0.0112]	[0.00420]	[0.0111]
Default +15	0.0332***	-0.0261	0.0316***	0.00495	0.000643	0.0128	0.00175	-0.00966
	[0.00869]	[0.0197]	[0.0101]	[0.0236]	[0.00434]	[0.0110]	[0.00422]	[0.0114]
Default +16	0.0309***	-0.0298	0.0250**	0.00655	-0.00587	0.0120	-0.00159	-0.0116
	[0.00864]	[0.0195]	[0.0102]	[0.0240]	[0.00429]	[0.0109]	[0.00425]	[0.0115]
Supplier controls	No	No	Yes	Yes	No	No	Yes	Yes
Client controls	No	No	Yes	Yes	No	No	Yes	Yes
Constant	0.588***	0.584***	0.646***	0.152***	0.162***	0.170***	-0.215***	-0.251***
	[0.000863]	[0.00256]	[0.0109]	[0.0557]	[0.000434]	[0.00139]	[0.00624]	[0.0299]
Observations	104,093	8,536	69,451	4,811	85,457	7,149	57,134	4,002
R-squared	0.000	0.006	0.013	0.072	0.001	0.008	0.282	0.311
No. of supp-cust pairs	3,095	510	2,553	378	2,535	422	2,101	317

The dependent variable is the proportion of sales to each customer as % of total sales of the supplier (col 1-4) and ratio of accounts receivables to long-term assets (col 5-8). Default + s is a dummy variable containing a 1 if the firm's client went into bankruptcy s periods after the period, 0 otherwise. Estimation period is from the first quarter of 1996 to the fourth quarter of 2007. Estimations are done over a supplier-customer pairs where the customer is non-bankrupt in odd-numbered columns, and where the customer went bankrupt in even columns. Non-bankrupt clients were randomly assigned to a bankrupt client in the same 2-digit SIC code industry to associate them with a bankruptcy dates. Specifications in columns 3, 4, 7, and 8 contain the following firm time-varying controls: log of total assets, sales growth, tangible assets to total assets, net profit margin, market to book value of equity, cash flows to total assets, and capital expenditures to total assets. All estimations contain supplier-customer fixed effects

Table 4: Evolution of sales and accounts receivables of suppliers.

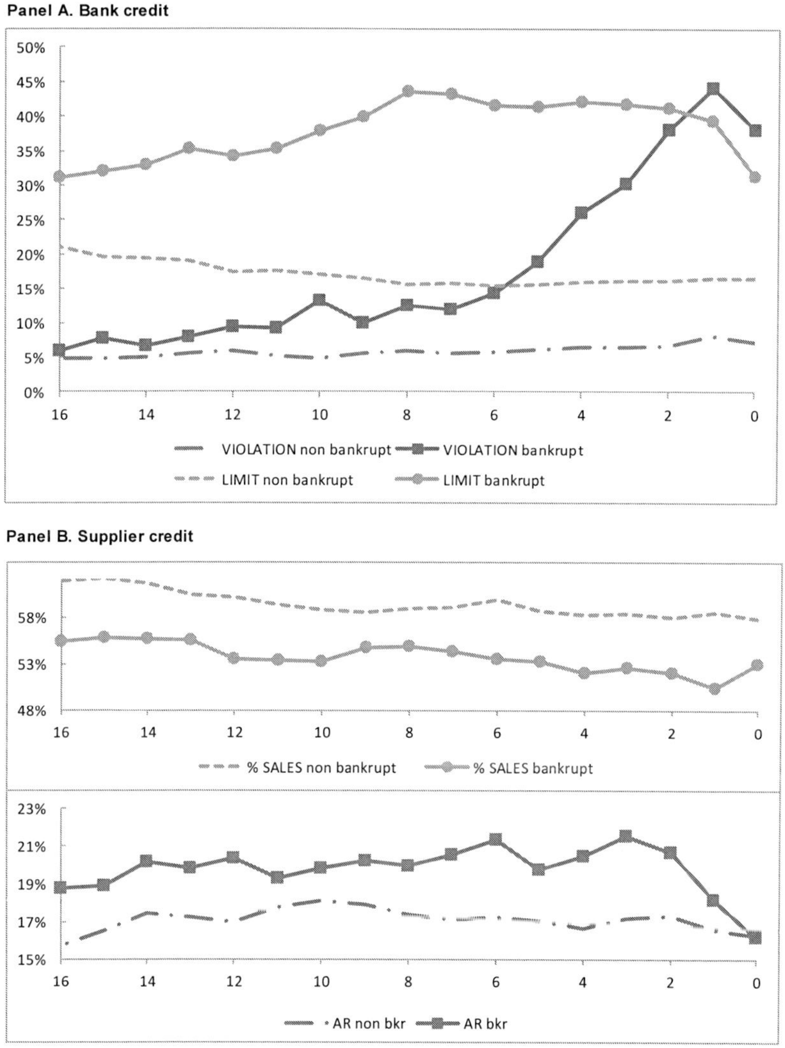

Panel A plots the constant term plus the estimated coefficients of the default coefficients in Table 3 (columns 1, 2, 5, and 6, respectively) and Panel B the corresponding values for Table 4. The horizontal axis is the time to bankruptcy. LIMIT is the limit on lines of credit, VIOLATION is a dummy for a violation on a financial covenant, AR is accounts receivable. % SALES is the sales, as % of total supplier sales, to the customer. LIMIT and AR are measured as percentage of long-term assets (i.e. assets 17 periods or more before bankruptcy)

Figure 2: Evolution of supply of credit in the periods leading to bankruptcy.

Panel A in Figure 2 also shows the evolution of covenant violations as firms approach bankruptcy. As far as 16 periods before bankruptcy, firms that eventually went bankrupt had a 1 to 2% higher propensity to violate covenants on their lines of credit, although these differences are not statistically significant. In fact, the observed decrease in limits roughly coincides with the period when the differences between covenant violations of bankrupt vs. non-bankrupt firms becomes statistically significant. This evidence is consistent with Roberts and Sufi's (2009) findings that banks are likely to renegotiate the terms of the loans after the first violation, and start to accelerate loans only after repeated violations.

Table 4 shows striking differences between banks and suppliers regarding the provision of credit to bankrupt firms. Sales to suppliers slowly fall by around 12% during the 16 quarters preceding bankruptcy, and the trend is always negative. In contrast, the proportion of sales to non-bankrupt firms is very stable. The ratio of accounts receivable to assets of supplier-customer pairs with a bankrupt customer also fall by a significant 7% over the periods leading to bankruptcy, contrasting with the stable long-term ratio of around 20% for supplier-customer pairs with healthy customers.

These results suggest that suppliers withdraw their support to distressed customers much earlier than banks do. This finding is consistent with two non-mutually exclusive explanations. One possibility is that suppliers have better or timelier information about the underlying credit quality of firms. Biais and Gollier (1997) exogenously assume that suppliers, by the mere nature of their business with clients, are more in contact with them and can therefore elicit information about their credit quality in a more timely manner than banks. Burkart and Ellingsen (2004) endogenize this information to the type of good lent by suppliers. Suppliers lend goods which cannot be diverted for private benefits (as opposed to cash lent by banks), but instead should be input for the production process of the firm. This means that suppliers learn from the orders of a given customer that he has the intention to produce.

Whether suppliers are better informed or not about the credit quality of their clients depends to a large extent on which type of banks the clients are dealing with. In fact, the relationship lending literature claims that through long relationships banks acquire soft information about their clients (e.g., Berger and Udell, 2002; Stein, 2002 and Berger et al, 2005). The features of the contract could also play a role on how informed banks are. For example, Rajan and Winton (1995) claim that covenants and collateral are introduced to debt contracts precisely as mechanisms to gather the information about deteriorating financial conditions of the firms. Our data does not have information about who the providers of the lines of credit are, so we cannot rule out completely the information advantage hypothesis. However, our results show that distressed firms are more likely to violate covenants on their debt, and still banks are increasing lines of credit. Thus, we believe that information advantage plays a limited role in the differences in behavior between different creditors.

The other explanation which is compatible with our results is that creditors have different incentives to support firms in financial difficulties due to differences in the contracts (implicit or explicit). We focus the remainder of the paper on examining the incentives of different types of suppliers to support the eventually failed firms.

IV. Creditor incentives under firm financial distress

In this section we focus on our sample of distressed firms that eventually end up in default, and analyze the incentives of different types of creditors to support their clients. We base our first hypothesis on theory by Wilner (2000), who shows that suppliers have an implicit equity stake in their clients which makes them dependent on future rents obtained from continuing the relationship. This dependence gives trade creditors larger incentives to grant concessions to customers in financial distress than a ceteris paribus supplier with no dependence relationship with their clients. Thus, our first hypothesis is the following:

H1: *All else equal, a supplier will provide more support to a client that purchases a higher proportion of his sales.*

In line with the idea that relationships are valuable, Cuñat (2007) shows that when clients are costly to replace suppliers increase trade credit provision to clients that are experiencing liquidity shocks. This model implies that in addition to the importance or dependence of the supplier on sales to a failed client, the concentration of the client's industry should also play a role. If the market of potential clients is very concentrated, it will become more difficult or costly to replace the failed client. This situation forces, as before, a supplier dependence on the client, which increases incentives to support the distressed clients. Our second hypothesis is therefore:

H2: *All else equal, suppliers with clients in concentrated markets are more likely to provide support to failed customers than suppliers that are in competitive markets.*

Following a different line of reasoning, a third stream of the literature finds that the characteristics of the supplied good determine the amount of credit that clients will receive from their suppliers. Differentiated goods, for example, have higher collateral value for the suppliers than for the general public as suppliers can redeploy them better than the general public (Franks and Maksimovic, 2005). This in turn may lead suppliers of differentiated goods to be more willing to support distressed firms. In the extreme, tailor-made goods for a specific customer could create a dependency of the suppliers on that particular customer of the type described before. These theories generate our third hypothesis, namely:

H3: *Suppliers of differentiated goods are more willing to support distressed firms than ceteris paribus suppliers of differentiated goods.*

To test the above hypotheses on our sample, we focus on the subsample of distressed firms and on suppliers' sales to each failed customer. The hypotheses suggest that when there is a dependency of the supplier on the failed customer, the supplier should have higher incentives to support the client for a longer period. We compare the evolution of the proportion of sales to a given customer and accounts receivables of suppliers under a dependency situation with their clients, relative to whenever there is not such a dependency relationship. For this purpose we estimate the following specification:

(2)

$$SuppVar_{ijt} = \alpha_{jt} + \beta_0 ClientDefault_{jt} + \sum_{s=0}^{3} \beta_s ClientDefYr_{jt+s}$$
$$+ \beta\delta_0 \left(Dep_{ij} * ClientDefault_{jt}\right) + \sum_{s=0}^{3} \delta_s (Dep_{ij} * ClientDefYr_{jt+s})$$
$$+ \Gamma * \mathrm{X}_{\mathrm{it}} + \Delta * Z_{jt} + \eta_{ijt}.$$

In this equation, the dependent variable $SuppVar_{ijt}$ refers to either the proportion of sales that supplier i purchases from client j, or the total accounts receivable of supplier i. $ClientDefault_{jt}$ is a dummy variable containing a one if client j defaulted in period t, or zero otherwise. $ClientDefYr_{jt+s}$ are four dummy variables containing a one if the customer default occurred in year s after the observation period (i.e., the dummy for year 0 takes the value of 1 if the default occurred 1, 2, 3, or 4 quarters after the observation period, and so on).[12] Dep_{ijt} measures the dependence of supplier i to client j in period t. Finally, X_{it} and Z_{jt} are matrices containing time-varying supplier and client characteristics, respectively. Whenever possible, we estimate equation (2) with client-quarter fixed effects in order to exploit the heterogeneity of suppliers that have relationships with the same client in the same quarter; otherwise we estimate the equation with client fixed effects.

We use three measures of the dependence of suppliers to specific clients. To test H1, our measure of dependence is a dummy taking the value of one whenever pre-default sales to client j by supplier i represent more than the median, zero otherwise. For H2, our dependent variable is a dummy taking a one whenever the suppliers deliver differentiated goods to the clients. To classify the industries of the supplier into differentiated goods, standardized goods, and services, we follow Burkart, Ellingsen and Giannetti (2011). Finally, to test H3, we classify a relationship as dependent whenever the Herfindahl index of market concentration for the client is above the median concentration. Because the temporal variation of the dependence measure for H3 depends on client characteristics, we cannot estimate the latter specification with client-quarter fixed effects; so we estimate it using client fixed effects.

The results of these estimations are found in Table 5; in each of Panels A, B, and C, respectively, we test hypotheses H1, H2, and H3. In general we find evidence to support each of our three hypotheses, as the interaction of the year to default dummies with the dependence variables are positive and significant in most cases. These results show that whenever there is a dependence relationship, the withdrawal of supplier support occurs later than for the average supplier relationship. Results are particularly strong whenever the client represented a large percentage of the supplier's sales, or the good provided by the supplier is differentiated. These results show that suppliers can be held up in some dependent relationships and forced to provide support to their clients.

[12] We cannot estimate these specifications using 17 quarter dummies as before due to sample restrictions: we do not have enough quarterly observations with balance sheet information of clients, suppliers, and their relationship. We separate the actual quarter of default because results in the previous sections show that behavior in this quarter is very different.

	Panel A. Dependence = Importance of Client						Panel B. Dependence = Differentiated goods					
	(1)	(2)	(3)	(4)	(5)	(6)	(7)	(8)	(9)	(10)	(11)	(12)
Dependent variable:	% Sales			AR / LT Assets			% Sales			AR / LT Assets		
Bankruptcy qtr	-0.0566	-0.111		-0.236*	-0.0181		-0.0514	-0.0753		-0.372*	-0.214	
	[0.0403]	[0.0903]		[0.123]	[0.0613]		[0.0398]	[0.0663]		[0.204]	[0.328]	
Year -1	-0.0848***	-0.0900**		-0.151***	-0.0291		-0.0811***	-0.0681***		-0.235***	-0.253*	
	[0.0182]	[0.0445]		[0.0553]	[0.0296]		[0.0180]	[0.0264]		[0.0903]	[0.132]	
Year -2	-0.0702***	-0.116**		-0.0387	-0.0519		-0.0631***	-0.0161		-0.0560	-0.213	
	[0.0163]	[0.0512]		[0.0499]	[0.0337]		[0.0161]	[0.0277]		[0.0800]	[0.140]	
Year -3	-0.0759***	-0.0497		-0.0299	-0.0181		-0.0716***	0.000792		-0.108	-0.304*	
	[0.0168]	[0.0768]		[0.0517]	[0.0574]		[0.0166]	[0.0314]		[0.0831]	[0.160]	
Year -4	-0.0410**	-0.0264		-0.0649	0.0568		-0.0359**	0.00255		-0.128	-0.301**	
	[0.0163]	[0.116]		[0.0496]	[0.113]		[0.0161]	[0.0306]		[0.0799]	[0.150]	
Dependent * (Bankruptcy qtr)		0.454***	0.770***		0.213**	0.359***		0.182*	0.0262		0.215	0.526
		[0.156]	[0.171]		[0.0949]	[0.127]		[0.0993]	[0.152]		[0.529]	[1.348]
Dependent * (Year -1)		0.239***	0.452***		0.0785	0.149**		0.146***	0.244***		0.295	0.596
		[0.0841]	[0.0941]		[0.0503]	[0.0721]		[0.0423]	[0.0598]		[0.219]	[0.424]
Dependent * (Year -2)		0.164	0.417*		0.0498	0.0458		0.0923**	0.130**		0.312	0.303
		[0.138]	[0.221]		[0.0804]	[0.160]		[0.0374]	[0.0530]		[0.191]	[0.327]
Dependent * (Year -3)		-0.199	-0.121		0.179**	0.189*		0.0399	0.0986*		0.353*	0.249
		[0.140]	[0.139]		[0.0882]	[0.104]		[0.0410]	[0.0583]		[0.206]	[0.328]
Dependent * (Year -4)		0.611***	0.544***		0.0198	0.126		0.0843**	0.0598		0.364*	0.375
		[0.182]	[0.167]		[0.138]	[0.127]		[0.0396]	[0.0525]		[0.195]	[0.308]
Supplier controls	No	Yes	No	No	Yes	No	No	Yes	Yes	No	Yes	Yes
Client controls	No	Yes	All	No	Yes	All	No	Yes	All	No	Yes	All
Observations	9,388	923	1,658	7,479	747	1,392	9,388	5,286	5,365	7,036	4,004	4,057
R-squared	0.005	0.131	0.060	0.002	0.179	0.023	0.029	0.104	0.122	0.006	0.030	0.035
Number of Clients	113	26		104	26		113	91		103	85	
Number of Client-quarters			738			680			1,416			1,273

	Panel C. Concentration of client market					
	(13)	(14)	(15)	(16)	(17)	(18)
Dependent variable:	% Sales			AR / LT Assets		
Bankruptcy qtr	-0.0354	-0.0358	0.0279	-0.175	-0.175	-0.0447
	[0.0405]	[0.0450]	[0.0553]	[0.204]	[0.237]	[0.290]
Year -1	-0.0611***	-0.0595***	0.00703	0.0129	0.0265	0.0687
	[0.0188]	[0.0207]	[0.0252]	[0.0927]	[0.107]	[0.127]
Year -2	-0.0628***	-0.0732***	0.0133	-0.00134	0.0159	-0.0429
	[0.0163]	[0.0178]	[0.0215]	[0.0796]	[0.0882]	[0.106]
Year -3	-0.0742***	-0.0792***	0.00874	-0.110	-0.0580	-0.0646
	[0.0168]	[0.0186]	[0.0234]	[0.0826]	[0.0933]	[0.115]
Year -4	-0.0422***	-0.0642***	0.0306	-0.144*	-0.112	-0.102
	[0.0163]	[0.0176]	[0.0221]	[0.0794]	[0.0866]	[0.107]
Dependent * (Bankruptcy qtr)		0.0227	-0.123		-0.0563	0.122
		[0.101]	[0.144]		[0.457]	[0.630]
Dependent * (Year -1)		0.0243	-0.00308		-0.119	-0.0176
		[0.0430]	[0.0553]		[0.191]	[0.245]
Dependent * (Year -2)		0.0814**	0.0563		-0.143	0.0774
		[0.0407]	[0.0538]		[0.187]	[0.245]
Dependent * (Year -3)		0.0504	0.0119		-0.270	-0.224
		[0.0417]	[0.0530]		[0.191]	[0.240]
Dependent * (Year -4)		0.161***	0.0505		-0.229	-0.108
		[0.0455]	[0.0553]		[0.211]	[0.252]
Supplier controls	No	No	Yes	No	No	Yes
Client controls	No	No	Yes	No	No	Yes
Observations	9,388	9,388	5,286	7,036	7,036	4,004
R-squared	0.008	0.010	0.055	0.018	0.019	0.033
Number of Clients	113	113	91	103	103	85

This table estimates the effect of dependent relationships on supplier support to a failed client. All estimations are done over the sample of suppliers with bankrupt clients. The dependent variables are the proportion of sales that a given supplier sells to the bankrupt client, as proportion of total supplier sales (% Sales), and the total accounts receivable to long term assets of the supplier. Bankruptcy qtr is a dummy containing a one for the quarter where bankruptcy occurred. Year -s is a dummy taking a one if the period occurred in year s leading to bankruptcy, zero otherwise. Dependent is a dummy variable taking a value of one whenever the supplier is dependent on the bankrupt client, according to the following definitions: Proportion of sales to the customer in Panel A, sales of differentiated goods in Panel B, and sales to client in concentrated market in Panel C. Supplier controls are the same as in Table 2. Client controls are log of total assets and net profit margin. All specifications control for client fixed effects except for those in columns 3, 6, 9, and 12, which control for client-quarter fixed effects.

Table 5: Supplier incentives in dependent relationships.

V. Conclusions

Using a sample of firms matched with their suppliers and detailed information on the use of bank lines of credit, we show that through lines of credit the average bank withdraws its financial support to clients in financial distress six quarters later than the average supplier. This is consistent with the non-contractual nature of trade credit, its consequent junior priority, the fact that trade credit is generally unsecured, and the lower diversification of suppliers' portfolios of clients. We also find that the average timing of withdrawal of bank support coincides with the period in which covenant violations for defaulted firms become statistically different to zero, consistent with banks withdrawing their support as soon as the signals provided by covenants about the financial situation of the firms become sufficiently informative. In contrast, the earlier withdrawal of supplier support is consistent with an information advantage of suppliers relative to banks (Biais and Gollier, 1997; Burkart and Ellingsen, 2004).

Under some situations, however, the supplier has an important implicit stake in its customer's business. These situations force suppliers to support their customers for a longer time period, and with larger financial commitments. This phenomenon is fully consistent with Wilner's (2000) and Cuñat's models which explain the higher equilibrium price of trade credit (relative to bank credit) with an insurance premium paid by the potentially benefitted customers. Our empirical findings show how such a dependency situation arises whenever the vendor sells a large fraction of its produce to one particular customer, whenever the market for the supplier's product is concentrated in a few clients, or whenever the product of the supplier is differentiated.

References

Andrade, G., and S. Kaplan. 1998. "How costly is financial (not economic) distress? Evidence from highly leveraged transactions that became distressed." *The Journal of Finance* 53: 1443-1493.

Araten, M., and M. Jacobs, Jr. 2001. "Loan equivalents for revolving credits and advised lines." *The Journal of the Risk Management Association* April: 34-39.

Baxter, N. D. 1967. "Leverage, risk of ruin and the cost of capital." *The Journal of Finance* 22: 395-403.

Berger, A. N., and G. F. Udell. 2002. "Small business credit availability and relationship lending: the importance of bank organizational structure." *Econ. J.* 112: 32–53.

Berger, A.N., N.H. Miller, M.A. Petersen, R.G. Rajan, and J.C. Stein. 2005. "Does function follow organizational form? Evidence from the lending practices of large and small banks." *Journal of Financial Economics* 76: 237–269.

Biais, B., and C. Gollier. 1997. "Trade credit and credit rationing." *Review of Financial Studies* 10: 903-937.

Burkart, M., and T. Ellingsen. 2004. "In-Kind Finance: A theory of trade credit." *American Economic Review* 94: 569-590.

Burkart, M., T. Ellingsen, and M. Giannetti. 2010. "What you sell is what you lend? Explaining trade credit contracts." *Review of Financial Studies* forthcoming.

Carbo Valverde, S., F. Rodríguez-Fernández, and U. Gregory F. 2008. "Bank Lending, Financing Constraints and SME Investment." *21st Australasian Finance and Banking Conference 2008 Paper*.

Cook, L. 1999. "Trade credit and bank finance: Financing small businesses in Russia." *Journal of Business Venturing* 14: 493-518.

Cuñat, V. 2007. "Trade credit: Suppliers as debt collectors and insurance providers." *Review of Financial Studies* 20 (2): 491-527.

Cuñat, V., and E. Garcia-Appendini. 2012. "Trade credit and its role in entrepreneurial finance", in "Handbook of Entrepreneurial Finance", edited by D. Cumming, *Oxford University Press*: 526-557.

Dahiya, S., A. Saunders, and A. Srinivasan. 2003. "Financial Distress and Bank Lending Relationships." *The Journal of Finance* 58 (1): 375-399.

Evans, J., and T. Koch. 2007. "Surviving chapter 11: Why small firms prefer supplier financing." *Journal of Economics and Finance* 31 (2): 186-206.

Franks, J., and K. Nyborg. 1996. "Control rights, debt structure, and the loss of private benefits: The case of the UK insolvency code." *Review of Financial Studies* 9 (4): 1165-1210.

Garcia-Appendini, E. 2010. "Supplier certification and trade credit." Working paper, Bocconi University.

Garcia-Appendini, E., and J. Montoriol-Garriga. 2012. "Firms as liquidity providers: Evidence from the 2007-2008 financial crisis." *Journal of Financial Economics*, forthcoming.

Garvin, L. T. 1996. "Credit, Information, and Trust in the Law of Sales: The Credit Seller's Right of Reclamation." *UCLA Law Review* 44: 247–360.

Giannetti, M. 2003. "Do Better Institutions Mitigate Agency Problems? Evidence from Corporate Finance Choices." *Journal of Financial and Quantitative Analysis* 38 (1): 185-212.

Hertzel, M. G., Z. L., Micah, S. Officer, and K. J. Rodgers. 2008. "Inter-firm linkages and the wealth effects of financial distress along the supply chain." *Journal of Financial Economics* 87: 374-387.

Jacobs, M. Jr., and P. Bag. 2011. "What do We Know About Exposure at Default on Contingent Credit Lines? – A Survey of the Literature, Empirical Analysis and Models." *Journal of Advanced Studies in FinanceVolume* 2 Issue 2 (1).

Jimenez, G., J. A. Lopez, and J. Saurina. 2009. "Emprical Analysis of Corporate Credit Lines." *Review of Financial Studies* 22 (12): 5069-5098.

Jorion, P., and G. Zhang. 2009. "Credit Contagion from Counterparty Risk." *The Journal of Finance* 64 (5): 2053-2087.

Longhofer, S. D., and J. A.C. Santos. 2000. "The Importance of Bank Seniority for Relationship Lending" *Journal of Financial Intermediation* 9: 57–89.

Longhofer, S. D., and J. A.C. Santos. 2003. "The paradox of priority." *Financial Management* Spring: 69-81.

McMillan, J., and C. Woodruff. 1999. "Interfirm Relationships and Informal Credit in Vietnam." *The Quarterly Journal of Economics* 114 (4): 1285-1320.

Molina, C. A., and L. A. Preve. 2012. "An Empirical Analysis of the Effect of Financial Distress on Trade Credit." *Financial Management* Spring: 187-205.

Petersen, M. A., and R. G. Rajan. 1997. "Trade credit: Theories and evidence." *Review of Financial Studies* 10: 661–691.

Rajan, R. G., and A. Winton. 1995. "Covenants and Collateral as Incentives to Monitor." *The Journal of Finance* 50 (4): 1113-1146.

Roberts, M. R., and A. Sufi. 2009. "Control rights and capital structure: An empirical investigation." *The Journal of Finance* 66(4): 1657-1695.

Stein, J. C. 2002. "Information production and capital allocation: decentralized versus hierarchical firms." *Journal of Finance* 57: 1891–1921.

Sufi, A. 2009. "Bank lines of credit in corporate finance: An empirical analysis." *Review of Financial Studies* 22: 1057-1088.

Titman, S., and R. Wessels. 1988. "The Determinants of Capital Structure Choice." *The Journal of Finance* 43 (1): 1-19.

Wilner, B. S. 2000. "The Exploitation of Relationships in Financial Distress: The Case of Trade Credit.'' *Journal of Finance* 55 (1).

CHAPTER SEVEN

CREDIT RISK MANAGEMENT AT BASLER KANTONALBANK: A PRACTITIONER'S VIEW

ARMIN LANDERER[1]

I. Introduction

Today's market environment is extraordinarily demanding for banks and their lending business. There are a lot of challenges, e.g. low interest rates, a fierce competition by banks in order to use their capacities built over years, companies generating high liquidity and large corporates increasingly tapping capital markets to finance their operations and investments and thus substituting banks as a refinancing source.

For Basler Kantonalbank, the lending business traditionally is a core activity and main source for generating income. The activities in the lending business comprise the following main customer groups:

- Mortgage financing for private customers
- Mortgage financing for professional investors
- Financing of small and mid-sized companies
- Financing of large / listed corporates in Switzerland

In the following, the article tries to give an overview of the implemented and planned activities by Basler Kantonalbank showing how we try to ensure a sustainable and profitable growth of volume and profit of the lending business as well as preserve and constantly improve the quality of the credit portfolio.

---

[1] The author is from Basler Kantonalbank, Güterstrasse 127, CH-4000 Basel, phone +41 61 266 29 20, mail: armin.landerer@bkb.ch.

Content

- Basler Kantonalbank – Key Figures
- Stakeholders in today's Lending Business
- Regulatory Environment in Switzerland regarding Credit Risk
- Credit Risk Management – Activities by Basler Kantonalbank
- Conclusion

II. Basler Kantonalbank – Key Figures

The Basler Kantonalbank group consists of the parent company Basler Kantonalbank and the subsidiary Bank Coop. Basler Kantonalbank currently holds 57,6 % of Bank Coop. Basler Kantonalbank is the 3rd largest Cantonal Bank in Switzerland with regard to total assets. The activities comprise mainly retail banking with 18 locations in the Canton of Basel Stadt, private banking, and corporate banking as well as the full range of securities and foreign exchange trading services for private and corporate clients. Bank Coop is primarily a retail bank with 33 locations all over Switzerland focusing mainly on mortgage financing.

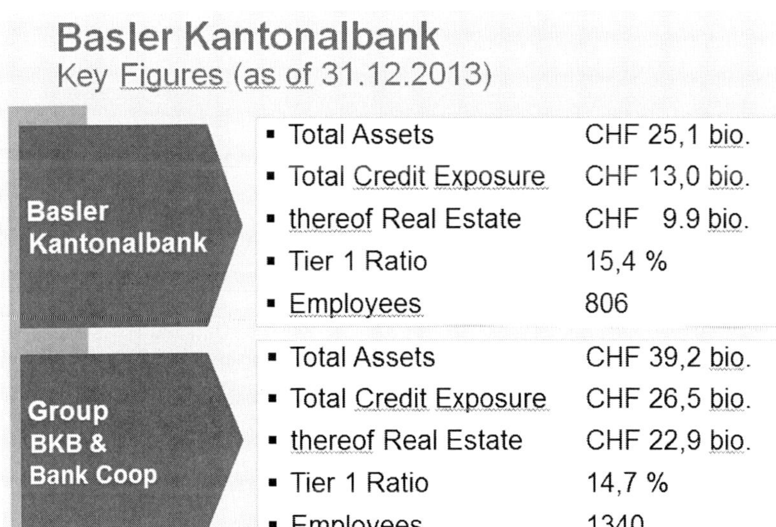

Figure 7-1: The respective key figures.

III. Stakeholders in today's Lending business

In the lending business there are several parties involved with opposed interests. The big challenge consists of finding an efficient and effective way to balance the quest to generate sustainable and profitable lending business growth on the one hand side and to conserve - or even better - to constantly improve credit portfolio quality on the other side.

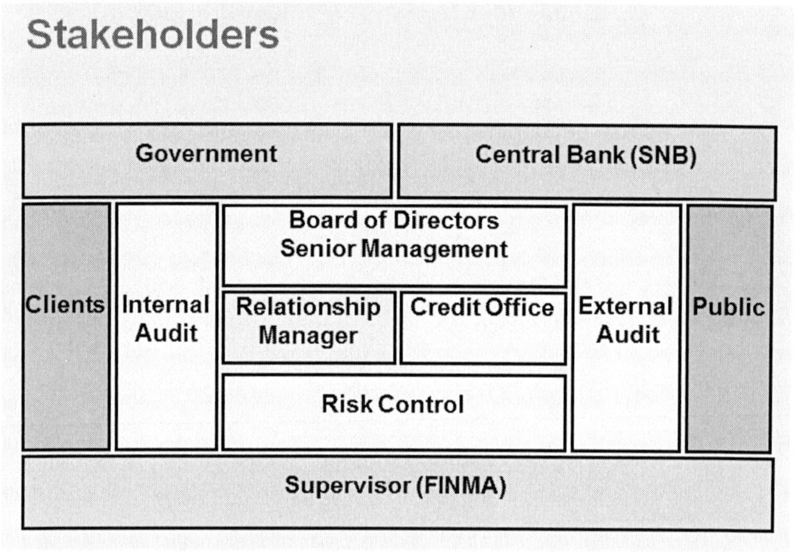

Figure 7-2: Following you can find an overview with the main stakeholders involved in the lending business:

Government, the Central Bank (Swiss National Bank) and especially the Supervisory Authority (Swiss Financial Market Supervisory Authority - FINMA) are the mayor players responsible for setting, overviewing and enforcing the regulatory framework.

Especially for a Cantonal Bank the expectations of the Public regarding functional and social responsibility as well as a risk conscience business guidance of the bank and its executives and staff are high.

The Client is in a powerful negotiation position vis-à-vis the bank regarding credit terms – if he has a good credit quality. Especially in a market environment with low interest rates and a very high liquidity allowing listed companies to tap capital markets for financing their operations and investments. This leads to the substitution of traditional bank financing by capital market transactions which creates additional pressure on credit terms and margins.

Then there are the stakeholders who are leading the process of analyzing, assessing, supervising and managing credit risk. Especially the Credit Office is the direct counterparty for the Client Advisor in order to find a suitable credit structure which adheres to the credit policy as well as to the business goals to generate profitable growth as set by Senior Management.

Risk Control checks data quality on a transaction level as well as the adherence to the internal credit regulations as set by the bank. Internal and External Audit periodically check the lending process regarding adherence to the internal and regulatory rules.

IV. Regulatory Environment in Switzerland regarding Credit Risk

In the following we show an overview of the main topics which are actually on the priority list of banks in order to comply with the necessary regulatory requirements as well as to further develop their credit risk management capabilities. There are intense activities by the regulatory authorities mainly regarding the following topics:

- Mortgage Lending for private individuals and professional investors
- Managing credit concentration risks - Large Corporate exposures
- Increasing demand for extensive data requirements

1. Mortgage Lending for private individuals and professional investors

Actually, the main concern by the regulatory authorities is the overheating of the real estate market in Switzerland. Especially, there are a few hot spots where the development of prices for private and commercial real estate have reached historically high levels and still tend to increase further. The high demand for real estate is mainly fueled by low interest rates and a high number of immigrants. To slow down the growth of real estate financing by banks and other financial institutions providing mortgage financing, regulatory authorities have implemented several decisive measures, e.g. higher equity requirements for the customer, imperative amortization of mortgages within certain time periods as well as additional capital requirements for the institution providing financing with the aim to increase financing costs for the banks as well as for the client.

A lot of banks in Switzerland still generate growth rates in mortgage financing which are well above market growth. Regulatory Authorities try to influence this development with distinctive measures in order to slow down the fast expansion of the growth of mortgage financing. Few of them have already been implemented. But there are other additional possible measures being discussed which would have different degrees of influence on the possible customer to buy real estate as well as on the financial institutions. Basically the two levers are increasing capital requirements for both parties involved (customer and financial institution) and tightening requirements regarding amortization.

The development of the prices in the Swiss real estate market is periodically shown by the two main indicators

- **UBS Swiss Real Estate Bubble Index** - published on a quarterly basis
- **Real Estate Report by the ETH Zurich and comparis.ch** – published on a bi-annual basis

In order to follow closely the real estate market in the region of Northwestern Switzerland – basically the home turf of Basler Kantonalbank – we have launched the

- **BKB Eigenheimindex Region Nordwestschweiz** (index for real estate in the region of northwestern Switzerland) – published on a bi-annual basis

allowing us and other interested parties, e.g. our customers, real estate investors and promoters, academic and economic publishers to get a clear picture of the development of the real estate market in our region.

2. Managing credit concentration risks - Large Corporate exposures

The main concern is to avoid concentration risks in the credit portfolio. There are different views on this subject. First of all, there is the regulatory perspective which allows regulatory concentration ceilings up to 25 % per counterparty. Secondly, there is the economic view which forces a bank to stipulate their maximum concentration risk in the credit policy. Thirdly, one can view concentration risks from a nominal perspective, meaning that credit concentrations have to be in a certain relation to the bank's nominal capital base. We at Basler Kantonalbank do not exploit the existing regulatory possibilities and we try to limit credit exposures in a healthy relation to the bank's nominal and economical capital base.

3. Increasing demand for extensive data requirements

Supervisory authorities are increasingly demanding data and reports regarding credit exposures, i.e. scope, quantity, granularity, periodicity and quality.

The banks must improve data management in order to

- better assess and report risk,
- better manage risk in case of market changes, and
- get relevant statistics for improvements in risk measurement.

This forces banks to strengthen their middle and back offices as well as Credit Risk and Risk Control units, both in terms of headcount and required skills. In order to face increased requirements, substantial investments in software and tools are necessary. As a consequence, this trend is accompanied by higher costs – one of the factors reducing revenue margins. The positive effect is that the data and reports required by the supervisory authorities is key information which also the bank needs in order to manage the credit portfolio.

V. Credit Risk Management – Activities by Basler Kantonalbank

At Basler Kantonalbank, in the lending business and credit risk management we focus on the following three main areas in order to assure a consistent and powerful credit risk management.

1. Managing the single lending transaction

- Rating system (every counterparty is being rated by a rating tool called 'Credit Master')
- Data quality on a transaction level (completeness, consistency, accuracy)
- Credit structuring (terms and conditions, covenants etc.)

- «Economic Value Added» view of the single transaction (risk-/reward profile)

2. Managing the Credit Portfolio

- Implementation of a Credit Portfolio Steering Tool allowing the bank to define strategic credit levels (risk appetite), e.g. maximum exposure per economic sector, maximum credit concentration in an economic sector and maximum exposure per client in an economic sector. Every single large credit transaction is being rated and debt capacity as well as the debt to equity ratio are being calculated. All these factors are then entered into a scoring system which supports the decision making bank authorities with the necessary data
- Implementation of an Early Warning System in order to monitor private clients as well as small and mid-sized companies and to identify a deterioration in the financial health of borrowers at a very early stage allowing the bank to define and implement appropriate measures together with our customer
- Stress testing of Credit Portfolio (in accordance with the criteria set by FINMA)
- Constant Optimization of Credit Portfolio quality by reduction of concentration risks, optimization of credit structures, refining rating assessments, increasing requirements of financial quality of borrowers, close supervision of Real Estate credit exposures in hot spots
- MbO-goal for every Client Advisor (supervision and management of his credit portfolio)

3. Optimisation of Processes

- Customer Segmentation (clear separation of private and corporate clients)
- Corporate Governance (main goal: ensure checks and balances between client advisor, credit officer and risk controller)
- Data Quality Management (addressed by a strategic project within the bank)
- Collection and Reporting of «Exceptions to Policy» (automated process in place)
- Central input of financial statements by the Credit Office thus ensuring data quality and consistency

VI. Conclusion

Today's regulatory environment in general and especially in the lending business is very demanding and challenging. We at Basler Kantonalbank have implemented various tools and systems in order to put us in a position to efficiently and effectively analyze, assess, supervise and manage credit risk. This is an on-going process which demands constant management attention and full engagement of all parties involved. Since credit risk is the main risk component in our bank we will continue our high engagement in further developing our systems and our capabilities of managing credit risk.

CHAPTER EIGHT

FORECASTING DISTRESS IN EUROPEAN SME PORTFOLIOS

DIMITRA MICHALA, THEOHARRY GRAMMATIKOS AND SARA FERREIRA FILIPE[1]

Abstract

SMEs play a crucial role in most economies. In the Organization for Economic Cooperation and Development (OECD) countries, SMEs account for 95% of all enterprises and generate two-thirds of employment. In the European Union in particular, SMEs represent 99% of all enterprises and contribute to more than half of the value-added created by businesses. Despite their importance, SME credit risk remains largely unexplored by the academic literature, mainly due to their information

---

[1] Dimitra Michala (dimitra.michala@uni.lu) is doctoral researcher in Luxembourg School of Finance at University of Luxembourg. Theoharry Grammatikos (theoharry.grammatikos@uni.lu) is Professor of Finance in Luxembourg School of Finance at University of Luxembourg. Sara Ferreira Filipe (sara.ferreira@uni.lu) is post-doctoral researcher in Luxembourg School of Finance at University of Luxembourg. We would like to thank Jos Van Bommel, Michel Dietsch (discussant), Federico Galizia, Ruben Garcia Cespedes (discussant), Victoria Golikova (discussant), Jean-Daniel Guigou, Helmut Kraemer-Eis, Edward Olding, and participants in the 6th Annual EIBURS Meeting, the LSF Internal Seminar series, the International Conference on Economic and Social Development (Moscow Higher School of Economics), the Second Credit Analysis and Risk Management Conference (University of Basel), and the XXI Finance Forum (IE Business School) for precious comments. Special thanks to Mounir Shal for help with the database. This research is financially supported by the European Investment Bank University Research Sponsorship Program. All errors are our own.

opaqueness and lack of available data. In this paper, we explore a unique dataset that allows new insights into the European SME sector and its credit risk characteristics. First, our sample includes a very high number of micro companies. This focus on the micro sector is important, as nine out of ten European SMEs are micro-enterprises. Second, we include SMEs from eight European economies and examine distress within regions, allowing for regional comparisons and uncovering regional vulnerabilities, unlike earlier studies of SME credit risk, which have focused on a single economy. Third, we consider systematic factors, such as the macro-economy, bank lending conditions, and legal aspects. Hence, we are able not only to compute individual distress probabilities, but also to capture changes in overall distress rates and co-movements during economic cycles.

Our paper therefore contributes to the overall literature on corporate credit risk, and on SME risk in particular. It is well known that, unlike larger corporations with easier access to capital markets, SMEs face more challenges in their credit risk modelling. In fact, widely used structural market-based models for credit evaluation, such as the distance-to-default measure inspired by Merton (1974), cannot be applied in the SME setting. Instead, empirical predictive models such as credit scoring approaches (i.e. Altman, 1968) are the most common.

In the early credit rating literature, academics mostly use accounting ratios to predict firm distress. The first credit scoring study that focuses on small businesses is Edminster (1972), who analyzes nineteen financial ratios and develops a model using multivariate discriminant analysis. Recently the need for SME-specific research has become pressing, in particular with the implications of Basel's II special treatment requirements for SME exposures and the high number of distressed SMEs during the crisis. In line with these new concerns, Altman and Sabato (2007) develop a one-year default prediction model for SMEs using only accounting information. They apply panel logit estimation on a sample of around 2,000 US firms over the period 1994-2002 and find that their model outperforms generic corporate models such as Altman's Z-score (Altman and Hotchkiss, 2005).

Moreover, Grunert et al. (2005) and other authors have noted the possibility of using qualitative variables in default prediction models to improve discrimination. Stein (2002) is the first to investigate the importance of "soft" information in borrower-bank relationships. Specifically in the case of SMEs, where there is usually a problem of scarcity of reliable "hard" financial information, such non-financial elements can be very useful in distress prediction. Altman et al. (2010)

combine both qualitative and financial information in a default prediction model for SMEs. By applying multi-period logit estimation to a large sample of UK SMEs for the period 2000-2007, they find that data relating to legal action by creditors, company filings, and audit reports/opinions significantly increase the performance of their model. Such information though is not always available well in advance to predict default in a timely manner.

Another strand of literature, though not focusing on SMEs, analyses the additional benefit of using macroeconomic variables to forecast distress. Carling et al. (2007) find that the output gap, the yield curve and consumers' expectation add significant predictive power to distress models. Duffie et al. (2007) incorporate macroeconomic covariates to estimate conditional probabilities of corporate default for a sample of US listed industrial firms. Similarly, Campbell et al. (2008) introduce the macroeconomic environment through financial market variables. Nam et al. (2008) use specifically the volatility of the exchange rate and Koopman et al. (2009) condition on business cycle effects, bank lending conditions and financial market variables. Jacobson et al. (2013) use a large Swedish dataset and find that macroeconomic variables are important for explaining the time-varying default likelihoods, whereas firm-specific variables rank firms according to their relative riskiness. Authors have also noted the importance of industry effects: For instance, Chava and Jarrow (2004) observe improving forecasting performance by including industry groupings in their models.

In an early study, Berger and Udell (1998) discuss the impact of the macroeconomic environment on small firms. Some years later, Glennon and Nigro (2005) and Altman et al. (2010) are the first to examine business cycle effects on SMEs defaults in particular. Glennon and Nigro (2005), using a dataset of US loans guaranteed by the Small Business Administration Scheme, include business cycle dummy variables, the industrial production index growth and rates of regional business bankruptcies to capture regional and industry economic conditions on the default hazard. They find that the success or failure of a small loan is closely related to both regional and industrial economic conditions. Altman et al. (2010) use sector-level failure rates and also report a significant relationship with failure probability. Our study differs from previous ones since we examine a larger variety of systematic factors, ranging from exchange rates to bank lending conditions, and use a wider sample that includes SMEs from different European countries, allowing for regional models and comparisons.

We follow Shumway (2001) and estimate the probability of distress over the next year using a multi-period logit model. We assume that the marginal probability of distress (or hazard rate) over next year follows a logistic distribution and is given by:

$$h(t|x_{i,t-1}) = P(Y_{i,t} = 1|x_{i,t-1}) = \frac{1}{1 + \exp(-\beta x_{i,t-1} - \gamma y_{t-1})} \quad (1)$$

where $Y_{i,t}$ is an indicator that equals one if the firm is distressed in year t, $\beta x_{i,t-1}$ is a function of firm-specific characteristics that includes a vector of firm-specific variables $x_{i,t-1}$ known at the end of the previous year and γy_{t-1} is the baseline hazard function that includes the systematic variables y_{t-1} (same for all firms in the same economy).

In order to estimate the multi-period logit model, we need an indicator of distress (dependent variable) and a set of predictors (independent variables). We use the Amadeus and Orbis Europe databases (both available from Bureau Van Dijk) to detect the status of each firm in each year and extract the raw data that include financial and qualitative information. Finally, we use the European Statistical Service's (Eurostat), the European Central Bank's (ECB), the World Bank and Datastream databases for the systematic variables.

Because of the European focus of the study, we adopt the European Commission's definition for SMEs, according to which SMEs are companies that have less than 250 employees and either annual turnover up to €50 million or total assets up to €43 million. Our estimation sample consists of 2,721,861 firm-years observations (644,234 firms) out of which 49,355 are distressed. SMEs come from eight European countries, namely Czech Republic, France, Germany, Italy, Poland, Portugal, Spain and the United Kingdom. We keep a random one tenth of the firms from each country as a hold-out sample. The hold-out sample consists of 304,037 firm-year observations (71,823 firms) out of which 5,487 are distressed.

A firm-year is "distressed" if the following two conditions are met: (i) it is the last firm-year for which we have available financial statements before the firm leaves the sample; and (ii) the firm appears with one of the following statuses: defaulted, in receivership, bankrupt, or in liquidation. If no status information is available, we consider only the cases where the firm leaving the sample has negative equity in its last year, following Boss's (2010) definition of stock-based insolvency and Davydenko's (2012) definition of economic default. A firm-year is "healthy" in all other cases (i.e., if a firm drops from the sample due to merger). We construct the distress indicator as follows: it equals one for the distressed firm-years and zero for the healthy ones.

Concerning the accounting data, we calculate financial ratios from nine categories: liquidity, profitability, interest coverage, leverage, activity, cash flow, growth, asset utilization and employees efficiency. We choose the ratios mainly based on suggestions from past literature, but we also test less established ones. The total number of ratios examined is 70. A list is available upon request. After we calculate the 70 candidate ratios, we follow univariate analysis, correlation analysis and a forward stepwise selection procedure to select the best performing ratios.

Recent studies though (Grunert et al., 2004; Altman et al., 2010) find that accounting ratios are not sufficient to predict SME distress risk and that including firm size and qualitative variables can improve predictive power. For this reason, we also account for size, industry type, number of shareholders, location, legal form and age.

As for the systematic dependencies, we use country-specific values and examine business cycle variables, bank lending conditions, the financial market and insolvency codes measures. Since these variables are usually reported with a higher than annual frequency (quarterly, monthly or daily), we need to annualize or take averages in some cases. Finally, we also form and examine interaction effects between industry dummies, systematic variables, firm size, and systematic variables.

We estimate five models for the period 2000-2009. Model I includes only the idiosyncratic variables (accounting ratios, size, dummy for SMEs with more than two shareholders and dummy for SMEs in urban areas), model II includes both the idiosyncratic and the systematic variables, model III includes additionally the industry dummies, model IV includes some interaction terms, and, finally, model V includes age (available for a smaller sample). Panel A of Table 5 presents the estimated coefficients and chi-square values for the five alternative model specifications.

Table 1

Distress Prediction Models

Panel A. Estimation Results

The models are estimated for 2000-2009 data with yearly observations using the multi-period logit technique. All firm-specific variables are lagged by one year. The data set includes SMEs from eight European economies. Parameter estimates are given first followed by chi-square values in parentheses.

	Model I		Model II		Model III		Model IV		Model V	
Earnings before taxes to total assets	-0.755***	(-15.65)	-0.770***	(-15.89)	-0.763***	(-15.53)	-0.779***	(-15.99)	-0.777***	(-14.92)
EBITDA to interest expenses	-0.0000453***	(-14.98)	-0.0000450***	(-14.49)	-0.0000451***	(-14.58)	-0.0000441***	(-14.38)	-0.000045***	(-14.20)
Current liabilities to total assets	1.381***	(101.27)	1.420***	(103.81)	1.417***	(102.97)	1.409***	(101.04)	1.38***	(95.92)
Cash flow to current liabilities	-0.480***	(-8.99)	-0.485***	(-9.14)	-0.491***	(-9.16)	-0.475***	(-9.00)	-0.517***	(-9.22)
Turnover to total liabilities	-0.182***	(-36.96)	-0.177***	(-36.08)	-0.176***	(-35.56)	-0.182***	(-35.56)	-0.187***	(-35.64)
Size (ln(totals assets))	-0.127***	(-30.88)	-0.0940***	(-22.95)	-0.0913***	(-22.14)	-0.109***	(-23.13)	-0.097***	(-20.18)
Dummy equal to 1 if shareholders are more than 2	-0.291***	(-23.53)	-0.274***	(-21.99)	-0.272***	(-21.76)	-0.270***	(-21.50)	-0.225***	(-17.54)
Dummy equal to 1 if SME is located in an urban area	0.132***	(10.24)	0.141***	(10.85)	0.144***	(11.01)	0.153***	(11.54)	0.175***	(13.01)
FX rate (% change)			-1,686.8***	(-59.04)	-1,689.9***	(-59.01)	-2,627.20***	(-68.63)	-2,695.82***	(-69.51)
Unemployment			1.883***	(12.39)	1.914***	(12.58)	4.802***	(28.84)	4.345***	(25.82)
Economic sentiment indicator			-0.0259***	(-35.03)	-0.0258***	(-34.90)	-0.0388***	(-48.72)	-0.0386***	(-46.76)
Loans granted to non-financial sector (% change)			-4.414***	(-58.29)	-4.407***	(-58.07)	-5.246***	(-53.94)	-5.226***	(-54.84)
Years to resolve insolvency proceedings			0.0949***	(27.40)	0.0958***	(27.57)	0.1211***	(25.80)	0.1209***	(25.75)
Industry 1 (Agriculture, Mining, Manufacturing)							0.0442***	(3.48)	0.0938***	(7.26)
Industry 2 (Utilities, Transportation, Communication)					-0.0762***	(-3.56)				
Industry 3 (Construction)					0.0798***	(5.84)	0.1035***	(8.06)	0.0782***	(6.01)
Industry 4 (Trade)					-0.0295*	(-2.50)				
Industry 5 (Accommodation and Food)					0.212***	(10.18)	0.251***	(12.25)	0.3169***	(15.49)
Small firm* FX rate (% change)							1,796.63***	(35.16)	1,737.00***	(33.17)
Small firm* unemployment							-10.495***	(-37.76)	-10.591***	(-37.41)
Small firm* economic sentiment indicator							0.0146***	(30.15)	0.0151***	(30.47)
Small firm* loans to non-financial sector (% ch.)							1.771***	(10.93)	1.639***	(10.24)
Small firm* years to resolve insolvency proceedings							-0.0493***	(-6.79)	-0.0673***	(-8.95)
Medium firm* FX rate (% change)							1,936.71***	(20.51)	1,975.46***	(19.98)
Medium firm* unemployment							-11.241***	(-15.40)	-12.091***	(-15.97)
Medium firm* economic sentiment indicator							0.0174***	(16.96)	0.0196***	(18.36)
Medium firm* loans to non-financial sector (% ch.)							4.084***	(14.02)	3.766***	(12.94)
Medium firm* years to resolve insolvency proceedings							-0.1392***	(-9.81)	-0.1605***	(-10.94)
Age									-0.0133***	(-17.30)
Age (3-9)									0.5501***	(43.76)
Constant	-4.675***	(-140.65)	-2.479***	(-29.79)	-2.523***	(-30.26)	-1.6732***	(-19.07)	-1.9558***	(-21.45)

	Model I	Model II	Model III	Model IV	Model V
Firm-year observations	2,721,861	2,721,861	2,721,861	2,721,861	2,652,157
Firms	644,234	644,234	644,234	644,234	620,872
Distressed firms	49,355	49,355	49,355	49,355	47,841
Pseudo R-squared	0.147	0.171	0.171	0.178	0.187
Log likelihood	-210,601.30	-204,638.50	-204,538.30	202,880.11	194,837.44
Wald test	78,110.8***	84,259.5***	84,526.8***	85,305.9	81,789.3***
Likelihood ratio test		11,925.57***	200.45***	3,316.36	16,085.34***
* p<0.05, ** p<0.01, *** p<0.001					
Panel B. In-sample prediction tests					
Hosmer-Lemeshow test: Percentage of the 49,355 distressed firms predicted in each decile in the year of their distress.					
Decile					
1 to 5	11.38%	11.09%	10.96%	10.67%	10.24%
6	5.28%	5.16%	5.09%	5.01%	5.27%
7	7.50%	7.15%	7.28%	7.27%	7.33%
8	11.20%	11.16%	11.25%	10.91%	10.33%
9	17.46%	17.86%	17.84%	17.83%	17.34%
10	47.17%	47.58%	47.57%	48.32%	49.49%
8 to 10	75.83%	76.59%	76.66%	77.06%	77.16%
9 to 10	64.63%	65.44%	65.41%	66.15%	66.83%
Area under the ROC curve	0.8241	0.8382	0.8386	0.8431	0.8571
Panel C. Out-of-sample prediction tests					
A hold-out sample of 71,823 European SMEs (304,037 firm-year observations) is used.					
Hosmer-Lemeshow test: Percentage of the 5,487 distressed firms predicted in each decile in the year of their distress.					
Decile					
1 to 5	11.46%	11.35%	11.26%	10.30%	10.15%
6	5.41%	4.76%	4.59%	5.41%	5.39%
7	7.58%	7.62%	7.91%	6.74%	7.63%
8	11.24%	10.53%	10.66%	11.45%	10.71%
9	17.51%	18.70%	18.53%	18.15%	17.16%
10	46.78%	47.04%	47.04%	47.95%	48.95%
8 to 10	75.54%	76.27%	76.23%	77.55%	76.82%
9 to 10	64.30%	65.74%	65.57%	66.10%	66.11%
Area under the ROC curve	0.8234	0.8369	0.8373	0.8437	0.8472

In model I, all firm-specific variables are significant and have the expected signs. Specifically, the probability of distress is negatively related to profitability (earnings before taxes to total assets), coverage (EBITDA to interest expenses), cash flow (cash flow to current liabilities) and activity (turnover to total liabilities) and positively related to leverage (current liabilities to total assets). The probability of distress is a decreasing function of the firm size (natural logarithm of total assets), indicating that as the firms become larger, they are less likely to undergo distress. Two additional interesting findings are that SMEs with less than three shareholders and SMEs in urban areas are riskier on average. The vast majority of SMEs have less than three shareholders but it seems that SMEs with more shareholders receive higher capital support in difficult times. This effect dominates the higher administrative costs that the existence of more shareholders may entail. A possible explanation for the higher risk of SMEs in urban areas is that these companies face higher competition (due to geographical proximity) and pay higher rents than their counterparts in the countryside. These effects seem to dominate the larger customer base available for urban SMEs.[2]

In model II, the firm-specific variables retain their significance and signs once the systematic variables are added. We identify five systematic variables as doing the best overall job in predicting distress, namely the FX rate change, the unemployment, the economic sentiment indicator, and the change in bank lending. All systematic variables have significant coefficients and the expected signs. Specifically, an appreciation of the currency, an increase in the economic sentiment indicator and an increase in the lending by banks result in lower distress rates whereas an increase in unemployment and in the years to resolve insolvency result in higher distress rates.

The effect of currency appreciation can be explained since European SMEs are mainly local market players and most often import raw materials and other supplies instead of exporting goods. Thus, an appreciation of the local currency makes these imports cheaper. Concerning the economic sentiment indicator, it reflects current conditions across the business sectors of the local economy. Since an increase in the indicator means better economic climate, it is negatively related to the distress rate. A similar logic holds for bank lending. An increase in bank lending growth means better access to finance for SMEs. Concerning

---

[2] Dietsch and Petey (2006) show a similar effect. Specifically, they find evidence from French SMEs that more attractive and wealthy regions demonstrate higher distress rates on average.

unemployment, an increase in its rate signals a worsening economy and is positively related to distress.

At this point, we need to elaborate on the effect of the bankruptcy laws on distress risk. Davydenko and Franks (2008) examine defaults in France, Germany and the U.K. and find differences in bankruptcy codes among these countries to be important determinants of outcomes of the defaults. We find a positive relation between the length of proceedings and distress risk. The more years it takes to resolve an insolvency case, the less friendly the code is supposed to be and the less likely for the firm to survive during the process. This finding is in accordance with evidence from the World Bank that longer proceedings are usually associated with higher costs and reduce creditors' chances of recovering outstanding debt.

Moving to model III, the firm-specific and systematic variables retain both their signs and significance and all industry dummies, except for industry 1 (Agriculture, Mining, Manufacturing), enter with significant coefficients. Concerning the signs of the industry dummy coefficients, industries 2 (Utilities, Transportation, Communication) and 4 (Trade) are negatively related to distress and industry 3 (Construction) and 5 (Accommodation and Food) are positively related to distress. From the sizes of the estimated coefficients, we rank the industries according to their estimated probability of distress (from largest to smallest) as follows: industry 5 (Accommodation and Food), industry 3 (Construction), industry 6 (Other services), industry 4 (Trade), industry 2 (Utilities, Transportation, Communication).

In model IV, we report results with interaction effects, in addition to the variables of model III. Specifically, we first test interaction effects between systematic variables and industry dummies, between systematic variables and size, and finally, between industry dummies and size. We find that the interaction effects that are most important in terms of performance improvement are between systematic variables and size dummies and report only these results for reasons of parsimony. From the coefficients of the interaction effects it is obvious that the distress probability of relatively larger SMEs (small and medium firms) is less sensitive to the systematic factors than the distress probability of the smallest SMEs (micro firms). I.e., we investigate how the effect of a bank lending change differs for the small and medium firms compared to micro firms. When we introduce interaction effects, the negative coefficient of the bank lending change increases in absolute size, demonstrating the increased sensitivity of micro firms to such a change. On the other hand, the additional effect of the bank lending change for small firms is positive (but still lower in absolute terms), and even more positive for medium firms. Thus, for the relatively larger SMEs, the same change in bank lending influences their distress probability less (but to the same direction) compared to micro firms. All other interaction effects display similar patterns.

In model V, we introduce firm age and test its effect on distress probability for a slightly smaller sample for which we have available data on age. We find, in accordance with previous literature, that older firms are safer.

In order to evaluate the performance of our models, we perform in-sample and out-of-sample testing. We employ two widely used measures, the Hosmer and Lemeshow grouping based on estimated distress probabilities and the area under the Receiver Operating Characteristic (ROC) curve.

According to the Hosmer and Lemeshow method, the estimated distress probabilities for each year are ranked and divided into deciles. Out of the ten groups created (each one containing the 1/10 of the firms in that year), the first group has the smallest average estimated distress probability and the last the largest. Next, we aggregate the number of distressed firms in each decile for each year over 2000-2009 and calculate the corresponding percentages of the distressed firms in each decile. The area under the ROC curve (AUC) is constructed from the estimated distress probabilities versus the actual status of the firms in each year for all possible cut-off probability values. The AUC ranges from zero to one. We should note at this point that the Hosmer and Lemeshow method assesses mainly calibration and the AUC assesses discrimination. We believe that our models' accuracy should be evaluated by considering both calibration and discrimination and for this reason we employ both tests.

Panel B of Table 5 presents the results of the in-sample tests. According to the Hosmer and Lemeshow grouping, the percentage of distressed firms in the last three deciles increases from model I to model II (75.83% to 76.59%). Also, the percentage of distressed firms in the first five deciles drops (11.38% to 11.09%). This shows that adding the systematic variables improves performance both in terms of an increase in the correct classification of distressed firms and a decrease in the incorrect classification of healthy firms. AUC also increases from 0.8241 to 0.8382. This result is better than those achieved by previous studies in the literature. Specifically in Altman et al. (2010) this figure ranges between 0.78 and 0.80. When it comes to model III, it only modestly outperforms model II. Specifically, by taking industry effects into account, the AUC remains almost the same and the percentage of distressed firms in the last three deciles increases slightly (76.59% to 76.66%). Given these results, controlling for industry effects improves performance only marginally, once we have already accounted for systematic factors. When we add interaction effects between size and systematic factors, we notice a further increase in the percentage of distressed firms in the last three deciles (76.66% to 77.06%). AUC also increases from 0.8386 to 0.8431. Thus, once again, the involvement of systematic variables improves prediction accuracy. Moving to model V, it seems that age also helps slightly.

Panel C of Table 5 presents the results of the out-of-sample tests. Out-of-sample testing is challenging since improvements in the in-sample fit can be a result of over-fitting of the original data. We use the coefficients estimates from the original models to predict distress for the hold-out sample. Results follow the same pattern as before.

To further demonstrate the importance of systematic variables in distress prediction, Figure 1 plots the aggregate probability of distress for the whole sample period. The graph shows that in model I, where only firm-specific variables are included, the estimated probabilities of distress are relatively stable over time, following a smooth upward trend. It is the systematic variables (present in models II, III and IV) that shift the mean of the distress distribution and are able to capture distress clustering during recessions. When systematic variables are included, distress rates vary greatly with the business cycle, increasing on downturns and lowering on upturns. These findings are in accordance with Jacobson et al.'s (2013) study for Sweden. They show that firm-specific variables account for the cross-section of the default distribution while the macroeconomic variables shift its mean in each period. Also, they find that industry effects offer small gains in their models in terms of forecasting accuracy.

In unreported results, we split our sample in regional groups and find that SMEs across Europe are vulnerable to the same idiosyncratic factors but identify regional variations in the importance of macro variables. We also split our sample in four rolling window periods (each one lasting five years) and find that whereas sensitivities to idiosyncratic factors remain relatively stable over time, coefficients of systematic variables are more volatile, responding to changes in the prevailing macroeconomic conditions. Industry effects in many cases yield insignificant and rather unstable coefficients. Finally, we test the performance of our models with a battery of out-of-sample tests.

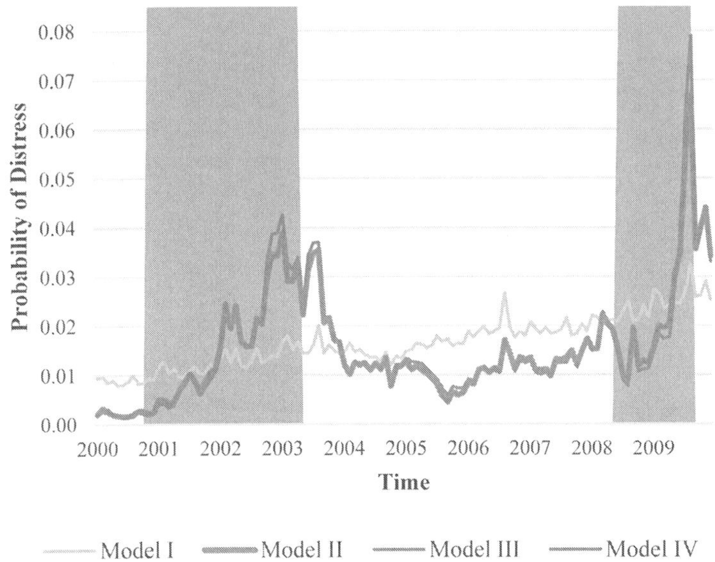

Figure 8-1. Aggregate probability of distress. The figure plots the aggregate probability of distress for firms in the overall sample. We define it as the simple average probability of distress of all firms. The columns denote recession periods in the Euro area, as indicated by OECD.

References

Altman, E. I. 1968. "Financial Ratios, Discriminant Analysis and the Prediction of Corporate Bankruptcy." *The Journal of Finance* 23 (4): 589-609.

Altman, E. I., and E. Hotchkiss. 2005. *Corporate Financial Distress and Bankruptcy*. 3rd ed. Wiley.

Altman, E. I., and G. Sabato. 2007. "Modelling Credit Risk for SMEs: Evidence from the U.S. Market." *Abacus* 43 (3): 332-357.

Altman, E. I., G. Sabato, and N. Wilson. 2010. "The Value of Non-Financial Information in SME Risk Management." *Journal of Credit Risk* 6 (2): 95-127.

Berger, A. N., and G. F. Udell. 2006. "A More Complete Conceptual Framework about SME Finance." *Journal of Banking & Finance* 301 (1): 2945-2966.

Campbell, J. Y., J. Hilscher, and J. Szilagyi. 2008. "In Search of Distress Risk." *The Journal of Finance* 63 (6): 2899-2939.

Carling, K., T. Jacobson, J. Lindé, and K. Roszbach. 2007. "Corporate Credit Risk Modeling and the Macroeconomy." *Journal of Banking & Finance* 31 (3): 845–868.

Chava, S., and R. Jarrow. 2004. "Bankruptcy Prediction with Industry Effects." *Review of Finance* 8 (4): 537–569.

Davydenko, S. A. 2012. "When Do Firms Default? A Study of the Default Boundary." Working Paper.

Davydenko, S. A., and J. R. Franks. 2008. "Do Bankruptcy Codes Matter? A Study of Defaults in France, Germany, and the U.K." *The Journal of Finance* 63 (2): 568-608.

Dietsch, M., and J. Petey. 2004. "Should SME Exposures be treated as Retail or Corporate Exposures? A Comparative Analysis of Default Probabilities and Asset Correlations in French and German SMEs." *Journal of Banking & Finance* 28 (4): 773-788.

Duffie, D., L. Saita, and K. Wang. 2007. "Multi-period Corporate Default Prediction with Stochastic Covariates." *Journal of Financial Economics* 83 (3): 635–665.

Edminster, R. O. 1972. "An Empirical Test of Financial Ratio Analysis for Small Business Failure Prediction." *The Journal of Financial and Quantitative Analysis* 7 (2): 1477-1493.

Glennon, D., and P. Nigro. 2005. "Measuring the Default Risk of Small Business Loans: A Survival Analysis Approach." *Journal of Money, Credit and Banking* 37 (5): 923–947.

Grunert J., L. Norden, and M. Weber. 2005. "The role of non-financial factors in internal credit ratings." *Journal of Banking & Finance* 29 (2): 509-531.

Jacobson, T., J. Lindé, and K. Roszbach. 2013. "Firm Default and Aggregate Fluctuations." *Journal of the European Economic Association* 11 (4): 942-972.

Koopman, S. J., R. Kräussl, A. Lucas, and A. B. Monteiro. 2009. "Credit Cycles and Macrofundamentals." *Journal of Empirical Finance* 16 (1): 42-54.

Merton, R. C. 1974. "On the Pricing of Corporate Debt: The Risk Structure of Interest Rates." *The Journal of Finance* 29(2): 449–470.

Nam, C. W., T. S. Kim, N. J. Park, and H. K. Lee. 2008. "Bankruptcy Prediction Using a Discrete-Time Duration Model Incorporating Temporal and Macroeconomic Dependencies." *Journal of Forecasting* 27 (6): 493–506.

Stein, J. C. 2002. “Information Production and Capital Allocation: Decentralized versus Hierarchical Firms.” *The Journal of Finance* 57 (5): 1891-1921.

CHAPTER NINE

SUMMARY OF "AN EMPIRICAL ANALYSIS OF PRICED SYSTEMATIC RISK ON BONDS AND MARKET SEGMENTATION"

AUSTIN MURPHY, TERRY BENZSCHAWEL AND LIANG FU[1]

Abstract

This research investigates the existence of market segmentation between the equity and credit markets in terms of pricing systematic risk. It discovers risk-adjusted net returns of about 5% above Treasury rates could have been earned over the 2003-2011 interval from a strategy of buying (selling) non-distressed bonds with higher (lower) contributions to the risk of portfolios consisting of only fixed-income instruments. In particular, the high arbitrage profits are found when a portfolio is formed consisting of long (short) positions on bonds having ex-ante measured return co-variances with an index of pure fixed-income instrument in the highest (lowest) quartile. The investment alphas are statistically significant from zero whether risk is measured by Sharpe's (1964) traditional Capital Asset Pricing Model (CAPM) betas or by Fama and French's (1995) 3-factor model.

The positive significant alphas for this strategy for arbitraging bond market segmentation are also found using a new measure of systematic risk that adjusts for the survival bias caused by still existing bonds never having displayed the market return co-variation associated with an actual default. The new measure of systematic risk is based on research by

[1] Austin Murphy (Ph.D. Finance, University of Georgia) is a Professor of Finance at Oakland University. Terry Benzschawel is Managing Director of Bond Portfolio Analysis (Citibank), and Liang Fu (Ph.D. Accounting, University of Florida) is an Assistant Professor of Accounting at Oakland University.

Murphy, Fu, and Benzschawel (2013), who have shown this survivorship bias can result in large underestimates of bonds' true systematic risk. Those investigators have developed several procedures for adjusting for this problem that are utilized in this research to ensure the arbitrage opportunities are indeed feasible and not just an artifact of biased statistical tests.

Kapudia and Pu (2012) have previously discovered evidence of temporally varying lead-lag relationships between the stocks and bonds of individual firms, but they left it to future research to determine if risk-adjusted profits can be earned for such a lack of contemporaneous market integration. It is hypothesized here that such relationships reflect temporal variation in the compensation required for the contribution to the risk of pure credit portfolios and to more diversified asset groups that include equities. In particular, the yield premiums required for credit market risk may diverge daily and weekly from those required by diversified investors in patterns which could be predictable. This particular hypothesis merits the investigation that is carried out in the research summarized here.

The empirical examination of this study focuses on an 8-year horizon of 2003-2011 using monthly observations on both yield spreads and bond returns. The findings indicate that the abnormal returns available from buying (selling) bonds with greater (lower) contributions to the risk of pure fixed-income portfolios are statistically significant only for non-distressed bonds. It is hypothesized that distressed debts are generally not held by the institutional investors like banks that are largely restricted to investing in non-distressed credit instruments, and thus the contribution of distressed bonds to the risk of pure fixed-income portfolios is not priced in the market because they tend to be held by more diversified investors.

The study finds the higher (lower) risk-adjusted returns on non-distressed bonds with higher (lower) credit betas are not statistically significant over the 2003-2007 subinterval. This finding implies a high level of confidence in generating arbitrage profits from arbitraging the market segmentation might only exist over longer holding periods.

However, the insignificant 2003-2007 results might also stem from phenomena that were unique to that time interval. For instance, Murphy (2011) has shown that inadequate regulation and disclosure in the market for credit default swaps (CDSs) motivated large financial institutions to maximize the systematic risk of the CDS debt insurance they sold because their counterparties were unaware of their resulting default risk and because those fixed-income investors didn't have to bear the full losses from systematic risk due to their limited liability and the possibility of government bailouts. This incentive for profitable risk maximization might lead to the underpricing of CDSs on debts with greater co-movement with bond indexes that would be similar to those institutions' investment positions. Arbitrage would then cause the debts underlying those CDSs with artificially low insurance premiums to have lower yield spreads than otherwise. Such effects might offset the impact of other investors constrained to pure fixed-income portfolios bidding down (up) the prices of those bonds contributing more (less) to their own risk, thereby explaining the statistically insignificant results over that earliest subinterval. On the other hand, the existence of significantly higher yields and risk-adjusted returns to bonds with higher betas measured relative to pure fixed-income portfolios over the second subinterval might stem from increased regulator and counterparty monitoring of the CDS market after the financial crisis that may have reduced the incentive to risk maximization for CDS sellers.

In conclusion, it does appear that diversified investors should maximize (minimize) their fixed-income holding of bonds with higher (lower) pure credit betas in order to maximize their risk-adjusted returns, at least long term. To eliminate any higher taxation of such assets held by individual investors subject to tax, they might optimally be held in tax-exempt accounts like 401ks.

This strategy might also apply to publically-traded financial institutions such as banks which have shareholders diversified into both the equity and credit markets. Those institutions might optimally mitigate the risk and costs of bankruptcy by using hedging techniques that are independent of the market segmentation found in this study. For instance, they could purchase put options on their own stock, thereby enabling them to increase their equity capital during any adverse scenario (Murphy, 1997). The latter strategy has already been used in a limited modified fashion by some banks which issued reverse convertibles allowing the issuer to put stock to their bondholders if the share price fell below a specified strike price.

Sufficient arbitrage of the market segmentation found in this research would eventually eliminate the abnormal returns available from such strategies. However, as indicated by Peters (2003), it is always uncertain whether inefficient pricing in the market might disappear. Thus, arbitrage trading based on past return relationships may not always persist.

References

Eugene F., and K. French. 1995. "Size and Book-to-Market Factors in Earnings and Stock Returns." *Journal of Finance* 50: 131-155.

Nikong K., and X. Pu. 2012. "Limited Arbitrage between Equity and Credit Markets." *Journal of Financial Economics* 105: 542-564.

Murphy A. 1997. "Buying Put Options to Insure Against Bankruptcy." *Journal of Financial Engineering* 6: 307-320.

Murphy A. 2000. *Scientific Investment Analysis*. Quorum Books: Westport.

Murphy A. 2011. "The Effect of Allowing Unregulated Credit Default Swaps." *International Review of Applied Financial Issues and Policy* 2: 620-631.

Murphy A., L. Fu, and T. Benzschawel. 2013. "Systematic Risk and Yield Premiums in the Bond Market." SSRN working paper, http://ssrn.com/abstract=2303970.

Peters E. 2003. "Simple and Complex Market Inefficiencies: Integrating Efficient Markets, Behavioral Finance, and Complexity." *Journal of Behavioral Finance* 4.

Sharpe W. 1964. "Capital Asset Prices: A Theory of Market Equilibrium under Conditions of Risk." *Journal of Finance* 19: 425-442.

CHAPTER TEN

THE FINANCIAL STABILITY BOARD (FSB) WORK AGENDA AND ITS LINK TO CREDIT RISK

IMENE RAHMOUNI-ROUSSEAU[1]

I. Introduction

Over the past five years, the Financial Stability Board (FSB) has co-ordinated a range of reforms addressing the fault lines from the crisis. When fully implemented, these reforms will considerably improve the resilience of financial systems and increase financial stability globally. They strengthen financial institutions, in particular systemic ones, and create the conditions for well-functioning markets. They take a holistic view of regulation by targeting not only banks but also other non-bank financial institutions. Overall, the cross-country, cross-sector view of the FSB and its wide reach[2] contribute to reduce the potential for regulatory arbitrage.

In addition, because regulation, no matter how sophisticated, cannot anticipate all situations and incentives leading to a build-up of risks, another important pillar of the FSB is its forward-looking process of identification of vulnerabilities in the global financial system. Credit risk is among the most scrutinised elements of the vulnerabilities assessment, owing to its asymmetric nature and its potential to interact with other risks, such as interest rate risk, market risk and liquidity risk.

---

[1] Imene Rahmouni-Rousseau is a member of the Financial Stability Board Secretariat. The views expressed here are solely those of the author and do not in any way represent the views of the Financial Stability Board.

[2] In addition to its wide membership, the FSB also has six Regional Consultative Groups (RCGs) involving jurisdictions that are outside of the FSB membership. The RCGs aim at increasing inclusiveness in the development of global financial policy initiatives.

As the repair of the financial system draws nearer to completion and the financial cycle swings further towards risk taking, monitoring financial innovation and changes in market structures and credit intermediation channels is essential to detect at an early stage the vulnerabilities that could lead to future financial instability.

II. The FSB regulatory work agenda: past and present

1. What is the FSB?

The FSB was re-established in 2009 to co-ordinate at the international level the work of national financial authorities and international standard setting bodies in the field of regulation, supervision and other financial sector policies[3]. The high degree of integration and interconnectedness of modern financial systems created the strong need for a co-ordinating body for global financial regulation. Indeed, failure to coordinate effectively national policies would lead to financial fragmentation and regulatory arbitrage, which would in turn increase future financial stability risks and adversely impact economic growth.

In contrast with larger international organisations, the FSB has remained a lean organisation, with around 25 staff members working in its Basel-based Secretariat, but the FSB can in turn leverage on a number of unique strengths:

- *Membership*: The FSB membership is particularly inclusive. It is composed of national financial authorities – central banks, banking and market supervisors, ministries of finance - from 24 jurisdictions, as well as international financial institutions such as the IMF, the World Bank, the OECD and the Bank for International Settlements, as well as international standard setting bodies such as the Basel Committee.
- *Working methods*: The FSB uses the knowledge and expertise of its 70 member agencies, which provides it with access to several thousand economists and financial sector experts. These experts are mobilised through an array of technical working groups which are supported by the FSB Secretariat.
- *Decision making*: the FSB operates by consensus. Its decisions result from a process where experts from member institutions are closely

[3] FSB (2009), "Financial Stability Board Charter", subsequently amended and restated in 2012. Both documents are available on www.financialstabilityboard.org.

associated through the technical working groups, facilitating collective ownership of proposals.

- *Follow-up process:* While the FSB decisions are not legally binding, there are several mechanisms in place, including continuous implementation monitoring and a programme of peer reviews, to ensure that members adhere to international standards.

2. Strengthening the resilience of financial institutions

In the run-up to the financial crisis, banks became severely undercapitalised relative to the risks they were taking and paid insufficient attention to liquidity risk. When the crisis hit, these vulnerabilities left the banks unable to cope with financial stress and made the recourse to official capital and liquidity backstops unavoidable. An essential element of post-crisis reforms therefore mandates higher capital and liquidity buffers for banks, to protect the system against shocks that cannot be anticipated.

The Basel 3 standards agreed in 2010 substantially raise the quantity and quality of capital required from banks. In addition, the counter-cyclical buffer introduces an additional capital buffer that can be built up during booms and drawn down in times of stress in order to mitigate pro-cyclicality and influence bank risk taking behaviour. The new leverage ratio will act as a backstop to mitigate the uncertainties related to the calibration of risk weights, and avoid that banks use internal models in order to lower artificially their capital requirements. Finally, Basel 3 also introduces for the first time global liquidity standards for liquidity that will apply to banks in all key markets.

3. Ending Too Big To Fail (TBTF)

The "too-big-to-fail" problem arises when the threatened failure of a financial institution forces public authorities to bail it out to avoid large-scale financial instability and long-lasting economic damage. Beyond being costly in the short-term, the use of taxpayer money for bank bail-outs distorts incentives and creates moral hazard in the long-term. The FSB has designed a three-pronged agenda to address the TBTF problem, including higher loss-absorbency, credible resolution and more intensive supervision:

- *Higher loss absorbency:* financial institutions that are designated as systemically important will need to hold additional capital buffers, that are commensurate with the greater economic impact of their failure compared with institutions that are smaller and less central to the system. The FSB regularly publishes lists of global systemically important financial institutions[4].

- *Supervision:* systemically important institutions should be subject to more intensive and effective supervisory oversight. Since regulation takes time to adapt, stronger supervision is needed to support regulatory changes on an ongoing basis as the financial system evolves and innovates. The FSB reports on Supervisory Intensity and Effectiveness highlight the features and the progress towards this new approach to supervision[5].
- *Resolution:* Authorities should be in a position to resolve financial institutions in an orderly manner without bailing them out and while maintaining continuity of their vital economic functions. To be credible, orderly resolution requires changes in national legal frameworks to enact the necessary tools and powers for authorities, as well as changes in the financial institutions, in particular changes to their organisational structure and cross-border operations to make them more resolvable. The FSB Key Attributes set out the essential features that should be part of the resolution regimes of all jurisdictions[6].

4. Discouraging regulatory arbitrage

Regulations that are narrowly designed are prone to regulatory arbitrage. Thanks to its cross-sector membership, the FSB has taken a keen interest in ensuring the cross-sector consistency of regulation as well as expanding, as needed, the regulatory perimeter. Two key examples of international policy development illustrate this approach:

- *Cross-sector approach to TBTF:* While the last crisis mostly featured large failures in the banking system, there is the potential for other types of financial institutions, including insurance companies, asset managers and financial market infrastructure, such as central counterparties, to create systemic risk in the future. Therefore, the FSB TBTF policies have extended to each of these key sectors. While

---

[4] FSB (2013), "2013 update of group of global systemically important banks (G-SIBs)" available on www.financialstabilityboard.org. Updates are posted on publications/ policy areas/ systemically important financial institutions (SIFIs).

[5] These reports are available on www.financialstabilityboard.org under Publications/ Policy Areas/ Supervision.

[6] FSB (2011), "Key Attributes of Effective Resolution Regimes for Financial Institutions", available on www.financialstabilityboard.org, section publications/ policy areas/ resolution planning.

the assessment of systemic importance and the policy measures recommended can vary across sectors to reflect the nature and degree of risks posed to the global financial system, the overarching objective is to reduce the negative externalities from the distress or disorderly failure of financial institutions, regardless of the institutional sector in which risky activities are undertaken[7].

- *Shadow Banking:* The "shadow banking system" can broadly be described as credit intermediation involving entities and activities (fully or partially) outside the regular banking system or non-bank credit intermediation in short. Such intermediation, appropriately conducted, provides a valuable alternative to bank funding that supports real economic activity. But experience from the crisis demonstrates the capacity for some non-bank entities to operate on a large scale in ways that create bank-like risks to financial stability. The FSB has put in place an annual monitoring process that screens non-bank financial intermediation globally in order to identify and measure shadow banking risks[8]. In addition, a policy framework is being developed to contain risks related to shadow banking activities, with a focus on money market funds, securitisation, securities financing operations, and other shadow banking entities[9].

5. Creating the conditions for well-functioning markets

A move to market-based finance emphasises the importance of having continuously-functioning markets. The goal is to ensure that markets remain liquid and their participants well protected against default by one of their participants, so that markets can be sources of strength rather than weakness, even at times of stress. Three examples of reforms that contribute to increase market resilience are:

---

[7] FSB (2013), "Global systemically important insurers (G-SIIs) and the policy measures that will apply to them" and FSB (2014), "Consultative Document: Assessment Methodologies for Identifying Non-Bank Non-Insurer Global Systemically Important Financial Institutions", both available on www.financialstabilityboard.org , publications/ policy areas/ systemically important financial institutions (SIFIs).

[8] FSB (2013), "Global Shadow Banking Monitoring Report 2013" and other annual reports available on www.financialstabilityboard.org, publications/ policy areas/ shadow banking.

[9] FSB (2013), "Strengthening Oversight and Regulation of Shadow Banking: An Overview of Policy Recommendations", available on www.financialstabilityboard.org, publications/ policy areas/ shadow banking.

- *Transparency*: Market discipline only works if there is sufficient transparency about risk exposures, so that market participants can develop their own informed assessment of risks. As an example, the Enhanced Disclosure Task Force (EDTF), in which the FSB brought together banks, investors and other stakeholders, aims at improving the risk disclosures made by banks to investors and counterparties[10].
- *Data architecture*: Similarly, a sound data infrastructure supports an accurate measurement of risks and ultimately better market functioning. FSB-sponsored initiatives in this area include, for example, the global Legal Entity Identifier (LEI) for uniquely identifying counterparties to financial transactions and the systematic reporting of all derivative transactions to trade repositories.
- *OTC derivatives*: The global financial crisis of 2008 highlighted structural deficiencies in the lightly regulated and mostly opaque over-the-counter derivatives market. New requirements to trade on organised platforms and report transactions to trade repositories increase market-wide transparency. The potential for contagion through interconnectedness of participants on derivatives markets will also be reduced by mandating the use of central counterparties. These entities interpose themselves between the two participants to a standardised derivative transaction, and apply minimum capital and margining requirements to these transactions[11]. Finally, transactions that by nature cannot be centrally cleared will also attract minimum capital and margining requirements to discourage regulatory arbitrage.

III. Future risks: the FSB analysis of vulnerabilities and the role of credit risk

While a lot has been done to make the regulatory framework more comprehensive, more effective and less prone to regulatory arbitrage, it is inevitable that a highly dynamic and complex financial system creates its own future challenges and tends to leave regulatory design in permanent catch-up mode. This puts a premium on having a forward looking, thorough and comprehensive process for identifying vulnerabilities in the financial system, as well as the genuine capacity and willingness to act upon the identified vulnerabilities. As the economic recovery takes hold,

[10] Enhanced Disclosure Task Force (2012), "Enhancing the risk disclosure of banks", available on www.financialstabilityboard.org

[11] Of course, this in turn puts a premium on policies to ensure that core financial infrastructure, such as central counterparties, does not itself become a source of systemic risk.

financing needs expand and markets become more complacent about risks, financial authorities need to remain ahead of the curve and be able to adapt their supervisory and regulatory responses to emerging risks.

1. The FSB process to identify vulnerabilities

The main FSB mechanism for identifying and assessing risks and vulnerabilities in the financial system is through the Standing Committee on Assessment of Vulnerabilities (SCAV). The focus of the SCAV assessment comprises conjunctural macrofinancial risks (e.g. the build-up of excessive leverage, credit growth, and maturity mismatching that over time heighten the potential for crisis), and risks arising from structural weaknesses or fault lines in the financial system (such as misaligned incentives or other forms of market failure which can lead to shocks being amplified).

The SCAV's functions are to:

- monitor and assess vulnerabilities affecting the global financial system and propose to the Plenary actions needed to address them
- monitor and advise on market and systemic developments, and their implications for regulatory policy;
- provide input for the Early Warning Exercise conducted in collaboration with the IMF; and
- since 2011, conduct the annual shadow banking monitoring exercise.

The SCAV reports its findings to the FSB Plenary as well as to the FSB Standing Committee on Supervisory and Regulatory Cooperation (SRC). Based on SCAV's analysis, the Plenary decides whether specific vulnerabilities require a policy response in the areas of the FSB's competence, namely policies to strengthen the robustness of the financial system such as supervision, regulation, standards or design features of market infrastructure.

Relative to the risk assessments conducted in national authorities and other international financial institutions, the comparative advantages of the FSB process lie in its inclusiveness and in the direct link provided through the FSB Plenary to those authorities that can take action to mitigate identified vulnerabilities. The SCAV leverages on the risk assessments conducted in the major central banks and international financial institutions in different regions, pools the knowledge, compares and contrasts experiences, assesses the materiality of concerns and helps to spread warning signals. Its analysis is therefore less prone to gaps. Furthermore, the SCAV assessments are designed to propose recommendations for early remedial actions in the areas where vulnerabilities are building up. Having supervisory authorities and standard setting bodies "under one roof" in the FSB umbrella helps to engage with them on the follow-up actions. Finally, the FSB Standing Committees working in the area of supervision and regulation and in the area of standards implementation can also ask the SCAV to conduct risk assessments on, for instance, the impact of regulatory reforms on the functioning of markets, so that there is a two-way process.

2. Highlights from the analysis of financial system vulnerabilities

The credit risk legacy from the crisis

The banking system today is significantly better capitalized today than after the crisis. Still, bank repair is incomplete and uneven in some financial systems, in particular in Europe. First the financial crisis and then the recession together had a strong impact on the situation of the European banking system in a variety of ways. In particular, the combined effects of stagnation in the real economy and the weak situation of sovereigns have increased credit risk in the balance sheet of banks. Forbearance by banks may have contributed to conceal the problems faced by certain borrowers.

In order to restart bank lending and strengthen economic growth, it is essential that the legacy of the last crisis is addressed without delay. The European Central Bank has undertaken a comprehensive assessment of banks prior to assuming its new supervisory role. The exercise will include an Asset Quality Review looking specifically at individual asset items and individual exposures and probing their valuation, risk classification, potential forbearance and provisioning levels. The transparency provided by this exercise should contribute to foster confidence in the banks and overcome the crisis legacy.

Vulnerabilities from the necessary adjustment to higher interest rates

Since the crisis, financial systems and institutions around the world have operated in a very low interest rate environment for an extended period of time. This period may be coming to an end, with the US Federal Reserve starting to exit its unconventional monetary policy. As financial conditions normalise, a number of vulnerabilities could come to the forefront.

Despite a welcome decline in the leverage of banking systems, leverage in a broader sense has increased globally across G20 economies since the crisis, particularly corporate and government debt. This large debt overhang makes economies particularly vulnerable to shocks. According to BIS data, the total non-financial debt in G20 economies has increased from 100 trillion dollars in 2007 to 135 trillion dollars in 2012.

Taking a global view of debt stocks and their sensitivity to interest rates is particularly important as shocks are unlikely to happen in isolation. Interest rate shocks in key financial markets such as the US markets could trigger widespread spill overs to long term rates in the rest of the world, as was the case in May and June 2013, with emerging market bond yields exhibiting a particularly strong sensitivity.

Furthermore, the understanding of system-wide effects of large increases in interest rates remains incomplete for a variety of reasons:

- Stress tests can lead to a false sense of security as feedback effects are not incorporated into the models. A number of factors can amplify the impact of interest rate increases, one of them being rising liquidity risk. Secondary market liquidity for bonds has suffered a structural decline across a range of markets, as the ratio of dealer bond inventories to total bonds outstanding has fallen by over 75% since 2007.
- Not only banks but also non-banks are sensitive to interest rates. In particular, hedge funds and other leveraged investors such as US mortgage Real Estate Investment Trusts (mREITS) that rely heavily on short-term repos could face margin calls that would in turn lead to fire sales of assets and self-fulfilling market dynamics.
- There are indirect effects on financial institutions through the vulnerability of households, non-financial corporations, and sovereigns to interest rate increases. Sovereigns have accumulated heavy debt burdens that will take a long time to reduce with current low levels of economic growth. In some countries, non-financial corporations are highly leveraged and could become unable to service their debt should their interest rate payments increase rapidly.

Search for yield and credit risk

The continuation of the low interest rate environment leads to a stronger search for yield behaviour, whereby investors are forced to target assets with an ever higher credit risk, usually combined with other risks such as liquidity risk and duration risk, in order to maintain a fixed rate of return over time. This can lead to excessive risk taking in some market segments and an underestimation of risks that can translate into large unanticipated losses as financial conditions tighten. There are many examples of this in the current environment:

- Lending standards to non-financial corporations at the higher end of the credit risk spectrum continue to weaken. In the leveraged loan and high yield markets, the share of issuers with low credit ratings or very short credit histories (e.g. first time issuers) is on the rise. In addition, the increase in covenant-lite loans surpassed in 2013 their pre-crisis levels (Graph 1).
- Equity buffers included in Leveraged Buy-Out (LBO) deals are eroding and debt burdens are rising. As shown on graph 2, the equity proportion of deals in the US market has declined to 30%, very close to pre-crisis levels.
- While investment grade corporations are in good health and have high cash buffers, leverage of high yield corporates – the riskier ones – is rising rapidly

Issuance of Cov-lite loans

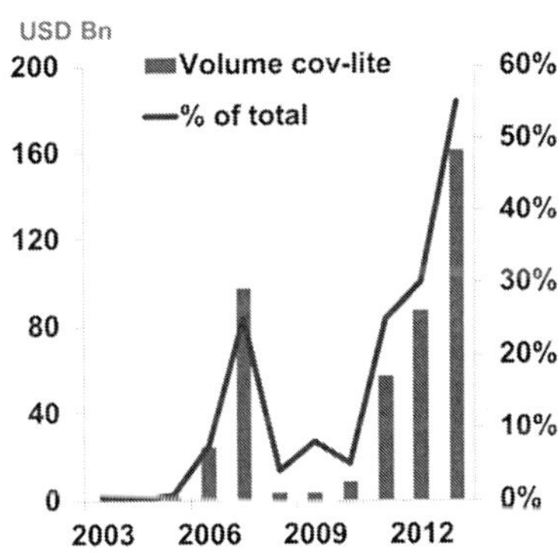

Source: S&P LCD

Proportion of equity in Leveraged Buy-Outs (LBOs)

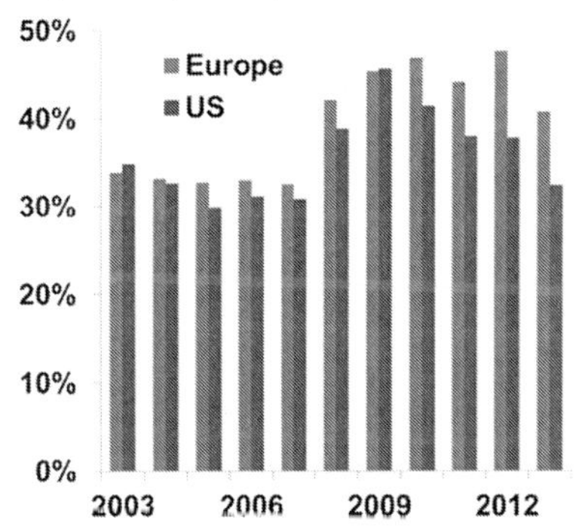

Source: S&P LCD

Figure 10-1: Issuance of Cov-lite loans. Figure 10-2: Proportion of equity in Leveraged Buy-Outs (LBOs).

Strong credit growth in Emerging Markets (EMs)

Underpinned by high levels of foreign capital inflows and robust economic growth, credit growth has also been growing well above trend in most EM economies since the crisis, in particular Asia and Latin America as shown in Graph 3. Emerging Europe is a notable exception, as credit growth has slowed markedly, perhaps related to the broader European context. Data collected by the FSB for the annual Shadow Banking monitoring report[12] highlight that some of this credit growth takes place in the non-bank financial sector. Shadow Banking activities in some EMs are growing strongly – albeit from a smaller base than most advanced economies.

Credit to GDP ratios vs. long-term trend

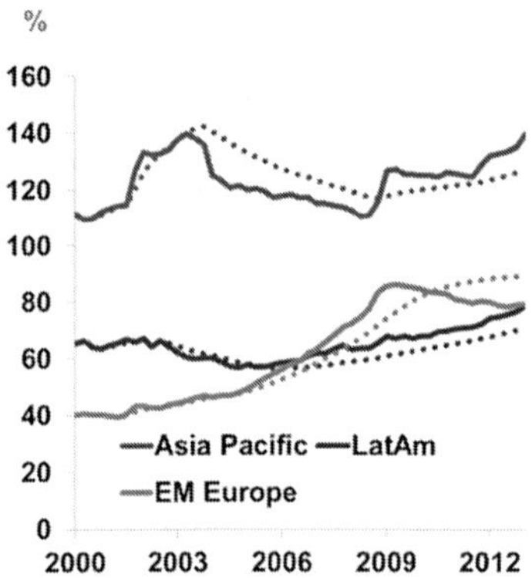

Source: BIS

Growth of non-bank sector (2012)

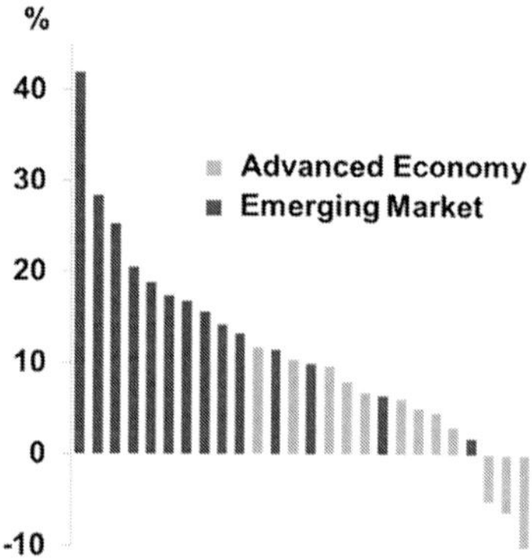

Source: FSB

Figure 10-3: Credit to GDP ratios vs. long-term trend. Figure 10-4: Growth of non-bank sector (2012).

IV. Conclusion

The completion of the FSB regulatory agenda and the full, timely and consistent implementation of agreed reforms will not only build more resilient national systems but also support a more effective and open global financial system. Important elements of this work agenda include strengthening financial institutions, ending Too Big To Fail, discouraging regulatory arbitrage, and creating the conditions for well-functioning markets. However, as financial systems and their interlinkages grow more complex, new challenges and risks to financial stability will arise. This puts a premium on having a forward looking, thorough and comprehensive process for identifying vulnerabilities in the global financial system, as

[12] FSB (2013), "Global Shadow Banking Monitoring Report 2013"

well as the genuine capacity and willingness to act upon the identified vulnerabilities. In a macro financial environment where the legacy credit risks from the crisis have not been fully addressed, new vulnerabilities could build up in a number of risk areas. Examples of potential vulnerabilities include those from the necessary adjustment to higher interest rate, from investor search for yield and the related weakening of credit standards, and from unexpected losses from the current strong credit growth in Emerging Markets (EMs).

References

Enhanced Disclosure Task Force. 2012. "Enhancing the risk disclosure of banks." available on www.financialstabilityboard.org.

FSB. 2009. "Financial Stability Board Charter" subsequently amended and restated in 2012. Both documents are available on www.financialstabilityboard.org.

FSB. 2013. "Global systemically important insurers (G-SIIs) and the policy measures that will apply to them", available on www.financialstabilityboard.org , publications/ policy areas/ systemically important financial institutions (SIFIs).

FSB. 2013. "Global Shadow Banking Monitoring Report 2013" and other annual reports available on www.financialstabilityboard.org, publications/policy areas/ shadow banking.

FSB. 2013. "Strengthening Oversight and Regulation of Shadow Banking: An Overview of Policy Recommendations", available on www.financialstabilityboard.org , publications/ policy areas/ shadow banking.

FSB. 2014. "Consultative Document: Assessment Methodologies for Identifying Non-Bank Non-Insurer Global Systemically Important Financial Institutions", available on www.financialstabilityboard.org , publications/ policy areas/ systemically important financial institutions (SIFIs).

CHAPTER ELEVEN

INTERNAL RATING MODELS FOR SME: PITFALLS AND LESSONS

MATTHIAS SCHALLER AND MARKUS HEUSLER[1]

Abstract

Credit rating models face certain more or less severe problems in current banking practice. This article focuses on internal rating models, drawing attention to five different issues concerning their design and application, in particular within the context of SME: 1) Being designed for the identification of short-term default risk, statistical rating models are in practice expected to differentiate between inherently sound companies as well; a task deemed to fail as long as it is not appropriately addressed during the model building process. 2) Developed on SME samples being strongly dominated by small companies, statistical models are likely to fit their predictive power towards this subsample. However, there is less reason to expect that the models perceive their performance when the comfort zone is left, that is, when they are applied to medium-sized or even large companies. 3) When confronted with risk-adjusted lending conditions, clients become interested in the underlying rating models and, in particular, in how they can improve their rating. Discussing the results of internal rating models with SME clients is, however, difficult to reconcile with the fundamental purpose of internal risk models and is, therefore, not particularly conductive for improving the client-bank relationship. 4) Whether or not internal credit ratings move with the economic cycle depends on various factors and can, in general, not be

[1] Matthias Schaller holds a Ph.D. in Business Administration from the University of St. Gallen and is data responsible at RSN. Markus Heusler holds a Ph.D. and a Titular Professorship in Theoretical Physics from the University of Zurich and is CEO at RSN. RSN Risk Solution Network AG, located in Zurich, is the leading credit risk platform for medium sized Banks in Switzerland.

predicted without knowing the model details and even the principles on which the model building was based upon. In fact, the expectations concerning the temporal behavior of internal rating models tend to be biased by the experience with external ratings rather than to result from the analysis of data and methods. 5) Developing models for credit portfolios mainly consisting of SME and mortgage clients is a different task than building credit portfolio models for traded credits and derivatives: In particular, when it comes to correlations, the character of the credit portfolio defines whether the counterparties are directly (causally) correlated or simply depend in a similar way on external drivers – a difference having fundamental consequences for the choice of the model architecture.

I. Introduction

The financial crisis at the end of the last decade very forcefully revealed several limitations of credit rating models in both theory and practical application. Several banking sectors and, subsequently, entire economies were reminded the hard way that using the past for predicting the future might only work as long as the past and the future are sufficiently similar. Moreover, the crisis has taught us once again, that delegating responsibility to models – either due to naivety or against better knowledge – is not a good idea.

With constantly changing circumstances, rating models might still be able to draw a relatively accurate picture of the risk situation of a single household or company. Assuming, however, that this holds also true for complex structured financial products probably stretches the trust in these models too far. And with estimated total costs between 40% and 90% of one's year economic output in the USA (Luttrell, Atkinson, Rosenblum 2013), this was a rather expensive lesson. Taking a less global view, this article intends to shed light on several less extensively studied pitfalls from credit rating modeling, drawn from the experience with internal rating models for SME, as applied by Swiss banks for more than fifteen years.

The Swiss market for credit risk solutions is dominated by two different approaches: A few large banks use their proprietary data and in-house know-how, built up during the last two decades, allowing them to work with their own credit risk models, embedded within their proprietary IT solutions. Most medium-sized banks, in contrast, pool their data and have outsourced both the methodological know-how required for model building and the implementation of the credit risk software to a dedicated provider. Swiss credit risk is constituted by about 2/3 of the outstanding credit volume to private households and 1/3 to corporates and SME, where 57% of the firms have less than 10 employees, 15% between 10 and 49, 15% between 50 and 249, and only 13% over 250 employees (SNB 2014). Within the sample of corporates and SME there is, thus, a strong preponderance of "small SME".

Developing credit risk solutions for the majority of medium sized Swiss banks provided several insights concerning the design and application of internal rating models. In this short essay, each section is devoted to one particular issue that we stumbled upon in the course of recent years: The "extrapolation issue" in section two discusses the trade-off associated with the different tasks of identifying risk vs. assessing opportunities of prospective debtors. The "quick-ratio issue", in section three, gets to the cause of the fact, that short-term liquidity indicators are most of the time too strongly represented in internal rating models for SME. Section four is devoted to the "communication issue" and draws the attention on potential hazards arising when banks are getting involved in discussions on internal rating results with their clients. Section five gives a brief discussion of the behavior of internal SME ratings during the economic cycle. Finally, section six intends to provoke thought concerning the "correlation issue", in particular within the context of credit portfolio models for typical counterparty portfolios of most Swiss banks.

II. The Extrapolation Issue – Risk and Opportunities

In horse racing, knowing that very overweight horses will most probably be among the slowest, one would not beg on the skinniest horse to win the race. Similarly, statistical credit rating models are optimized to identify failure potential (i.e., not even to recognize the slowest horse, but rather the one that is most likely to stumble over before making it to the finish line). Even though winning and stumbling are the two extreme realizations of the same outcome variable, it is obvious that the criteria that most accurately indicates failure will, in general, not provide the best indicator for predicting success. During the development of statistical rating models, one typically tries to find the optimal – i.e. maximally separating and stable – combination of factors that predict failure. When applying credit rating models, however, the focus lies by far not only on identifying the most risky debtors, but also on classifying the large majority of remaining debtors in an accurate manner. Within the standard approach, success potential is, however, measured by the same criteria (same model) as default risk. This inadmissible extrapolation, in consequence, results in unreliable rating classifications and unsatisfying pricing recommendations for SME clients with low risk.

One way to remedy the extrapolation problem is to apply hybrid rating systems: In the first step, a standard statistical model is used to obtain a primary classification measuring short-term risk. As elaborated in a later part of this article, this primary assessment typically focusses on the liquidity situation of the company, as on a short-term horizon, default is most likely to occur due to draining cash (at least for small companies). In the second step, a different model is used to differentiate between those debtors that do not show significant signs of short-term risk. This secondary assessment should, of course, emphasize on the profitability and sustainability of the client.

The two-step approach outlined above also opens the possibility to take account of the client's industry affiliation, as the criteria applied within the secondary assessment can be assessed with respect to the relevant peers. In fact, when it comes to scoring the ratios of financially healthy companies, absolute values are of limited use, as it is the ability to outperform the competitors in the medium to long run that makes the difference.

Even though the hybrid approach outlined above deviates from the original goal of rating modelling – which is predicting the likelihood of default –, the application of internal models broadened, and so needs the methodological approach. Even more so, as differentiations among better rating classes based on default probabilities in most circumstances simply lack the statistical power required.

III. The Quick-Ratio Issue – Identifying Short-Term Risk

Typically, credit rating models are designed to predict default within a horizon of 12 or 24 months. Developing rating models for SME by multivariate optimization of financial ratios typically results in the liquidity situation being the dominating indicator for default risk. In contrast, information based on the profitability, rentability, or debt situation generally receives less weight by the algorithms. This "quick-ratio problem" – i.e. the over-dependency of rating results on the most prominent key figure in the liquidity area – has not turned out to be of particular help when trying to create acceptance in internal rating models with credit experts.

The above issue is especially relevant, as SME represent all but a homogenous group: Employing a split along the two dimensions "industry" (measured as production versus trade & service companies) and "size" (measured in terms of annual turnover), it is obvious that, even within SME, there are significant differences – in particular between small production and large trading companies. Having eventually had access to sufficient default data within each of the four segments, revealed that short-term risk indicators vary massively over size and industry – thereby matching the economic intuition: With increasing turnover and increasing commercial activity, ratios from the P&L statement gain separation power, while ratios from the balance sheet – in particular liquidity rations – lose indication power for short-term risk. For smaller companies, as expected, default typically results from cash running out: Small companies usually do not make use of a professional cash management and typically do not have ready access to additional sources of funds when required. Larger trading companies, in contrast, rarely suffer from draining cash, but rather default if margins are not suitable for sustaining profitability on an ongoing basis.

So, why tend internal rating models for SME to focus too strongly on liquidity ratios? By design, credit rating models based on statistical analysis of separation power assign equal value to every observation in the sample. In most economies the number of small companies is simply larger than the number of bigger companies and, in addition, the former default more frequently than the latter. When optimizing a default prediction model for a typical SME sample, the resulting model will thus automatically be fitted towards small companies, being, in general, most heavily represented in the sample and providing, in particular, the most default observations. While the solution – building different statistical models for different industries, sizes, etc. – seems straightforward, its realization is usually prevented by the lack of data. The extent to which the statistical models built for the four SME sub-segments described above differ from each other shows that the tradeoff between data availability and segmentation depth must be handled with most care. If not, the short-term risk of entire portfolio segments will be measured by the wrong indicators.

IV. The Communication Issue – Statistical Models and Risk-Adjusted Pricing

Pricing loans is the prototypical lemon problem (Akerlof 1970): Banks offering loans to their clients for the same interest rates will inevitably attract the bad debtors, driving the good clients to the competitor offering risk-adjusted prices. Pricing credit transactions on internal risk models banks might, in addition, be inclined to communicate not only the offered rates, but also the underlying rating result – or even rating model.

From a methodological point-of-view, discussing internal rating results with clients is, however, a rather formidable challenge as, in most clients understanding, risk-adjusted means "client-adjusted". The fact is, however, that risk-adjusted conditions result from statistical concepts (e.g. default probabilities), while "client-adjusted" certainly suggests individuality. Adopting an individual perspective, it is thus hard – if not impossible – to argue that risk-adjusted prices are fair, as – by construction – this is not their purpose. Risk-adjusted pricing is an "insurance instrument" – serving for risk provisioning based on statistical methods – and not marketing tools. "Client-adjusted" pricing, on the other hand, would require a detailed analysis of all internal and external factors being relevant for the individual case – a task going way beyond the claim and possibilities of internal statistical models.

Hence, arguing on details of internal rating results with clients drives the discussion in the wrong direction, as both sides are usually not sufficiently aware of the fundamental issue addressed above. Even worse, too much insight into the bank's internal models might mislead the client and, in addition, open up the possibility of future window-dressing activities.

If necessary at all, internal rating results should be communicated along with the explanation, that they are based on a couple of factors having proved to be reliable statistical indicators when defining risk categories for the bank's risk provision (like insurance companies communicate the criteria, obtained from statistical analysis of past damages, on which their premiums are based upon). Apart from this, both the analysis of the expert and the discussion with the client should not focus on the internal model, but rather on the client's individual business. In doing so, the bank also takes the opportunity to signalize that it does not delegate the responsibility for the client relationship to a statistical system.

V. The Cyclicality Issue – Internal Ratings and Economic Development

It is an almost philosophical question whether or not internal credit ratings should move with the economic development, i.e. better ratings on average during boom periods and worse ratings during periods of bust. While banks typically, and for good reason, expect credit ratings to follow – or even indicate – the economic cycle, it is all but self-evident why internal SME ratings should behave in the same way.

In a typical sample of SME not all companies are equally affected by the economic development. A currency crisis, for example, might challenge the exporting industry, while domestic industries usually benefit. As internal rating models are generally developed on heterogenic SME samples, causal dependencies between economic developments and rating distributions can, at best, be expected for models specifically designed for individual industries. For this reason, the impact of a crisis on the overall rating distribution strongly depends on the characteristics of the particular crisis and the composition of the bank's credit portfolio.

Moreover, internal rating models are typically based on ratios of key figures. The behavior of these ratios, in turn, depends on the relative development of the respective nominators and denominators. During an economic upswing, for example, both turnover and investments tend to increase, potentially moving profit margins in either direction. Moreover, even if it the behavior of each single ratio was clear, the behavior of their weighted combination – i.e. the rating – is again not obvious and, of course, model dependent.

On the other side, if internal rating models were constructed using default information from different economic cycles – ideally spanning several phases of up- and downturns – then there would be some reason to expect that the rating distributions might follow the economic development to a certain extent: As SME defaults will cluster around periods of crises, the resulting statistical models will, at least, automatically assign higher weights to the financial figures moving the most during the crises.

It is – in general, and in particular within the context addressed in this section – a naïve undertaking to extrapolate form the experience with external credit ratings to the behavior of internal rating models. The two types of models are developed on the basis of different input information, by different methods, and for different purposes.

VI. The Correlation Issue – Portfolio Models for SME

Finally, while assessing default probabilities and loss severities to single counterparties and transactions is the primary task, the secondary challenge consists in measuring the risk of the entire loan portfolio. One of the key issues in this context concerns the implementation of correlations. The basic observation concerns the fact that one has to distinguish between two types of correlations: The first – and for many applications relevant – cause for correlated behavior is due to external influences having the same impact on groups of debtors; while the second cause is due to direct influences between debtors. To illustrate the difference on may visualize a swarm of fishes, moving either in the same way due to strong water currents or due to direct interactions between the individuals. In both cases the behavior is correlated, however, the modeling requires completely different knowledge and methods.

While externally induced correlations should be studied by sensitivity- and stress analyses, modeling direct correlations impacts the details of the portfolio model. When modelling risk for SME and mortgage portfolios, one has to be aware of the fact, that the majority of clients are actually not correlated in a direct (causal) sense, but rather due to the fact, that certain segments are subject to the similar external influences, like, e.g., changes in the interest rate environment or other macroeconomic drivers.

It is, for this reason, not conductive to apply portfolio models developed for traded credits and derivatives to counterparty portfolios consisting mainly of SME and mortgage clients, being – apart from legal or economic entities – mostly not causally correlated. Hence, within the present context, the preference has to be given to semi-analytic methods, such as the default approach of Credit Risk +. Even more, as market prizes for SME loans generally do not exist, value based models like Credit Metrics seem less appropriate for this segment.

Finally, it is worth noticing that induced correlations lead to increasing default rates and, in consequence, to shifts of the loss distribution towards higher losses, while only direct (default) correlations lead to fatter tails.

VII. Conclusion

Credit rating models are at the crossroads: Having suffered credibility problems in recent years, the ongoing introduction of risk-adjusted loan rates even broadened the application range of rating models. Focusing on internal models only, this article addresses five issues concerning both the design and the application of this kind of models. Having gained experiences with internal models for meanwhile almost two decades, the time has come to challenge both methodological basics and practical application. This is all the more the case since, above all, todays availability of internal data allows to put the assumptions to the best, on which one had to rely in the pioneering era of the subject.

References

Akerlof, G. 1970. "The Market for Lemons: Quality Uncertainty and the Market Mechanism." *Quarterly Journal of Economics* 84 (3): 488–500.

Luttrell, D., T. Atkinson, and H. Rosenblum. 2013. "Assessing the Costs and Consequences of the 2007-2009 Financial Crisis and its Aftermath." *Economic Letter, FRB Dalls* 8 (7): 1-4.

Schweizerische Nationalbank. 2013. "Bankenstatistisches Monatsheft" Juni 2014.

CHAPTER TWELVE

LENDING METHODOLOGIES AND SOCIO-ECONOMIC FACTORS IN MICROFINANCE

PATRICK SCHEURLE, PETER FANCONI AND ANDREA STAUDACHER[1]

I. Introduction

Microfinance has experienced rapid growth during the last decade and is becoming a broadly recognized asset class. Originally, primarily used by development institutions, microfinance investments enjoy increased popularity among private investors such as pension funds, insurance companies, corporations, foundations, family offices but also private individuals. Hand in hand with its growth, the industry has professionalized and investors show a keen interest in understanding the mechanics in detail. In addition, advancements in research methodologies and improving data availability have produced new insights into the industry in general and in credit risk related aspects in particular.

This chapter intends to link this hunger for a detailed understanding by practitioners with the latest insights from academic research. Concretely, the article discusses frequently applied state of the art lending methodologies in microfinance in the context of traditional credit theory and provides an overview of the latest findings on credit risk relevant aspects across these methodologies. The focus will be on the intersection between microfinance institutions and end-borrowers.

Following this introduction, a brief description with key information on the microfinance industry and its value chain are presented in order to set the grounds for a common understanding of the coming sections. Section three outlines frequently applied lending methodologies in

---

[1] Dr. Patrick Scheurle is CFO/COO, Peter Fanconi CEO, and Andrea Staudacher a research professional at BlueOrchard Finance S.A.

microfinance which form the basis for a more in-depth discussion of important socio-economic factors, such as gender and habitat in Section four. The article concludes with an outlook.

II. The Microfinance Market

The roots of microfinance date back at least to the 14th century and the pawn shops of Franciscan monks. However, the success of "modern" microfinance may be particularly linked to two names – Muhammad Yunus and Kofi Annan. Muhammad Yunus was awarded with the Nobel Peace Prize in 2006 for developing the micro credit market as an instrument to reduce poverty through the supply of financial resources to entrepreneurs and small businesses. Kofi Annan, former General Secretary of the United Nations identified microfinance as an important instrument to achieve the Millennium Development Goals and in this context created awareness for this sector on a larger scale.

A recent study shows that microfinance assets pooled in investments vehicles amount to roughly USD 9 Billion .[2] Total assets deployed by the industry, including those not pooled in investment vehicles, are estimated at around USD 70 Billion to USD 100 Billion. Investments span global developing and frontier markets. The most significant volumes can be found in Latin America and Eastern Europe & Central Asia. However, East Asia & Pacific as well as Middle East & North Africa are fast growing regions.

Figure 12-1 shows that nowadays the microfinance industry is highly specialized and typically characterized by four relevant elements. Investors fund investment vehicles which provide capital to so called microfinance institutions (MFIs). MFIs in turn lend money to microentrepreneurs who use these financial resources for productive activities.

Investors can broadly be divided into two groups: public and private. Public investors include for example supranational institutions such as the Worldbank, KfW or other development institutions. Private investors span the entire range from large institutions like pension funds to private individuals.

Investment vehicles are pooling instruments and are essential for efficient and effective deployment of the collected funds. Many investment vehicles are incorporated in Luxembourg or the US due to the quality of the financial infrastructure in these locations. Investment vehicles usually

[2] Microrate (2013): The State of Microfinance Investment 2013.

appoint an external asset manager or advisor specialized in microfinance providing expertise as well as on-site infrastructure.

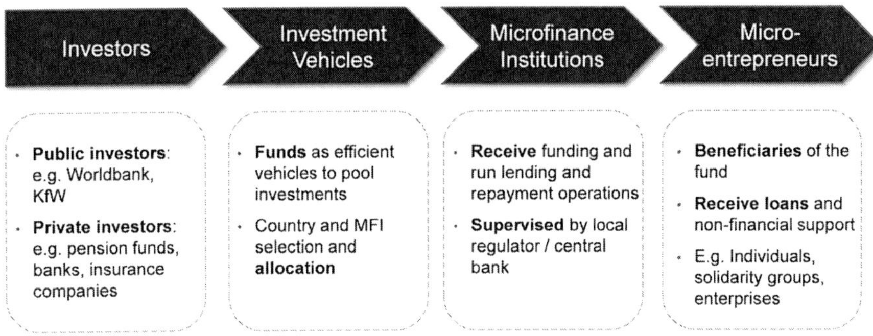

Figure 12-4: The microfinance value chain: Connecting capital markets to microfinance

Microfinance institutions receive funding by the investment vehicles and run the lending and repayment operations on the ground, thereby representing the link between the funding pool and the microentrepreneurs that are the end-borrowers. MFIs are highly heterogeneous in terms of size and setup. Some MFIs are multinational corporations or banks with balance sheets of several billion dollars. Other MFIs are NGOs or cooperatives with only a few employees providing credit but do not take deposits at all.

The microentrepreneurs are the ultimate beneficiaries of the funds. They receive loans provided by the MFIs and typically engage in productive activities with the capital they receive. Moreover, non-financial benefits can be granted to debtors, such as education and health care support.

Figure 12-1 shows that capital flows initially from the left to the right and from the right to the left when amortizations or interest rate payments occur. This highlights the fact that credit risk in microfinance is a multistage process. The investment vehicle is exposed to credit risk of the underlying loans provided to MFIs.[3] The MFIs themselves are exposed to credit risk of the underlying loans given to microentrepreneurs. This relationship between MFIs and microentrepreneurs will be the focus of the further discussion below.

---

[3] Investment vehicles provide equity and debt to MFIs. However, with a share of about 80%, debt investments are the dominant funding source for MFIs.

III. Traditional Credit Theory and Microfinance Lending Methodologies

Traditional credit analysis is based on Stiglitz and Weiss` (1981) model of credit rationing. In addition, loans are generally granted based on interest rates and collateral requirements to protect lenders from asymmetric information and moral hazard (see Akerlof`s market for "lemons", 1970). In general, riskier entrepreneurs pay higher interest rates and have to provide more collateral due to a higher probability of default than safer borrowers. The riskiness of borrowers and hence the required amount of collateral is usually determined by credit ratings. There are situations where clients` demand for credit is rationed. There will be no lending without collateral and credit rating due to information asymmetries between borrower and lender. A key requirement in traditional credit theory is the posting of collateral which has two major benefits: On the one hand, it makes credits more affordable to the borrower in case of a high default probability. On the other hand, it can compensate for difficulties and uncertainties with respect to the determination of the probability of default. However, the poor are hardly in a situation which allows them to post collateral. Microfinance is an approach which does not rely on traditional lending methodologies but addresses the presence of asymmetric information and lack of collateral by trust (Hartarska and Holtmann, 2006; Meyer and Nagarajan, 2006; Zeller, 2006).

Microfinance is an approach to lend financial resources by creating a network of trust between families, friends or even strangers where they support each other in order to gain access to financial resources (Barboza and Trejos, 2009). In practice, these principles are implemented through a number of concrete lending methodologies and instruments.

The most important lending methodologies in microfinance are discussed below in detail. These are joint liability, peer surveillance, progressive lending and frequent meetings with the MFI (Armendáriz de Aghion, 1999; Armendáriz de Aghion and Mordoch, 2005; Barboza and Barreto, 2006; Barboza and Trejos, 2009; Morduch, 1999; Stiglitz, 1990; Stiglitz and Weiss, 1981; Van Tassel, 1999; Varian, 1990, among others).

First, a significant success of microfinance lending is attributable to a group`s joint liability, which reduces the amount of private information not known to the lender or at least the impact of the information asymmetry between lender and borrower(s). Group loans or individual loans under joint liability create peer-pressure among members to share skills, knowledge and private information. Furthermore, there are cultural norms why people individually are willing to repay the loan because if borrowers cannot meet their debts, they will "lose their face". Although information asymmetries still prevail between borrowers and lenders the risks associated with it are almost eliminated (Barboza and Trejos, 2009; Kropp et. al, 2009).

Second, joint liability also creates learning effects between the members of the association, since they share and compare their experiences with each other. Because borrowers are all liable for the debt of other group members, they monitor and mentor each other to make sure that there is no default or delay of the interest and principal loan amount. Additionally, good performers want to gain access to new loans and hence train, monitor and support group members that are likely to fall behind (Armendáriz de Aghion, 1999; Barboza and Trejos, 2009; Besley and Coate, 1995; Ghatak and Guinnane, 1999; Kropp et. al, 2009; Stiglitz, 1990; Stiglitz and Weiss, 1981; Van Tassel, 1999; Varian, 1990).

Third, Barboza and Trejos (2009) proved empirically that repayments become less volatile when moving up the progressing loan structure. As a whole, entrepreneurs with successful repayments of the first, second etc. tranche move up the progressing loan ladder. The lower repayment rates of groups in lower level loans indicate that newcomers are still in the process of sharing and acquiring relevant business and financial knowledge. Members of higher loan levels, on the other hand, show a stable and continuously improving performance. This illustrates that learning affects group dynamics and ensures high repayment rates.

Fourth, frequent meetings with the MFI take place to collect interest due. This allows the MFI to closely monitor business projects and provide clients practical financial knowhow and useful skills early on before the client's situation deteriorates.

IV. Socio-economic factors that influence repayment rates

Besides the lending methodology, research increasingly sheds light on the importance of some socio-economic factors on repayment rates whereby two attributes have attracted particular attention by practitioners as well as academics: the borrower's habitat and gender.

1. Urban vs. Rural

Regarding the total microfinance market, approximately 50% of total loans are granted to people living in an urban environment, 45% and 5% of loans are granted to the rural population and semi-urban population, respectively. Two important factors that characterize these microfinance environments are the availability and distance from markets.

In general, performance of loans is in favor of urban compared to rural debtors. This is because they have access to more information and higher value-added production activities. The convenient access to markets leads to a steady cash flow from which interest rate and principal can be paid continuously (Barboza and Trejos, 2009). MFIs that are mostly invested in the rural environment usually face more challenges than in the urban setting. This is because clients located in the rural area usually concentrate their effort in low value added production activities. Since frequent visits to markets are expensive, clients want to minimize transportation cost per unit by solely going to the market when they produced sufficient pieces. Clients involved in agricultural production activities can realize yield and cash flows by the time it has been harvested. As a result, cash flow is not generated constantly and it is further challenging for these clients to make repayments on a regular basis. The close proximity to markets is a necessity for clients to generate continuous cash flows and to enhance the probability of success of lending institutions (Barboza and Trejos, 2009).

2. Gender

Roughly two thirds of all loans granted by MFIs are given to women compared to approximately one third which is granted to men. This perhaps counter-intuitive difference suggests that, for some reasons, gender is an important factor in microfinance. Further, the fact that most MFIs have included gender in their credit scoring model supports the hypothesis that gender is an informative element to assess creditworthiness of a potential borrower. Thereby, female loan applicants are typically treated with a bonus by the scoring models and male applicants with a penalty, i.e., there is a clear discrimination which takes place on the supply side rather than the demand side. It can therefore be concluded from a practical perspective that women are perceived as less risky borrowers compared to men. Why is that?

Recent research found that female clients do not only have a higher social impact compared to male clients, but also reduce financial risk for the MFI (Armendáriz de Aghion and Morduch, 2005). Female characteristics, such as chastity, modesty, discretion and discipline are mainly traced back to cultural norms where it was observed that women are the guardians of the honor of family, lineage and clan. Blumberg`s (1991) research illustrates that women hold back less income for personal use. This is reflected in several studies focusing on spending behavior between gender roles. Since women are usually in charge of the family household and hence control income and expenditure, they invest proportionally more income on family education, nutrition, health care and children`s needs, whereas men spend more for their own consumption, such as entertainment and luxury items (Armendiáriz de Aghion and Morduch, 2005). Moreover, Karim (2011) explains the microfinance market as an "economy of shame", which draws on mutual monitoring between borrowers to which women are more receptive. In addition, women participate more frequently and more intense in group meetings. Consequently, social and moral pressures are higher among female debtors leading to higher repayment rates in general. A second explanation is that women tend to be more risk averse than men when starting an own business or making financial decisions. Several studies suggest that women are more cautious than men in their financial decisions, less opportunistic and more likely to cooperate, which reduces information asymmetry and moral hazard (Hartmann-Wendels et al., 2009; Todd, 1996). Since women are more risk averse than men, they are less likely to request loans that exceed their repayment ability (Armendiáriz de Aghion and Morduch, 2005; Phillips and Bhatia-Panthaki, 2007). However, smaller loans increase operational cost.

As a whole, a customer base dominated by women is almost worldwide associated with lower risk of default (Remenyi, 2000). This effect remains statistically significant even after controlling for the nature of the loan (D´espallier et al., 2013). Although repayment rates are higher when lending to women, the amount of loans are generally smaller. The fix operational cost prevent MFIs from better performance when lending to women. D´espallier et al. (2013) showed that MFIs focusing on women are unfortunately not yet able to transfer the lower risk of default into a significantly better financial performance.

V. Conclusion

The Microfinance market grows rapidly and continuously. Today, investments in microfinance are not limited to development institutions, private investors are also increasingly developing interest as well as stake. Key beneficiaries are small entrepreneurs and businesses. Thereby, investment vehicles– mostly in the form of debt and equity funds as well as microfinance institutions play an essential role in the efficient allocation of the funds.

The lack of collateral has been a major barrier in lending to microentrepreneurs, since the poor do not have resources that they can post as collateral. In microfinance physical collateral is substituted by social collateral, namely trust, which provides access to financial markets in the form of microloans. There are different characteristics of loans and personalities that reduce information asymmetries by social collateral. Joint liability of debtors, for instance, creates pressure on each individual to pay back the loan on time as social norms force defaulted debtors to "lose their face". This results in continuous monitoring and mentoring of clients to prevent peers from default. Furthermore, the establishment of a progressive loan structure leads to adverse selection on higher levels, as only clients with high repayment rates can progress on the loan ladder. Last but not least, frequent meetings with the MFI reduce the amount of private information only known to the borrower.

Besides the characteristics of loans in microfinance, socio-economic factors influence repayment rates. Whereas clients living in urban areas usually have more constant cash flows due to the availability of a market to sell their products, borrowers in rural areas face difficulties in generating constant cash flows. This is mostly due to two circumstances. Rural clients are, on the one hand, involved in farming activities that do not allow for constant cash flows before harvesting. On the other hand, they are no matter what they produce, further away from markets. Attending markets regularly results in high transportation cost due to a lack of infrastructure as well as financial resources. Thus, debtors try to reduce transportation cost per unit sold which usually leads to rather volatile market attendances and consequently, volatile cash flows. In addition, gender characteristics play an important role in microfinance. Several empirical studies show that lending to women reduces the risk of default to the MFI. This is because women are more sensitive to family issues and are mostly in charge of their families` finances. Higher repayment rates of women are also associated with higher social and moral pressures of women compared to men. Moreover, women tend to be more risk averse than men, so that they are less likely to request a loan that exceed their payment abilities.

The success of microfinance today shows, that it is an established practice to reduce initial information asymmetries. By adopting long-term and sustainable strategies, microfinance is seen as an instrument to foster financial inclusion and fight poverty whereby social impact and wealth generation go hand in hand.

References

Akerlof, G. 1970. "The Market for Lemons: Quality Uncertainty and the Market Mechanism." *Quarterly Journal of Economics* 84(3): 488-500.

Armendáriz de Aghion, B. and J.Morduch. 2005. "The Economics of Microfinance." *Cambridge, MA: MIT Press.*

Armendáriz de Aghion, B. 1999. "On the Design of a Credit Agreement with Peer Monitoring." *Journal of Development Economics* 60 (1): 79-104.

Barboza, G and S. Trjos. 2009. "Micro Credit in Chiapas, Mexico: Poverty Reduction Through Group Lending." *Journal of Business Ethics* 88 (2): 283-299.

Barboza, G. and H. Barreto. 2006. "Learning by Association, Micro Credit in Chiapas, Mexico." *Contemporary Economic Policy* 24 (2): 316-331.

Besley, T. and S. Coate.1995. "Group Lending, Repayment Incentives and Social Collateral."*Journal of Development Economics* 46 (1): 1-18.

D´espallier, B., I. Guerin, and R.Mersland. 2013. "Focus on Women in Microfinance Institutions." *The Journal of Development Studies* 49 (5): 589-608.

Ghatak, M. and T. Guinnane. 1999. "The Economics of Lending with Joint Liability: Theory and Practice." *Journal of Development Economics* 60 (1): 195-228.

Hartarska, V. and M. Holtmann. 2006. "An overview of recent developments in the microfinance literature." *Agricultural Finance Review* 66 (2): 149-165.

Hartmann-Wendels, T. Mählmann, and T.Versen. 2009. "Determinants of banks` risk exposure to new account fraud. Evidence from Germany." *Journal of Banking & Finance* 33 (2): 347-357.

Kropp, J., C. Turvey, D. Just, R. Kong, and P. Guo. 2009. "Are the poor really more trustworthy? A micro-lending experiment." *Agricultural Finance Review* 69 (1): 67-87.

McDowell, M. 2006. "Microcredit in Europe: The Experience of the Savings Banks, Perspectives – World Savings Banks Institute." European Savings Banks Group, London.

Meyer, R. and G. Nagarajan. 2006. "Microfinance in developing countries: accomplishments, debates and future directions." *Agricultural Finance Review* 66: 167-194.

Morduch, J. 1999. "The Microfinance Promise." *Journal of Economic Literature* 37 (4): 1569-1614.

Phillips, C. and S. Bhatia-Panthaki. 2007. "Enterprise development in Zambia: reflections on the missing middle." *Journal of International Development* 19 (6): 793-802.

Remenyi, J. 2000. "Is there a `state of the art` in microfinance?" In *Microfinance and poverty alleviation: Case studies from Asia and the Pacific*, edited by J. Remenyi and B. Quinoñes, 25-61. London: Pinter.

Stiglitz, J. and A. Weiss. 1981. "Credit rationing with imperfect information." *American Economic Review* 71 (3): 393-410.

Stiglitz, J. 1990. "Peer Monitoring and Credit Markets." *The World Bank Economic Review* 4 (2): 351-366.

Todd, H. 1996. "Women at the Centre: Grameen Bank Borrowers after One Decade." *Dhaka, Bangladesh: Dhaka University Press.*

Van Tessel, E. 1999. "Group Lending Under Asymmetric Information." *Journal of Development Economics* 60 (1): 3-25.

Varian, H. 1990. "Monitoring Agents with Other Agents." *Journal of Institutional and Theoretical Economics* 146 (1): 153-174.

Zeller, M. 2006. "A comparative review of major types of rural microfinance institutions in developing countries." *Agricultural Finance Review* 66 (2): 195-214.

CHAPTER THIRTEEN

PERFORMANCE AND CONSISTENCY OF CREDIT RATINGS IN STRUCTURED FINANCE

ROMAN STEBLER[1]

Abstract

This study explores the relative performance and consistency of credit ratings in the run-up and during the subprime mortgage crisis. Using a unique record of monthly credit rating migration data from Standard & Poor's, Moody's, and Fitch on 154'608 U.S. residential mortgage-backed securities, we empirically investigate rating agencies' monitoring role by focusing on characteristics of estimated probabilities of default. The results are threefold: First, employing multivariate logit regression models we find that the predictive power of ratings in assessing credit default risk varies distinctively across rating agencies. Second, taking into account basic asset characteristics significantly improves model fit and performance statistics for all rating agencies, indicating that some determinants of credit default risk are underrepresented in prevalent rating methodologies. Third, the study provides suggestive evidence that rating agencies failed to account for rising real estate prices in their credit risk assessment, thereby creating a bias, which led to underestimated default risk and inconsistent credit ratings.

Overall, the findings contribute to the understanding of credit ratings in structured finance and highlight the limitations of their usefulness for

---

[1] The author is from the Institute for Finance, School of Business, University of Applied Sciences Northwestern Switzerland and University of St. Gallen, Switzerland. I am grateful to Thomas Nette from Moody's Analytics, and Markus Luehe and Mikhail Putkaradze from Fitch Solutions for supporting the research. I thank Simone Westerfeld and Stefan Morkötter for useful comments and discussion. I also thank Tanja Artiga Gonzalez for helping prepare the data.

comparing credit default risk within rating scales, but also across different rating agencies.

I. Introduction

Since the downturn of the structured finance market in 2007 and the subsequent financial crisis, there has been a growing focus on understanding the implications and complexity of structured products, but also on the relevance of credit ratings and the role of credit rating agencies. Credit ratings play an important part in international capital markets and are widely used for both regulatory and investment purposes. Especially in structured finance, where products exhibit complex architecture and increased asset opaqueness, credit rating agencies perform a key function as due diligence is usually delegated to them by investors and many mutual funds, governments, and private investors only buy instruments that have been rated by an acquainted agency.

Given the importance of credit ratings for monitoring credit default risk on behalf of investors, studies examining rating agencies' behavior have considerably gained in relevance over the past few years. However, actual empirical evidence on the performance of rating agencies in structured finance and in particular during the recent market turmoil remains rather limited. Despite comprehensive literature on credit risk and rating performance in the corporate bond market, to our knowledge, no previous work has undertaken a systematic empirical analysis of rating performance and consistency based on a combined rating migration record from Standard & Poor's, Moody's, and Fitch. In an effort to close this gap, this paper explores the monitoring role of credit ratings in structured finance and empirically investigates rating agencies' ability to track credit default risk in the run-up and during the subprime mortgage crisis. The purpose of this study is to provide empirical evidence on how well rating agencies reflect actual risk of failure, the extent to which rating performance varies between rating agencies, and the consistency of rating scales over time. Using an extensive rating migration record on 154'608 U.S. residential mortgage-backed securities from 1985 to 2012, we employ multivariate logit regression models to estimate probabilities of default. Receiver operating characteristic allow for a comparison of rating agencies' ability to discriminate with respect to credit default risk. We also perform post-estimations of margins to assess the impact across different subsamples and overall ordinal consistency of rating scales.

The results are threefold: First, the predictive power of ratings in assessing credit default risk varies distinctively across rating agencies.

Second, taking into account basic asset characteristics significantly improves model fit and performance statistics for all rating agencies, indicating that these determinants of credit default risk are underrepresented in prevalent rating methodologies. Third, the study provides suggestive evidence that rating agencies failed to account for rising real estate prices in their credit risk assessment, thereby creating a bias, which led to underestimated default risk and inconsistent credit ratings. Whereas these insights do not claim to preclude alternative theories, they provide a possible explanation for about 32.00% (S&P), 45.44% (Moody's), and 54.28% (Fitch) of total misclassified defaults in the sample. In line with prior research, the results further confirm credit risk to be significantly higher if a tranche is assigned a split rating at inception. Moreover, annual credit default risk is subject to gradual increase during the pre-crisis period, indicating a deterioration of the overall credit quality in the market well before the outburst of the crisis in late 2007. Overall, the findings contribute to the understanding of credit ratings in structured finance and the role of rating agencies in the subprime mortgage crisis. Notably, they highlight the limitations of credit rating's usefulness for comparing credit default risk within rating scales, but also across different rating agencies.

The remainder of this paper is structured as follows: Section II briefly introduces the basic terminology and practice in structured finance and outlines the special role of rating agencies in the process of securitization and subsequent monitoring phase of structured assets. Section III provides the motivation for the empirical analysis. In Section IV, we develop the hypotheses and discuss the most relevant related literature. Section V provides information on data, sample construction and summary statistics. The methodology and empirical results are presented in Section VI. Finally, Section VII summarizes the major findings and concludes with potential implications for further research.

II. The Role of Credit Ratings in Asset Securitization

In structured finance, the term securitization refers to the financial practice of pooling various types of contractual debt and selling the pooled debt as securities to investors, which in turn receive the interest and proceeds from the repayment of the underlying debt.[2] The practice

[2] There exists comprehensive literature on this topic, providing detailed discussion on the process and history of securitization. For a detailed overview see e.g.

typically applies to assets that are illiquid and is especially common in the real estate industry and the lending industry. The main types of structured finance instruments thus include securities backed by mortgage receivables such as residential mortgage-backed securities (RMBS) and commercial mortgage-backed securities (CMBS), whereas instruments backed by other types of receivables such as credit card debt, auto loans, or student loans are more broadly defined as asset-backed securities (ABS). Collateralized debt obligations (CDO) constitute a special type of securitized assets as they apply to the same concept but are typically backed by a portfolio of ABS or MBS. Motives driving financial intermediaries' issuance of securitized assets have included reduction of regulatory capital, access to new and cheaper sources of funding, and portfolio management. Investors' interest has been motivated by portfolio diversification and attractive risk-return profiles.

There are a number of players involved in the process of securitization. The *originator* (sometimes also referred to as issuer or sponsor) initially owns the assets engaged in the deal. These assets are pooled together and sold to a *special purpose vehicle* (SPV), a tax-exempt external legal entity formed for the specific purpose of funding the assets. In this way, the credit risk of the collateral asset pool is de-linked from the credit risk of the originator. Asset pools are then split into tranches of varying degrees of subordination and maturity through the use of credit support specified within the transaction structure to create securities with different risk-return profiles. The originator typically needs the help of an investment bank, the *underwriter* (or arranger), in setting up the structure of the transaction, marketing and selling tranches to investors, and providing liquidity support in the secondary trading market. In this process, underwriters work in close collaboration with *rating agencies*, which provide certification services to investors who need to carry out a due-diligence investigation of the underlying assets and evaluate the structure of the security. A key objectives of the tranching process is to create at least one class of tranches whose rating exceeds the average rating of the total collateral asset pool and to create rated securities from a pool of unrated assets. The common blueprint of each security thus includes a number of senior tranches, a class of subordinate tranches, and an unrated residual equity tranche which is typically retained by the underwriter. Senior tranches are often rated AAA, signifying the lowest bankruptcy likelihood, while subordinated classes receive lower credit ratings, as they are among the first to absorb potential losses in case of issuer default.

Cetorelli & Peristiani (2012), Lemke et al. (2013), Kravitt (2005), Sabarwal (2006), or Saunders & Cornett (2011).

Triggered by the downturn of the structured finance market and the subsequent financial crisis, there has been a growing focus on understanding the implications and complexity of structured products, but also on the relevance of credit ratings and the role of credit rating agencies. Credit ratings play an important part in international capital markets and are widely used for both regulatory and investment purposes. Yet, the rating agencies' activities have the potential of being particularly significant in situations where investors face relatively high costs in assessing the structure and credit risk profile of a given asset. This is particularly the case in structured finance. As noted by the Bank for International Settlement's Committee on the Global Financial System, the process of tranching contributes significantly to the complexity and risk properties of structured products. The variety of possible risk profiles generated through tranching can lead to substantial differences among tranches, and between tranches and ordinary bond portfolios, in terms of the ex-ante uncertainty about losses and their timing, even when the two instruments have the same expected loss (BIS, 2005). As a result of the complex architecture of structured products and the fact that information about the underlying credit portfolio is highly opaque, the balance of information is typically skewed towards the issuer of a security or product. Thus, credit rating agencies perform a key function as due diligence is delegated to them by investors and many mutual funds, governments, and private investors only buy instruments that have been rated by an acquainted agency.

The credit assessment process in structured finance diverges significantly from the rating process of corporate bonds. Unique features of the securitization market include the accessibility of rating tools used by the agencies and the close cooperation between agency and issuer during the negotiation phase. The latter being heavily discussed in the wake of the recent subprime crisis. Another specific feature of structured finance ratings is the fact that rating agencies apply different rating methodologies in assessing credit risk. Whereas S&P and Fitch ratings are based on probability of default (PD), Moody's credit models are based on expected loss (EL), reflecting both the likelihood of default and expected financial losses in the event of a default (loss given default). Peretyatkin and Perraudin (2002) argue that, as a result, certain tranche structures can lead to meaningful differences in the ratings assigned by the agencies. In particular, the authors suggest that ratings assigned on the basis of EL tend to be higher than PD-based ratings on senior tranches with high loss absorption capacity, and lower on mezzanine tranches with lower loss absorption capacity. These findings are also confirmed by Fender & Kiff (2005). This paper does not intend to discuss independency issues and differences in rating agencies' methodology. However, we proceed with the assumption that the credit rating process in securitizations features some aspects which are unique to this market and therefore potentially affect the interpretation and transferability of our results.

III. Motivation

The distribution of rating changes plays a crucial role in many credit risk models. As is well-known, these distributions vary across time, sectors, and different issuer types. Ignoring such dependencies may lead to inaccurate assessments of credit risk. Studies examining rating agencies' behavior have considerably gained in relevance over the past few years. The increasing use of ratings for benchmarking purposes, in particular, ratings-based capital requirements and the investment grade versus sub-investment grade dichotomy depending on the rating of an asset, have led to a de facto regulatory function of credit rating agencies in the operation of securities markets. The importance of credit ratings in structured finance is further accentuated by the industry's oligopolistic market structure which counts a total of ten nationally recognized statistical rating organizations (NRSRO) in the United States, but is to a large extent characterized by the three major players in the field: Standard & Poor's (37.81% market share), Moody's Investors Service (32.76%), and Fitch (20.34%), cumulatively providing more than nine out of ten outstanding credit ratings for securitized assets in 2012.[3]

Given the strong reliance on credit ratings for risk management and benchmarking purposes it is hardly surprising that, following the recent market downturn, rating agencies were subject to a wake of criticism. Much of this criticism centered on misguided incentive schemes and regulatory aspects of the credit rating process, raising the need for a change in regulation standards and increased scrutiny of rating agencies by the government. Researchers also argued that the one-dimensional nature of credit ratings based on expected loss or probability of default is not an adequate metric to fully gauge the riskiness of structured instruments (e.g. Pagano & Volpin, 2009). Several papers have been published on credit risk and performance-related aspects of credit ratings in the corporate bond market. Some of them focus on properties and uses of option based

---

[3] Annual Report on Nationally Recognized Statistical Rating Organizations, U.S. Securities and Exchange Commission (SEC), December 2012, p. 6.

estimates of risk neutral default probabilities obtained from Merton-type models. Others propose alternative measures of probability of default based on accounting data and stock market prices (see e.g. Shumway, 2001; Chava & Jarrow, 2004; Campbell et al., 2008). Yet, due to product complexity and opaqueness of the underlying asset portfolio, models estimating rating performance for corporate bonds hardly find application to structured finance instruments. In addition, the peculiarities of the structured finance market prevent transferability of results and implications from these approaches to a large extent. Thus, actual empirical evidence on the performance of rating agencies in structured finance, and in particular during the financial crisis, remains rather scarce. Although credit ratings of structured products have been the topic of a number of studies (e.g. Benmelech & Dlugosz, 2009; Bolton et al., 2012; Griffin & Tang, 2012), to our knowledge, no previous work has undertaken a systematic empirical analysis of rating performance and consistency based on a combined rating migration record from Standard & Poor's, Moody's, and Fitch.

Our motivation for analyzing rating performance in the context of residential mortgage-backed securities further stems from the fact that RMBS contributed significantly in exacerbating the financial crisis. RMBS constitute by far the most common type of structured assets. When the market was on its height by mid-2007, about 68.97% of all structured finance tranches with a rating from either S&P, Moody's, or Fitch were backed by residential mortgages, followed by general ABS with 11.56%. CMBS and CDO had a roughly equal market share of 10.31% and 9.15%, respectively. Like all fixed-income securities, the prices of (fixed-rate) structured instruments move in response to changes in interest rates, which may also affect the repayment on underlying loans. RMBS are particularly vulnerable in this respect as home equity loans tend to be the most sensitive to changes in interest rates, while credit cards, auto loans, or student loans are generally less prone to interest rate sensitivity. As a consequence, assets backed by residential mortgages suffered most severely during the subprime crisis and played a key role in creating a spillover effect by transitioning market frictions from the local mortgage lending sector to the global economy.

Following the criticism faced by rating agencies, legislators in the United States and other jurisdictions have commenced to reduce rating reliance in laws and regulations, thereby restraining the de facto regulatory function held by rating agencies (White, 2010). Interviews with large institutional investors in structured products further suggest that they do not rely on ratings as the sole source of information for their investment decisions, which limits the potential for misunderstood risk exposures (BIS, 2005). Nevertheless, credit ratings sustained little of their integral role in structured finance, and rating agency approval still appears to determine the marketability of a given structure to a wider market. Pension funds, banks, and insurance companies use the screening function of ratings to make investments and allocate regulatory capital. Central banks and governments enact regulations and guidelines which rely on credit ratings to define minimum standards for credit risk management. It is therefore not surprising that the Big Three rating agencies are still viewed by the Financial Crisis Inquiry Commission (FCIC) as key players in the process of mortgage securitization.[4] Based on these considerations, the next section will develop the research questions and formulate a set of different hypotheses which are tested in the empirical analysis.

IV. Hypothesis Development

The interpretation of credit ratings' informational content has been subject to some debate in recent years, especially in structured finance. Some researchers argue that, if ratings are to be informative indicators of credit risk they must reflect both idiosyncratic and systematic risk. Idiosyncratic credit risk is tied to the unique circumstances of a specific security, whereas systemic risk affects all securities in the market. For example, Hilscher & Wilson (2013) point out that diversified and risk-averse investors will care about both raw default probability and systematic risk, just as a corporate bond prices depends not only on expected payoff (which depends on its raw default probability) but also on its discount rate or risk premium (which depends on its systematic default risk). Credit ratings therefore ought to contain information about at least one and ideally both of these important attributes. On the other hand, Moody's argues that, in principle, credit ratings are intended to be accurate measures of relative credit risk as determined by each security's relative fundamental creditworthiness and without reference to explicit time horizons (Cantor & Mann, 2003). Beyond controversy, rating agencies frequently emphasize that the definitions of rating categories they employ are explicitly non-quantitative and not directly linked to explicit probabilities of underlying asset delinquency. In any case, relying on credit ratings as a major source of information for investment decisions

[4] The Financial Crisis Inquiry Report. National Commission on the Causes of the Financial and Economic Crisis in the United States. February 2011, pp. 43–44.

requires a sound understanding of their informative content and in particular, its differences across rating agencies. Investors are generally aware of the fact that, for example, Moody's tends to provide slightly more conservative assessments of credit risk compared to Standard & Poor's or Fitch. However from the perspective of legislators and regulatory authorities, credit ratings are largely treated as identical, based on the mapping process described in the previous section. In contrast, we argue that relative differences around the link between ratings and an asset's underlying probability of default are largely underestimated in current literature. From the perspective of investors and regulators in structured finance it is crucial to understand (i) how well rating agencies indicate actual risk of failure, (ii) the extent to which rating performance varies between rating agencies, and (iii) the consistency of rating scales over time and different subsamples. The performance of rating agencies is determined by how well they exert due diligence on behalf of investors. Relative agency performance can thus be assessed by comparing differences in correlations between ratings and defaults. Hence we can formulate the first hypothesis as follows:

$H1_0$: *Default prediction accuracy does not differ across agencies.*
$H1_A$: *Default prediction accuracy differs across agencies.*

Starting from the premise that Standard & Poor's, Moody's, and Fitch have access to the entirety of publicly available information, it can be assumed that all public information which is relevant to the creditworthiness of an asset is reflected in the rating. In addition, rating agencies might obtain superior knowledge through close collaboration with underwriter and originator which would also be considered in the credit assessment process. Based on these assumptions, classification accuracy may not be improved by factoring additional public information into the model. Based on these considerations, we hypothesize that:

$H2_0$: *Additional public information does not improve default prediction accuracy.*
$H2_A$: *Additional public information improves default prediction accuracy.*

Rating performance and consistency of rating scales are closely linked concepts in determining the overall success of a rating agency. By definition, high rating performance also implies strongly consistent credit ratings. Assuming consistency in rating scales, the likelihood of asset default should constantly increase along the rating scale from higher to lower ratings. Additionally, this pattern is required to prevail across different subsamples and time windows. Essentially, analyzing consistency in ratings is an alternative method in determining rating agencies' success. We can therefore test the following hypothesis:

$H3_0$: Rating scales are consistent with respect to predicted probabilities of default.
$H3_A$: Rating scales are not consistent with respect to predicted probabilities of default.

V. DATA

The main analysis is based on a dataset combining credit rating information from three different sources. The joint data comprises the complete monthly long-term credit rating migration of residential mortgage-backed securities rated by Standard & Poor's, Moody's Investors Service, and Fitch Ratings. Standard & Poor's ratings are obtained through the S&P Credit Ratings database on Wharton Research Data Services (WRDS). The global database uses the combined information of S&P RatingsXpress and Compustat fundamental and market data, providing the credit rating migration of 158'539 RMBS tranches issued between 1977 and 2012. Moody's credit ratings are taken from the Structured Finance Default Risk Services database (SF-DRS) which covers the credit histories and material impairment of all Moody's-rated structured finance products issued since 1982. As of 2012, the database includes historical changes in credit ratings of 94'216 RMBS tranches, segmented into 10'704 deals. Fitch credit ratings are provided by the Fitch Solutions Integrated Data Services (IDS) and include the global record of historical credit ratings since 1985 on both issuer- and tranche-level for the Fitch-rated structured finance universe offering detailed sub-level debt classification of each rated tranche. The available record up to 2012 comprises 79'305 RMBS tranches from 1'515 different originators.

Besides daily rating migration, numerous deal- and tranche-level characteristics are available for each data set. All three records commonly feature a number of tranche-level security identifiers along with tranche name, original amount, asset type, domicile of assets, debt currency, issue launch date, legal maturity date, sub-industry classification, and information on credit enhancement or specialized financial structuring. Rating migration data include daily long- and short-term credit ratings and rating changes from the respective rating agencies, as well as watch list and rating outlook indications where applicable. Moreover, S&P and Fitch provide additional information on issuer- and entity-level for each tranche alongside with interest rates paid on debt obligations. Moody's record on the other hand includes debt classification according to tranche seniority, impairment calculations for tranches in default, and several deal-level characteristics such as unique deal identification, deal name, and original sale amount.

From the raw data, the final sample is constructed; a tranche is included in the final sample if it cumulatively satisfies the following criteria:

(i) The tranche has to be identifiable by means of a unique security identifier code such as CUSIP, ISIN, or CINS;
(ii) The relevant tranche characteristics (original amount, asset type, domicile of assets, debt currency, issue launch date, legal maturity date, industry classification, and information on credit enhancement and collateral) have to be known;
(iii) In order to rule out currency- and country-specific effects, tranche's original amount is required to be denominated in U.S. Dollar and the majority of assets are domiciled in the United States;
(iv) A rating migration record of at least one long-term credit rating publication from either S&P, Moody's, or Fitch must be available.

After applying the above criteria, the final sample is obtained by matching tranches records from S&P, Moody's, and Fitch based on available security identifier codes. This enables the identification single-rated and multiple-rated (i.e. double- and triple-rated) tranches. In this study, the terms single-, double-, and triple-rated are referred to with respect to coverage by S&P, Moody's, and Fitch, as they cumulatively provide about 90.91% of total outstanding credit ratings in the structured finance market. However, we implicitly accept the possibility that some tranches might be rated by additional NRSRO or non-NRSRO certified rating agencies which are not covered by this sample.

Table 1: Summary Statistics

This table shows summary statistics and selected tranche characteristics of all available U.S. Dollar-denominated RMBS tranches issued between January 1985 and July 2012. The sample only includes securities whose underlying assets are predominantly domiciled in the United States. S&P ratings are obtained from the S&P Credit Ratings database in WRDS, Moody's ratings are from the Structured Finance Default Risk Services database (SF-DRS), and Fitch ratings are provided by Fitch Solutions Integrated Data Services (IDS).

Subsample	# of rated Tranches	Senior Tranches (in %)	Multiple Ratings (in %)	Legal Maturity (in Years)	Mean Volume (in USDm)	Mean Rating at Issuance	# of Defaults (≤ C)	in % of Subsample
Total	154'608	100.00%	72.41%	28.83	48.60	3.34	49'022	31.71%
Rating Agency								
S&P	125'498	81.17%	78.15%	28.96	52.10	3.13	41'949	33.43%
Moody's	88'955	57.54%	94.46%	29.05	59.20	2.96	31'855	35.81%
Fitch	72'917	47.16%	85.90%	28.97	46.70	3.02	22'836	31.32%
Subordination								
Senior (AAA)	97'599	63.13%	81.42%	28.34	72.10	1.02	14'942	15.31%
Subordinate	57'009	36.87%	56.99%	29.68	13.30	7.29	34'080	59.78%
Collateral								
First Mortgage	85'457	55.27%	78.72%	29.08	41.40	2.73	22'991	26.90%
Subprime Mortgage	35'246	22.80%	94.40%	28.80	67.20	4.08	15'469	43.89%
Other	33'905	21.93%	33.67%	28.23	45.20	4.07	10'562	31.15%
Vintage								
before 2000	37'211	24.07%	63.73%	26.18	41.00	2.24	594	1.60%
2000-2003	29'580	19.13%	75.61%	28.41	48.00	2.93	2'025	6.85%
2004-2006	63'387	41.00%	80.64%	30.11	54.10	4.07	32'884	51.88%
2007-2008	19'055	12.32%	76.50%	30.66	49.90	3.55	13'425	70.45%

Table 1 provides summary statistics of the final sample. It comprises a total of 154'608 tranches, of which 81.17% are rated by S&P, Moody's provides credit statements for 57.45% of tranches, and 47.16% have a Fitch rating assigned. The large majority of tranches are rated by more than one rating agency. Notably, Moody's ratings and tranches backed by subprime mortgages are rarely published on a standalone basis. In the case of Moody's ratings, this might be explained by the fact that Moody's is often viewed as being more conservative compared to its competitors (see e.g. Livingston et al., 2010). With respect to the borrower quality of securitized loans, the sample features mostly securities backed by prime-rate collaterals (55.27%), while roughly equal shares of tranches are collateralized by subprime loans (22.80%) and intermediate quality increments (21.93%) such Alt-A. Mean maturity denotes the period between issue launch date and the date on which the principal amount becomes due and payable. In general, tranche terms do not appear to vary substantially across subsamples, although mean maturity along with tranche original sales amount, have increased along with market growth.

Mean rating at issuance denotes the cross-sectional mean rating score of all tranches at the time of issuance. To calculate mean ratings, this paper follows convention and uses a numerical rating scale to convert ratings.[5] The numerical scores corresponding to the rating notches range from 1 for AAA/Aaa through 20 for CC/Ca. A score of 21 is used to indicate impaired ratings. A security is impaired when it is downgraded to C or D, or when it suffers a principal loss. However, ratings implying lower bankruptcy likelihood will still be referred to as 'higher' or 'better' ratings for the rest of this paper. We adjust for time lags between initial publications of rating for multiple-rated tranches, by calculating the respective means over the first date on which the ratings of all involved rating agencies are publicly available. Yet, the impact is found to be negligible as time lags typically do not exceed the period of three months. Ratings at issuance have been slightly deteriorating over the long term, but improved again shortly before the crisis.

Finally, number of defaults reports the count of tranches which have experienced a default during the sample period. In order to minimize the impact of inconsistencies between different rating scales and varying definitions of (near to) default, a tranche is considered impaired when it is downgraded to C or lower, or when it suffers a principal loss. As to be

[5] Despite its frequent application in financial literature for comparing different rating scales (see e.g. Cantor & Packer, 1997; Jewell & Livingston, 1999; Bongaerts et al., 2012, among others), the findings in Section IV illustrate that the results from this approach should be interpreted with due care.

expected, defaults are particularly common with tranches backed by subprime loans (43.89%) and subordinate tranches (59.78%), but also among more recent vintages, whose underlying loans did not benefit as much from rising real estate prices, leaving them much more vulnerable to impairment in case of adverse developments in the U.S. housing market.

Figure 1: Number of Tranches and Rating Distribution of U.S. RMBS

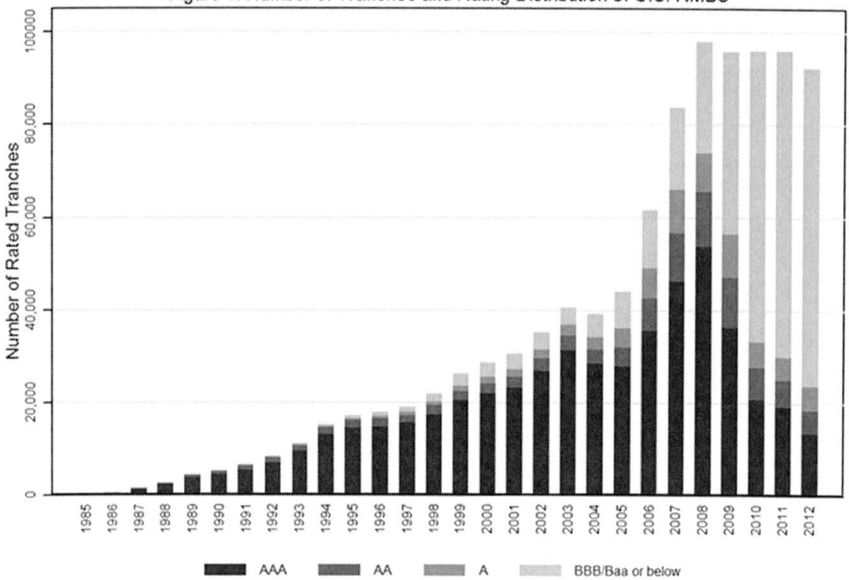

A more detailed overview on the evolution of the U.S. structured finance market is given in Figure 1. The chart reports the total number of tranches and mean rating distribution for tranches with an outstanding rating from S&P, Moody's, and/or Fitch. The RMBS market experienced rapid growth, especially during the post-millennial period. Several factors contributed to this development: Low interest rates, relaxed credit standards in combination with excessive lending have fuelled the real estate and mortgage market, especially for nonprime borrowers. Additionally, CDO issuers replaced troubled company debt with residential mortgages as their main source of collateral for their issues, following the crisis on high-yield corporate bonds between 2001 and 2003 (Croce et al., 2011). The dramatic rise in asset underwriting also became an increasingly important factor in the credit rating business. For example, within a decade Moody's revenues from structured finance ratings grew from $50 million in 1995 to just below $850 million in 2006.

Like the overall structured finance market, the RMBS sector has been dominated by AAA-rated tranches, when measured by number of tranches. When measured by dollar volume of issuance, the AAA share generally tends to be even higher. For example, in 2007, AAA-rated tranches accounted for approximately 50.72% of all RMBS by number of tranches and 82.82% by dollar volume. By comparison, tranches rated BBB/Baa or below comprised only a small fraction of the total issuance at roughly 2.86% in 2007, although they did account for 25.75% of all rated tranches in that year.

Figure 2: Monthly Mean Rating Levels of U.S. RMBS

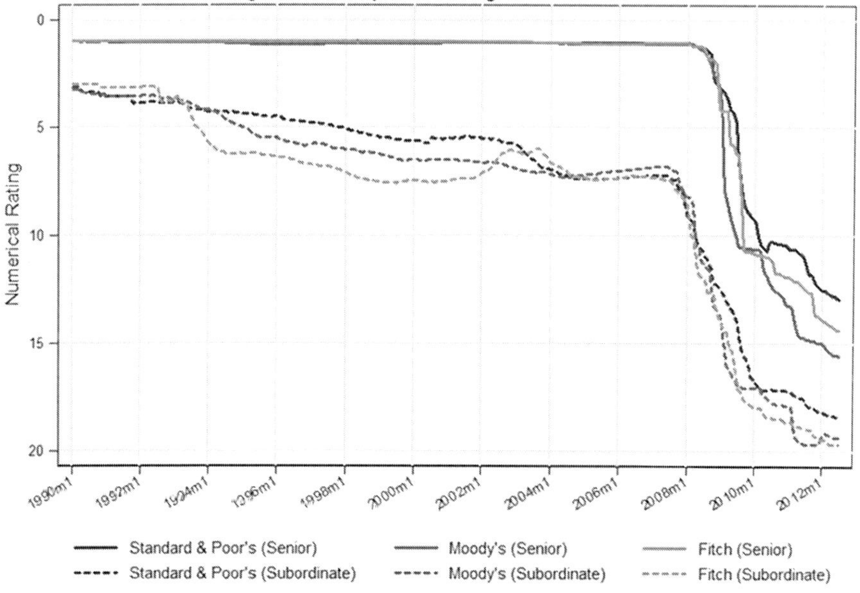

Figure 2 reports monthly mean numerical credit rating levels for Standard & Poor's, Moody's and Fitch. Notably, the differences in ratings between rating agencies among senior tranches have increased in the aftermath of the financial crisis, despite highly unanimous ratings in the years before. In general, the gap in rating-implied credit risk between senior and subordinate tranches has constantly widened since the origins of the market in the 1980s. Yet, senior tranches sustained a roughly similar decline in numerical rating notches between 2008 and 2012 as AAA-

subordination. Mean ratings of senior tranches across all rating agencies fell about 12.15 notches, whereas subordinate tranches lost about 11.30 notches during the same period.

When considering the variety of different risk-return profiles in rating agencies' monitoring portfolios, rating levels appear to be largely consistent. However, a direct comparison requires a common measure of credit risk to determine the relative performance of rating agencies. The next section will therefore introduce the methodology used in the empirical analysis and discuss the empirical results with respect to the three hypotheses.

VI. Methodology & Empirical Results

This paper uses estimated probability of default as identification strategy to evaluate and compare the performance of different rating systems. Estimates are predicted on the basis of pooled logit regression models and overall classification accuracy is quantified using receiver operating characteristic. Both applications are widely used measures in financial literature, and are commonly used in the context of credit ratings to predict default and assess a binary response model (e.g. Hilscher & Wilson, 2013; Kraemer & Guettler, 2008). To examine the consistency of rating scales we rely on a series of post-estimation analyses on margins to assess changes in default probabilities within each rating category that may occur over time.

1. Does Rating Performance Vary Across Rating Agencies?

To compare the performance of different rating agencies, practitioners can rely on rating transition probability matrices which are made publicly available by the rating agencies. Transition probability matrices indicate the probability of rating change to a lower (or higher) rating category, typically within the next twelve months. As such they provide a convenient means of comparing ratings of different agencies. However, several researchers have documented that transition matrices are highly sensitive to the business cycle[6], and the frequency of rating revision varies highly across rating agencies. Transition matrices therefore only constitute an imperfect means for performance comparisons. In order to compare rating agencies' ability to discriminate with respect to credit default risk, this paper relies on ex-post probabilities of default as a proxy for credit

---

[6] See e.g. Nickell et al. (2000), Bangia et al. (2002), Rösch & Scheule (2010), or Croce et al. (2011), among others.

risk. Probabilities of default are hereinafter defined as a security's ex post probability of encountering impairment, indicated by a downgrade to C or lower (equivalent to a score of 21 on the numerical rating scale) by the respective rating agency. Rating implied PD are calculated on annual basis over each rating category, and measure the likelihood of impairment within the next twelve months, conditional on the rating at the beginning of the year. Assuming that rating agencies take into account all available public and private information in the initial credit assessment and subsequent monitoring phase, credit ratings can be expected to provide a good approximation for an asset's inherent credit risk. We can thus operationalize the first research question by specify the following univariate baseline model to analyse the explanatory power of credit ratings with respect to predicting tranche default.

$$D_{i,t} = \beta_0 + \beta_1 Ratg_{i,t} + \varepsilon_i \qquad (1)$$

The dependent variable $D_{i,t}$ is binary and assumes 1 if tranche i entered into default in year t, and 0 otherwise. In response to the binary character of the dependent variable, we employ a pooled logit regression model which is estimated using maximum likelihood. Tranche rating is denoted by the variable *Tranche Rating (Ratg)* which refers to the numerical rating score of tranche i on the first business day of year t. The error term is assumed to be normally distributed with $\varepsilon_i \sim N(0, \sigma^2)$. Potential clusters on tranche level are accounted for by cluster-robust standard errors, which are a clustered version of Huber-White sandwich estimators.

The subsample results for each rating agency are presented in columns SP1, M1, and F1 of Table 2. As expected, coefficients for tranche rating are positive and statistically significant, indicating a strong relationship between an asset's credit rating and the likelihood of default. As the model uses logistic transformations, reported coefficients correspond to the expected change in log odds by a one-unit increase in the predictor variable. We can obtain the expected change in odds by exponentiating the coefficients, which for S&P yields an increase in odds of entering into default of 22.88% for a one-notch increase in rating scores. The corresponding changes in odds for Moody's and Fitch are 12.30% and 15.95%, respectively. From the analysis of coefficients we can already see that the difference in PD between units of measurement imposes a potential difficulty when comparing credit ratings from different rating agencies. For example, a downgrade by S&P to the next lower rating category roughly corresponds to a Moody's downgrade by almost two rating categories in order to equalize the expected change in PD.

Table 2: Classification Accuracy of Credit Ratings

This table provides the results of the pooled logistic regression for the three rating agencies estimated over annual tranche observations from 1985-2012. The dependent binary variable is *Default* and coded 1 if a tranche entered into default during a given year, and 0 otherwise. *Tranche Rating* refers to a tranches numerical long-term credit rating from the respective rating agency recorded at the beginning of the year. *Split Rating* indicates whether multiple ratings at issuance are consistent (1) or not (0). We further consider three control variables which improve the model fit: *Residual Maturity* indicates a tranche's remaining time to maturity, denominated in months. *Collateral* captures borrower quality of a tranche's underlying mortgage pool, and assumes 1 for tranches backed by prime-rate mortgages and 0 for more inferior capital quality such as Alt-A and subprime. *Multiple Ratings* is binary and assumes 1 if a tranche has an additional second or third rating, and 0 otherwise. Cluster-robust standard errors are a clustered version of Huber-White sandwich estimators and account for potential clusters on tranche level. Additionally, the receiver operating characteristic (ROC) and McFadden's adjusted R^2 are reported for each regression.

Dependent:	Standard & Poor's		Moody's		Fitch	
Default (Rating ≤ C)	(SP1)	(SP2)	(M1)	(M2)	(F1)	(F2)
Tranche Rating	0.206***	0.183***	0.116***	0.057***	0.148***	0.112***
	(0.0008)	(0.0011)	(0.0007)	(0.0010)	(0.0009)	(0.0011)
Split Rating		0.102***		0.262***		0.051***
		(0.0083)		(0.0093)		(0.0108)
Controls (3)	No	Yes	No	Yes	No	Yes
Cluster-robust SE	Yes	Yes	Yes	Yes	Yes	Yes
Method	Logit	Logit	Logit	Logit	Logit	Logit
AUROC	0.845	0.870	0.769	0.844	0.793	0.833
Sensitivity	90.94%	93.84%	84.97%	88.38%	84.38%	91.94%
McFadden's adj. R^2	0.241	0.253	0.103	0.190	0.171	0.200
Observations	695'043	695'043	493'281	493'281	408'737	408'737

Robust standard errors in parentheses, *** $p<0.01$, ** $p<0.05$, * $p<0.1$

A number of test statistics is employed to evaluate overall model fit. Receiver operating characteristic (ROC) provides a quantitative measure of the accuracy of diagnostic markers (credit rating) to discriminate between two states or conditions (default and non-default). The ROC curve depicts the relationship between the fractions of positive cases correctly classified (true positive rate) and that of positive cases incorrectly classified (false positive rate), for a range of probability thresholds. The true-positive rate is also called sensitivity, while specificity is the true-negative rate. The measure 1–specificity is also called the false-positive rate. Hence, for every cut-off value the ROC curve indicates the relationship between the true positive rate (sensitivity) and the false-positive rate (1–specificity). Accordingly, the larger the ROC statistics, the most accurate is the diagnostic marker to discriminate between default and non-default. The area under the ROC curve, or AURCO, can then be used as a summary measure for each rating agency to identify differences in the predictive power of credit ratings. The angle bisecting line, also called reference line represents a random model, in which case the marker provides no discriminatory power in ex ante distinguishing between default and non-default. A value between 0.5 (random model) and 1 (perfect foresight) indicates that the true-positive rate is higher than the false-positive rate and the model generates meaningful default predictions. In addition to the AUROC measure, sensitivity or true-positive rate, and McFadden's adjusted R-squared are reported for each regression. Sensitivity is calculated based on a cutoff score equal to the share of default observations in the subsample. As regards SP1, M1, and F1, all regression diagnostics unanimously point towards Standard & Poor's ratings for having the highest classification accuracy of predicting a default. The area under the ROC curve of 0.845 indicates considerable discriminatory power which is significantly[7] higher compared to Moody's (-0.076) and Fitch (-0.052). With respect to Hypothesis 1, the above results allow us to reject the null hypothesis and not reject the alternative hypothesis. Notably, S&P's R-squared of 0.241 indicates a fairly good fit compared to Moody's R-squared of 0.103, which by this metric cannot be considered a very strong model. The predictive accuracy of Fitch ratings appears to range somewhere in between, although the true-positive rate of Moody's is slightly higher.

---

[7] Areas under the ROC curve are compared using an algorithm suggested by DeLong et al. (1988). The chi-squared test yields a significance probability < 0.01 for all three combinations of test modalities, suggesting that there is significant difference in classification accuracies between all three areas.

2. Do Credit Ratings Reflect All Relevant Public Information?

Assuming that credit ratings incorporate all major determinants of credit default risk, including additional rating characteristics should ceteris paribus not result in an improvement of model fit and performance statistics. In a next step, we can therefore check for omitted or underrepresented factors in rating agencies' credit rating methodology by introducing some basic asset characteristics to the baseline model:

$$D_{i,t} = \beta_0 + \beta_1 Ratg_{i,t} + \beta_2 TTM_{i,T-t} + \beta_3 Coll_i + \beta_4 Mult_i + \beta_5 Split_i + \varepsilon_i \qquad (2)$$

First, we account for the fact that the likelihood of impairment typically decreases as tranches approach final maturity (T). *Time to Maturity (TTM)* therefore denotes remaining tranche lifetime in months defined as $T - t$. The variable *Collateral (Coll)* refers to borrower quality of a tranche's underlying mortgage pool and assumes 1 for tranches backed by prime-rate mortgages and 0 for more inferior capital quality such as Alt-A and subprime. *Multiple Ratings (Mult)* is a zero-one variable coded 1 if a tranche is rated by more than one rating agency, and 0 otherwise. Evidence from the corporate bond market shows, that firms with more asset opaqueness problems are more likely to receive split bond ratings (Livingston et al., 2007). The authors also show that split rated bonds are more likely to have rating changes in the future, implying a causal link between asset opaqueness, split ratings and rating changes. Provided this link also holds with structured assets, split ratings might indicate elevated uncertainty with respect to assets' inherent credit risk. This information is incremental as it cannot be produced by information from either rating agency alone. Consequently, a tranche with multiple consistent ratings is expected to be less risky than a tranche with the same average rating, but consisting of multiple dissenting ratings. The model set up in equation 2 directly allows us to test whether split rated tranches experience higher credit risk compared to non-split rated tranches by including *Split Rating (Split)* which is binary and captures whether multiple ratings at inception are consistent, i.e. whether they received the same numerical rating score from each affiliated rating agency (1), or not (0). In addition, the natural logarithm of tranche original amount, denominated in U.S. Dollar, was supposed to account for effects related to tranche size but did not display any statistical significance and has therefore been excluded from the models.

The results of the multivariate regression models are reported in columns SP2, M2, and F2 of Table 2. Interestingly, all regression diagnostics improve significantly compared to the baseline models. R-squared statistics increase only moderately for Standard & Poor's, implying that S&P ratings already incorporate the above factors to a large extent. On the other hand, R^2 for regression M2 nearly doubles compared to M1 which indicates that the additional variables add considerable explanatory power to the model. Accordingly, the analysis suggests that these factors might be underrepresented in Moody's current rating methodology. The area under the ROC curve generally confirms this view. However, chi-squared tests for equality of areas against the univariate models yield significance probabilities below 0.01 for all rating agencies. When considering the true-positive rate, differences between S&P (+2.90%) and Moody's (+3.41%) are less pronounced, and Fitch appears to gain most in terms of classification accuracy compared to the baseline model (+7.56%). The results allow us to reject $H2_0$ and not reject the alternative hypothesis. Tranche characteristics and additional public information prove to provide incremental explanatory power on the likelihood of tranche default, although the precise contribution varies across rating agencies. In addition, odds for experiencing default are between 5.23% (Fitch) and 29.95% (Moody's) higher for tranches which received a split rating upon inception. In line with Livingstone et al. (2007) the results further extend the link between split ratings and rating changes, suggesting that split rated tranches are more likely to suffer impairment compared to non-split rated tranches.

3. Are Rating Scales Consistent With Predicted Credit Risk?

To get a more nuanced view on the evolution of rating-implied probabilities of default and their overall consistency with rating scales, a series of margin post-estimations are calculated based on regressions SP2, M2, and F2. Margins are frequently used in Epidemiology and Biostatistics, but recently also in Economics[8] as an informative means for summarizing how the value of a response variable is related to different values of one or more covariates, holding the remaining variables at their means. In the context of logit or probit models we thus obtain the predicted probabilities associated with covariates or subsamples at predefined values. The coefficients from the baseline models further merely represent the average change in log odds for a rating change to the next adjacent category. It

[8] For a detailed discussion of margins and marginal effects see e.g. Long (1997), Long & Freese (2005), Bartus (2005), or Cameron & Trivedi (2010).

Table 2.1: Predicted One-Year Probability of Default by Year

This table reports the margins of predicted one-year default probabilities calculated from the logistic regression models (SP1, M1, F1) for selected rating categories and sample periods. Additional covariates in the model include the numerical tranche rating at the beginning of the period, tranche size, remaining time to maturity, and zero-one variables for tranche seniority and collateral quality.

Credit Rating (selected)	Period (selected)	Conditional Margins S&P		Conditional Margins Moody's		Conditional Margins Fitch	
		Predicted PD	Std. Err.	Predicted PD	Std. Err.	Predicted PD	Std. Err.
AAA / Aaa	before 2000	0.0017***	5.59E-05	0.0047***	7.38E-05	0.0036***	7.53E-05
AAA / Aaa	2000	0.0023***	5.39E-05	0.0069***	9.06E-05	0.0052***	9.22E-05
AAA / Aaa	2002	0.0028***	5.20E-05	0.0104***	1.23E-04	0.0064***	1.01E-04
AAA / Aaa	2004	0.0042***	6.23E-05	0.0219***	2.68E-04	0.0127***	1.71E-04
AAA / Aaa	2006	0.0053***	8.68E-05	0.0291***	3.68E-04	0.0194***	3.04E-04
AAA / Aaa	2008-2011	0.0056***	9.87E-05	0.0355***	4.69E-04	0.0219***	3.68E-04
AA / Aa2	before 2000	0.0025***	8.12E-05	0.0053***	8.03E-05	0.0045***	9.39E-05
AA / Aa2	2000	0.0033***	7.73E-05	0.0077***	9.49E-05	0.0064***	1.12E-04
AA / Aa2	2002	0.0040***	7.28E-05	0.0117***	1.22E-04	0.0080***	1.20E-04
AA / Aa2	2004	0.0060***	7.95E-05	0.0244***	2.54E-04	0.0158***	1.83E-04
AA / Aa2	2006	0.0075***	1.09E-04	0.0324***	3.48E-04	0.0241***	3.25E-04
AA / Aa2	2008-2011	0.0080***	1.25E-04	0.0395***	4.46E-04	0.0272***	3.97E-04
A / A2	before 2000	0.0043***	1.43E-04	0.0063***	9.40E-05	0.0063***	1.33E-04
A / A2	2000	0.0057***	1.35E-04	0.0091***	1.06E-04	0.0090***	1.56E-04
A / A2	2002	0.0069***	1.23E-04	0.0138***	1.23E-04	0.0111***	1.61E-04
A / A2	2004	0.0104***	1.14E-04	0.0287***	2.25E-04	0.0219***	1.99E-04
A / A2	2006	0.0129***	1.48E-04	0.0380***	3.05E-04	0.0333***	3.44E-04
A / A2	2008-2011	0.0138***	1.72E-04	0.0462***	3.96E-04	0.0375***	4.26E-04
BBB / Baa2	before 2000	0.0074***	2.53E-04	0.0074***	1.15E-04	0.0088***	1.94E-04
BBB / Baa2	2000	0.0098***	2.38E-04	0.0108***	1.26E-04	0.0124***	2.23E-04
BBB / Baa2	2002	0.0119***	2.15E-04	0.0162***	1.35E-04	0.0155***	2.27E-04
BBB / Baa2	2004	0.0178***	1.65E-04	0.0338***	1.94E-04	0.0303***	2.20E-04
BBB / Baa2	2006	0.0221***	1.89E-04	0.0445***	2.53E-04	0.0458***	3.35E-04
BBB / Baa2	2008-2011	0.0236***	2.22E-04	0.0540***	3.30E-04	0.0515***	4.27E-04

Delta-method standard errors in parentheses, *** $p<0.01$, ** $p<0.05$, * $p<0.1$

therefore implicitly assumes a linear increase in PD across rating scales. Yet, this might not necessarily be the case. On that account, we calculate the predicted probabilities of default for each rating category and different time windows.

The results for selected rating categories are presented in Table 2.1 and a graphical illustration of the entire sample, alongside with 95% confidence intervals is provided in Figures 3.1, 3.2, and 3.3. Several peculiarities deserve to be highlighted in this context. First, predicted probabilities of default seem consistent with rating scales in the sense that for each time period, PD increases towards the next lower rating category. Second, we can also note that the overall level of credit risk has constantly increased in the run-up of the subprime crisis, indicating a deterioration of the overall credit quality in the market well before the outburst of the crisis. Third, along with the rise overall credit risk we can observe an increase in the discriminative ability of credit ratings over the observation period, as indicated by relatively steeper slopes of graphs for more recent year. For example, whereas the difference in predicted PD between AAA/Aaa and BBB/Baa2 only amounted to 0.75% (S&P), 0.39% (Moody's), and 0.72% (Fitch) in 2000, it increased within six years to 1.68%, 1.54%, and 2.64% respectively. The figures also visualize that Moody's rating scale follows a linear increase in PD whereas S&P and Fitch scales exhibit a more convex relationship with predicted PD. Fourth, when comparing one-year PD across rating agencies it becomes evident that for example in 2006, a Fitch AA rating much rather corresponded to a S&P BBB rating than an 'equivalent' AA rating by S&P. Based on the latter it can be argued, that the standard approach for comparing ratings from different agencies might be problematic, as rating-implied probabilities of default might differ substantially across rating agencies. A further breakdown of this analysis to the subsamples of single-, double-, and triple-rated tranches has revealed that differences among rating agencies are less prevalent among multiple-rated tranches. This suggests that different credit ratings on the same asset have a tendency to converge, whereas rating-implied PD can be entirely different for single-rated tranches. However, the implications from this analysis may be interpreted with caution as one must also consider that rating agencies employ different methodologies in determining the overall creditworthiness of an instrument (EL approach by Moody's, PD approach by S&P and Fitch). Moreover, different definitions of the state of default might also prevent a clear-cut conclusion from this analysis.

Figure 3.1: S&P Predicted One-Year PD by Year

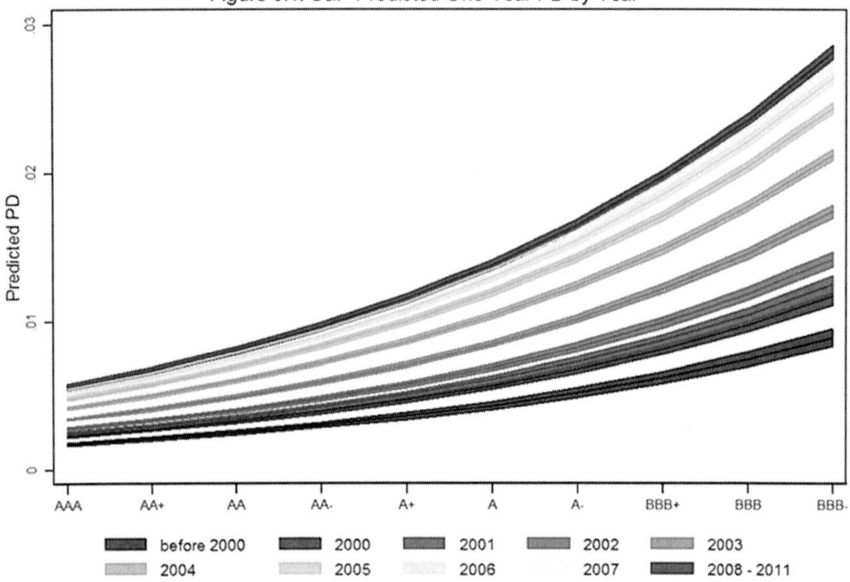

Figure 3.2: Moody's Predicted One-Year PD by Year

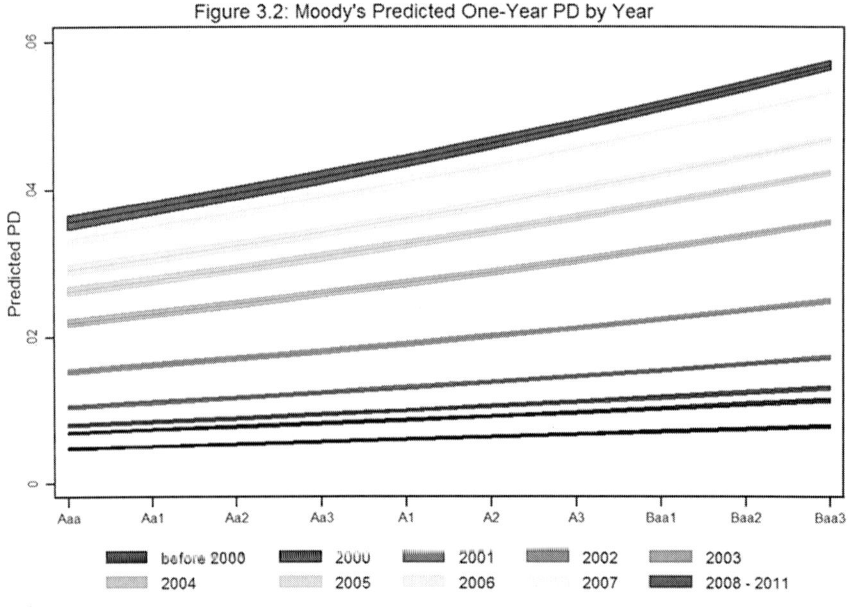

Figure 3.3: Fitch Predicted One-Year PD by Year

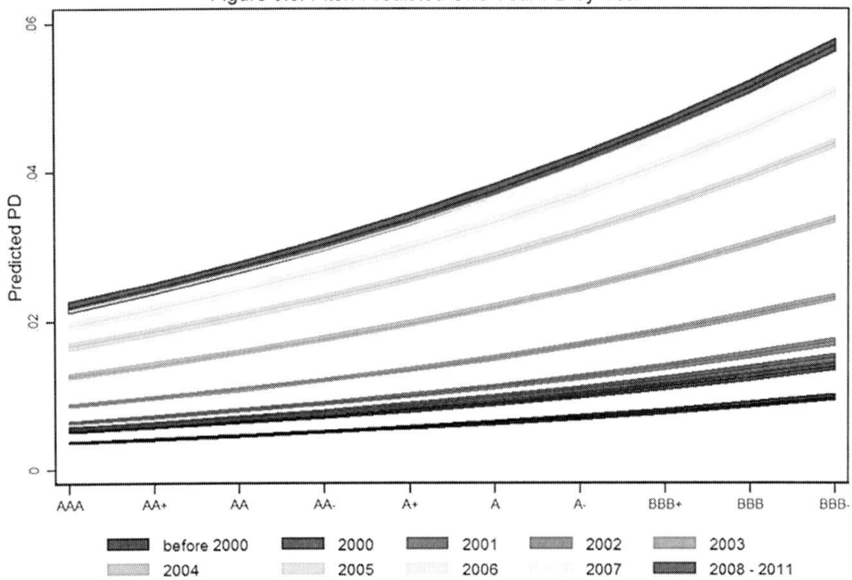

From the summary statistics we have seen that the number of defaults appears to be positively related to tranche vintage, i.e. the time of tranche issuance. As outlined in Section 4 of this paper, we hypothesize that the strong increase in PD among recent vintages might, however, constitute a potential source for inconsistencies within rating scales. We therefore conduct a second post-estimation analysis for different combinations of rating categories and tranche vintage on a reduced[9] crisis sample which includes pooled ratings and default observations from 2008 and 2009. Again, the condensed results are presented in Table 2.2 and a graphical illustration of the total sample is provided in Figures 4.1, 4.2, and 4.3.

[9] A reduced crisis sample is used for this analysis because as prior analysis has shown that default rates change over time, this bias is constrained by reducing the observation period. As for this analysis, we are mainly interested in variation of PD across different vintages. In addition, the number of defaults is particularly high during this period, and thus potential flaws in credit risk assessment are likely to have a strong impact on the rating scale. As a robustness check, the analysis is also conducted on the total sample, but found to yield only negligible variation in results.

Table 2.2: Predicted One-Year Probability of Default by Vintage

This table reports the margins of the pooled predicted one-year default probabilities calculated from the logistic regression models (SP1, M1, F1) for a reduced crisis sample (2008-2009) and selected rating categories and tranche vintage. Additional covariates in the model include the numerical tranche rating at the beginning of the period, tranche size, remaining time to maturity, and zero-one variables for tranche seniority and collateral quality.

Credit Rating (selected)	Vintage (selected)	Conditional Margins S&P		Conditional Margins Moody's		Conditional Margins Fitch	
		Predicted PD	Std. Err.	Predicted PD	Std. Err.	Predicted PD	Std. Err.
AAA / Aaa	2000	0.0030***	1.19E-04	0.0413***	9.06E-04	0.0226***	7.18E-04
AAA / Aaa	2002	0.0033***	1.22E-04	0.0468***	9.28E-04	0.0246***	6.22E-04
AAA / Aaa	2004	0.0040***	1.42E-04	0.0589***	1.09E-03	0.0358***	7.25E-04
AAA / Aaa	2006	0.0050***	1.76E-04	0.0823***	1.41E-03	0.0517***	1.06E-03
AA / Aa2	2000	0.0053***	1.87E-04	0.0482***	9.24E-04	0.0304***	8.90E-04
AA / Aa2	2002	0.0058***	1.90E-04	0.0544***	9.21E-04	0.0330***	7.50E-04
AA / Aa2	2004	0.0070***	2.16E-04	0.0683***	1.05E-03	0.0478***	8.02E-04
AA / Aa2	2006	0.0087***	2.67E-04	0.0941***	1.32E-03	0.0686***	1.15E-03
A / A2	2000	0.0122***	3.64E-04	0.0605***	9.46E-04	0.0471***	1.24E-03
A / A2	2002	0.0133***	3.58E-04	0.0680***	8.91E-04	0.0511***	1.01E-03
A / A2	2004	0.0162***	3.90E-04	0.0846***	9.31E-04	0.0730***	9.09E-04
A / A2	2006	0.0199***	4.74E-04	0.1140***	1.11E-03	0.1034***	1.21E-03
BBB / Baa2	2000	0.0277***	6.97E-04	0.0755***	9.95E-04	0.0720***	1.76E-03
BBB / Baa2	2002	0.0302***	6.57E-04	0.0842***	8.81E-04	0.0782***	1.42E-03
BBB / Baa2	2004	0.0365***	6.59E-04	0.1040***	7.91E-04	0.1098***	1.11E-03
BBB / Baa2	2006	0.0443***	7.71E-04	0.1366***	8.59E-04	0.1526***	1.29E-03

Delta-method standard errors in parentheses, *** $p<0.01$, ** $p<0.05$, * $p<0.1$

As we can easily see from the figures, rating scales display no more time-consistency with implied credit risk. Likewise, we can see from the table that Moody's Aaa-rated tranches issued in 2006 (PD 8.23%) were more likely to default during the crisis than Baa2-rated tranches from the 2000 vintage (PD 7.55%). Similarly, AAA-rated tranches issued in 2004 (PD 3.58%) were still more likely to default than AA-rated tranches issued four years earlier (PD 3.04%), according to Fitch. Considering the importance of credit ratings, these results point towards a major weakness in the credit rating system which deserves further investigation. Notably, with the exception of minor overlaps in adjacent rating categories, Standard & Poor's, unlike its competitors, remains largely consistent within its own rating scale. Still, with respect to the third hypothesis the results allow to reject the null hypothesis and not reject the alternative hypothesis.

Overall, the post-estimation analysis of predicted probabilities of default has revealed potential sources of error when comparing credit risk by solely relying on credit ratings. Rating-implied PD varies distinctively over time and across different tranche characteristics. In particular, effects related to a tranche's time of inception appear to have a strong impact on credit risk and constitute a major source of inconsistence for Moody's and Fitch ratings.

Figure 4.1: S&P Predicted One-Year PD by Vintage

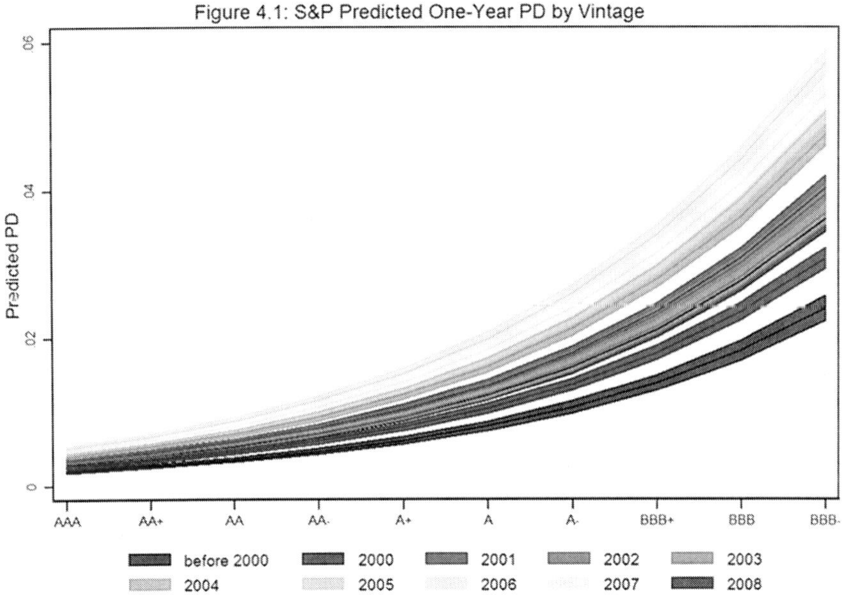

Figure 4.3: Fitch Predicted One-Year PD by Vintage

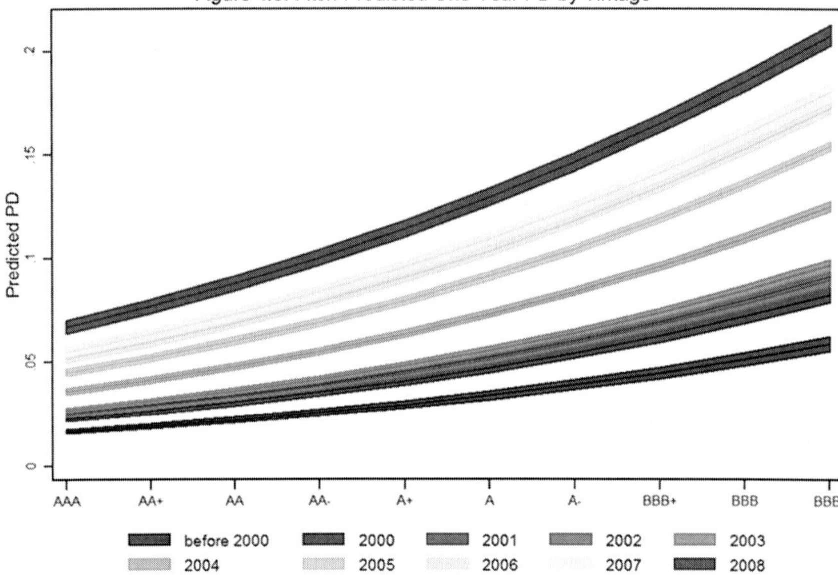

Figure 4.2: Moody's Predicted One-Year PD by Vintage

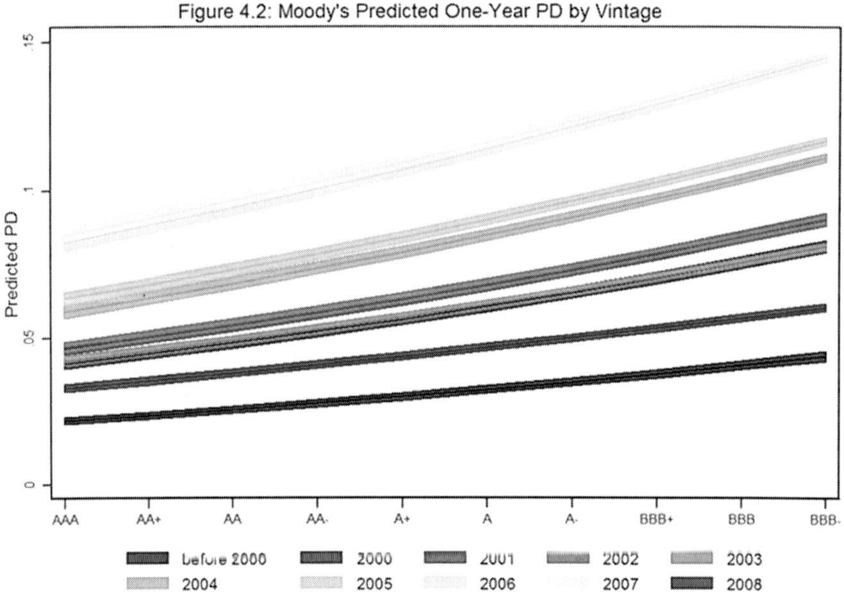

4. Does Neglected Change In Housing Prices Explain Flawed Risk Assessment?

In this section, we provide a potential explanation for the puzzling observation that rating agencies failed to estimate credit risk consistently within their own ordinal rating scales. Flaws in risk assessment processes are especially prevalent when PD of different vintages is compared. A more detailed view on the heterogeneity of residential mortgage-backed securities with respect to the time of inception is given in Figure 5, which depicts monthly mean ratings of all senior tranches in the sample, segmented by vintage. Senior tranches are typically rated AAA at inception. However, although most of these tranches are still attested unabated credit quality in the beginning of 2008, they are not affected all in the same way by the subsequent breakdown of the market. Whereas older vintages appear to perform relatively well during the crisis and post-crisis period, more recently issued tranches suffer much more severely with mean rating levels of tranches issued after 2004 dropping well below investment grade.

Indeed, this observed heterogeneity in credit risk might be explained by the appreciation in real estate prices between 1996 and 2006. The mortgage loans in a tranche's underlying portfolio are usually collateralized by the property. This increases the solidity of the payment guarantees and deters borrower default. Tranches issued in earlier years thus benefit from rising housing prices in the sense that collateralized properties become more valuable as house prices appreciate. The development in the real estate market thus, to some degree, provided insurance against the adverse shift which eventually hit the market in 2006. On the contrary, tranches issued shortly before these events were much more vulnerable, as the values of their collaterals were highly inflated.

Given different market conditions, the overall level of credit risk might be subject to change over time. Yet, consistent rating scales imply that tranches within each rating category are subject to roughly the same credit risk at the same time. But as we have already seen earlier, this is not supported by the empirical data. Figure 6 confirms these findings by exemplarily visualizing annual probabilities of default of AAA/Aaa-rated tranches, predicted by the baseline models for the reduced sample used in Figure 2.1. Contrary to the demands on consistency in rating scales, the high fluctuations in predicted PD supposedly point towards one or more omitted variables in the credit risk assessment. The figure now relates estimated PD to the development of the overall level of housing prices in

Figure 5: Mean Rating of Senior U.S. RMBS Tranches by Vintage

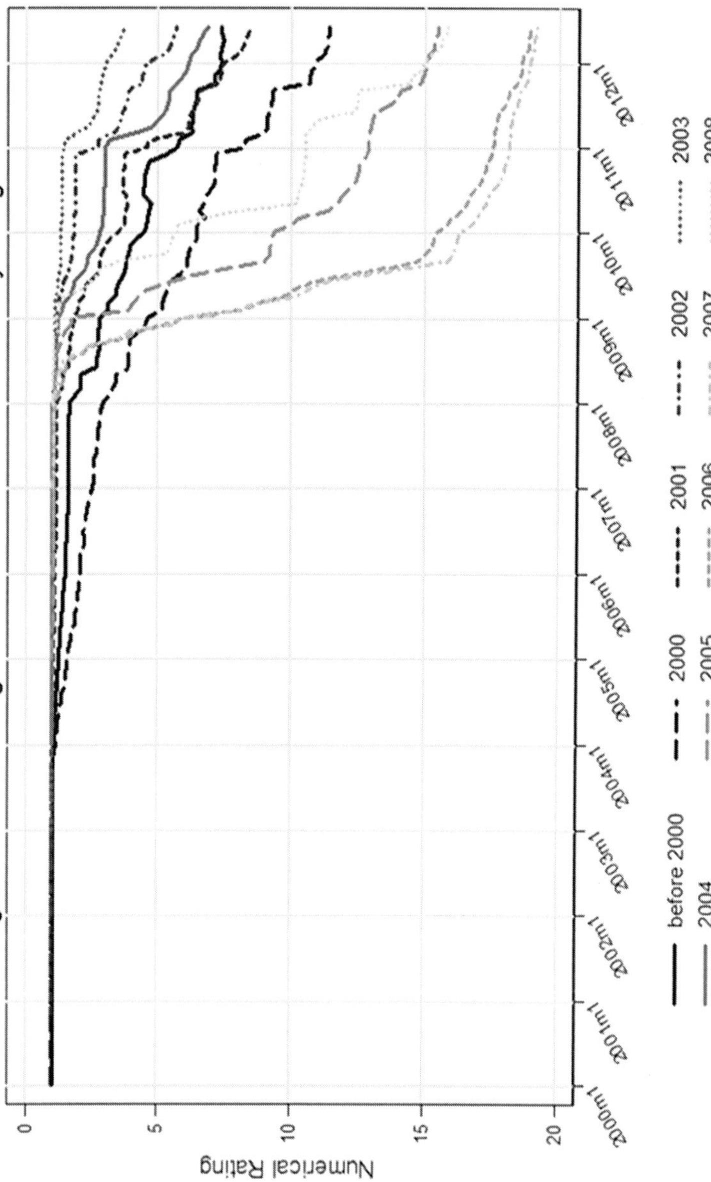

the U.S. as approximated by the S&P/Case-Shiller Home Price Indices. They measure the average change in home prices given a constant level of quality and cover 10 (CSI Composite 10) or 20 (CSI Composite 20) major metropolitan areas in the U.S. The indices are calculated monthly, using a three-month moving average algorithm. Home sales pairs are accumulated in rolling three-month periods, on which the repeat sales methodology is applied. The index point for each reporting month is based on sales pairs found for that month and the preceding two months. This averaging methodology is used to offset delays that can occur in the flow of sales price data from county deed recorders and to keep sample sizes large enough to create meaningful price change averages. Changes in the types and sizes of houses or changes in the physical characteristics of houses are specifically excluded from the calculations to avoid incorrectly affecting index values (Standard & Poor's, 2014).

Figure 6: One-Year PD for AAA/Aaa rated Tranches by Vintage

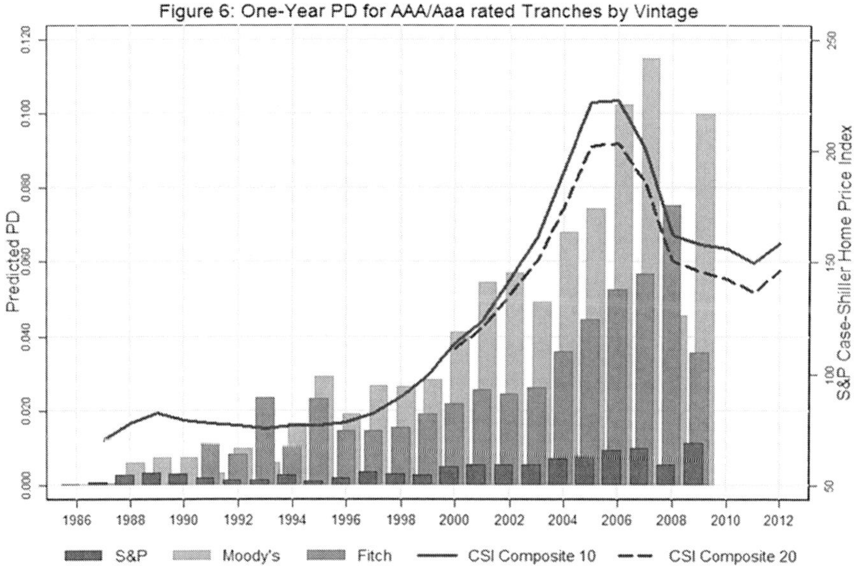

Interestingly, home prices display a strong co-movement with estimated PD throughout vintages, suggesting a link between the overall price level of homes at tranche inception and the likelihood of impairment. Though, the distinctiveness of this relationship again varies across rating agencies. In contrast to Moody's and Fitch, Standard & Poor's appears to be relatively more consistent in its credit assessment, and less prone to the home price bias. Supported by the fact that overall rating levels remained very high throughout the run-up of the crisis, it can, however, be hypothesized that rating agencies, either wittingly or unwittingly, failed to account for the effect of changes in housing prices in their credit risk assessment. In order to check on this notion we extend the logit models 1 and 2 introduced earlier by including the price level in the U.S. housing market as an additional predictor variable. This gives us the regression equations

$$D_{i,t} = \beta_0 + \beta_1 Ratg_{i,t} + \beta_2 CSI_{i,t-t_0} + \varepsilon_i \quad (3)$$

And

$$D_{i,t} = \beta_0 + \beta_1 Ratg_{i,t} + \beta_2 TTM_{i,T-t} + \beta_3\, COLL_i + \beta_4 Mult_i + \beta_5 Split_i + \beta_6 CSI_{i,t-t_0} + \varepsilon_i \quad (4)$$

where *CSI Composite 10 (CSI)* denotes the absolute change in the CSI Composite 10 Index between issuance of tranche i at time t_0 and the beginning of year t. Alternatively, we checked to controlling for the level of home prices by including raw CSI values at tranche inception as a predictor variable for default. However, using changes in index values yields largely superior results in terms of prediction accuracy. This makes also sense from a theoretical perspective, as it sets price levels at inception in relation to current price levels and thus provides a measure for how much a tranche's collateral has been able to build up insurance through appreciation.

The results of the extended models are presented in Table 3. Coefficients for *CSI Composite 10* are negative and strongly significant, thus confirming the notion that tranches which experienced a strong appreciation of real estate prices during their lifetime are less likely to enter into default and that this relationship is only poorly incorporated in credit ratings, if at all. Without exception, regression diagnostics improve considerably after controlling for changes in housing prices. For example, ROC measures gain +0.057 (S&P), +0.052 (Moody's), and +0.069 (Fitch) compared to the baseline models, and chi-squared tests on equality of areas are again highly significant. But also R-squared statistics indicate clearly improved model fit (+6.9%, +5.8%, and +6.7%, respectively).

Table 3: Impact of Housing Prices on Classification Accuracy

This table provides the results of the pooled logistic regression for the three rating agencies estimated over annual tranche observations from 1985-2012. The dependent binary variable is *Default* and coded 1 if a tranche entered into default during a given year, and 0 otherwise. *Tranche Rating* refers to a tranches numerical long-term credit rating from the respective rating agency recorded at the beginning of the year. *Multiple Ratings* is binary and assumes 1 if a tranche has an additional second or third rating, and 0 otherwise. *Split Rating* indicates whether multiple ratings at issuance are consistent (1) or not (0). *CSI Composite 10* is based on the S&P Case-Shiller Home Price Index covering 10 major metropolitan areas. The variable is calculated as the index difference between tranche inception and point of measurement. We further consider three control variables which improve the model fit: *Seniority* is a zero-one variable differentiating between senior (1) and AAA-subordinate tranches. *Residual Maturity* indicates a tranche's remaining time to maturity, denominated in months. *Collateral* captures borrower quality of a tranche's underlying mortgage pool, and assumes 1 for tranches backed by prime-rate mortgages and 0 for more inferior capital quality such as Alt-A and subprime. Cluster-robust standard errors are a clustered version of Huber-White sandwich estimators and account for potential clusters on tranche level. Additionally, the receiver operating characteristic (ROC) and McFadden's adjusted R^2 are reported for each regression.

Dependent:	S&P		Moody's		Fitch	
Default (Rating ≤ C)	(SP3)	(SP4)	(M3)	(M4)	(F3)	(F4)
Tranche Rating	0.161***	0.145***	0.067***	0.013***	0.095***	0.083***
	(0.0010)	(0.0011)	(0.0009)	(0.0012)	(0.0010)	(0.0011)
Split Rating		0.021**		0.153***		-0.057***
		(0.0086)		(0.0093)		(0.0111)
CSI Composite 10	-0.028***	-0.029***	-0.023***	-0.025***	-0.023***	-0.021***
	(0.0002)	(0.0002)	(0.0002)	(0.0002)	(0.0002)	(0.0002)
Controls (4)	No	Yes	No	Yes	No	Yes
Cluster-robust SE	Yes	Yes	Yes	Yes	Yes	Yes
Method	Logit	Logit	Logit	Logit	Logit	Logit
AUROC	0.902	0.910	0.821	0.874	0.862	0.870
Sensitivity	92.34%	93.94%	91.80%	86.87%	90.81%	92.86%
McFadden's adj. R^2	0.310	0.318	0.161	0.244	0.238	0.244
Observations	695'043	695'043	493'281	493'281	408'737	408'737

Robust standard errors in parentheses, *** p<0.01, ** p<0.05, * p<0.1

The above results contribute to explain the observed inconsistency between credit ratings and rating-implied default risk by introducing the change in housing prices the as a potentially omitted variable in rating agencies' credit rating methodologies. Although the resulting bias appears to be less pronounced for Standard & Poor's compared to Moody's and Fitch, controlling for it significantly improves the predicted classification accuracy of ratings from all rating agencies.

VII. Conclusion

This paper examines relative performance and consistency of credit ratings in structured finance using an extensive rating migration record on U.S. residential mortgage-backed securities from Standard & Poor's, Moody's, and Fitch. We argue that while investors are generally aware of marginal differences between rating agencies, the relative differences around the link between ratings and probability of default are largely underestimated in current literature. In particular, we aim to provide empirical evidence on how well rating agencies indicate actual risk of failure, the extent to which rating performance varies between rating agencies, and the consistency of rating scales over time and different subsamples. In order to test our hypotheses, we specify pooled logit regression models to estimate one-year probabilities of tranche default to assess the predictive power and consistency of different rating systems by analyzing how well rating agencies discriminate with respect to credit risk.

We find that the predictive power of ratings in assessing credit default risk varies distinctively across rating agencies, and that Standard & Poor's appears to outperform Moody's and Fitch in terms of rating classification accuracy. Taking into account additional public information significantly improves model fit and performance statistics for all rating agencies, indicating that these determinants of credit default risk are underrepresented in prevalent rating methodologies. In addition, the study provides suggestive evidence that rating agencies failed to account for rising real estate prices in their credit risk assessment, thereby creating a bias, which led to underestimated default risk and inconsistent credit ratings. Overall, the findings provide a possible explanation for about 32.00% (S&P), 45.44% (Moody's), and 54.28% (Fitch) of total misclassified defaults in the sample. In line with prior research, the results further confirm credit risk to be significantly higher if a tranche is assigned a split rating at inception. Finally, annual credit default risk is subject to gradual increase during the pre-crisis period, indicating a deterioration of the overall credit quality in the market well before the outburst of the crisis in late 2007. The implications of our results are relevant to all market participants who engage in structured finance, but in particular to investors, regulators, and policymakers. Despite that fact that credit rating processes and methodologies in structured finance are distinctive to this market segment, the lessons learned from this analysis may also find application to other markets which rely on credit ratings.

Overall, the findings of this paper contribute to the understanding of credit ratings in structured finance and the role of rating agencies in the subprime mortgage crisis. Notably, they highlight the limitations of credit rating's usefulness for comparing credit default risk within rating scales, but also across different rating agencies.

References

Bartus, T. (2005). "Estimation of marginal effects using magreff." *The Stata Journal*, 5 (3): 309-329.

Bangia, A., F.X. Diebold, and T. Schuermann. 2002. "Ratings migration and the business cycle, with applications to credit portfolio stress testing." *Journal of Banking & Finance* 26 (2): 445-474.

Cameron, A. C., and P. K. Trivedi. 2010. "Microeconometrics using Stata, Revised Edition." *StataCorp LP*.

Campbell, J.Y., J. Hilscher, and J. Szilagyi. 2008. "In search of distress risk." *Journal of Finance* 63 (6): 2899-2939.

Cantor, R., and C. Mann. 2003. "Measuring the Performance of Corporate Bond Ratings." *Moody's Special Comment* April 2003.

Cantor, R., and F. Packer. 1997. "Differences of opinion and selection bias in the credit rating industry." *Journal of Banking & Finance* 26 (10): 1395-1417.

Chava, S., and R.A. Jarrow. 2004. "Bankruptcy prediction with industry effects." *Review of Finance* 8 (4): 537-569.

Cetorelli, N., and S. Peristiani. 2012. "The Role of Banks in Asset Securitization." *Federal Reserve Bank of New York Economic Policy Review* 18 (2): 47-64.

Croce, A., S. Lugo, and R.W. Faff. 2011. "Rating Alignment, Rating Shopping and Reputation of Credit Rating Agencies: Evidence from the Subprime Crisis." Working Paper. Retrieved January 21, 2013, from www.ssrn.com.

Delianedis, G. and R. Geske. 1998. "Credit risk and risk neutral default probabilities: information about rating migrations and defaults." Bank of England, UK.

DeLong, E. R., D.M. DeLong, and D.L. Clarke-Pearson. 1988. "Comparing the areas under two or more correlated receiver operating characteristic curves: A nonparametric approach." *Biometrics* 44 (3): 837–845.

Fender, I., and J. Kiff. 2005. "CDO Rating Methodology: Some Thoughts on Model Risk and Its Implications." *Journal of Credit Risk* 1 (3): 37-58.

Fitch Ratings (2014). Definitions of Ratings and Other Forms of Opinion. Retrieved January 21, 2013, from http://www.fitchratings.com.

Griffin, J.M., and D.J. Tang. 2012. "Did Subjectivity Play a Role in CDO Credit Ratings?" *Journal of Finance* 67 (4): 1293-1328.

Güttler, A., and M. Wahrenburg. 2007. "The Adjustment of Credit Ratings in Advance of Defaults." *Journal of Banking & Finance* 31 (3): 751-767.

Hilscher, J., and M. Wilson. 2013. "Credit Ratings and Credit Risk: Is One Measure Enough?" AFA 2013 San Diego Meetings Paper.

Jewell, J., and M. Livingston. 1999. "A Comparison of Bond Ratings from Moody's S&P and Fitch IBCA." *Financial Markets, Institutions & Instruments* 8 (4): 1–45.

Kravitt, J.H.P. 2005. Securitization of Financial Assets, Second Edition. Aspen Publishers, New York.

Kraemer, W., and A. Guettler. 2008. "On comparing the accuracy of default predictions in the rating industry." *Empirical Economics* 34 (2): 343-356.

Lemke, T., G. Lins, and M. Picard. 2013. Mortgage-Backed Securities, 2013-2014 ed. (Securities Law Handbook Series). Thomson West, New York.

Livingston, M., A. Naranjo, and L. Zhou. 2007. "Asset Opaqueness and Split Bond Ratings." *Financial Management* 36 (3): 49–62.

Livingston, M., J. Wei, and L. Zhou. 2010. "Moody's and S&P Ratings: Are They Equivalent? Conservative Ratings and Split Rated Bond Yields." *Journal of Money, Credit and Banking* 42 (7): 1267–1293.

Long, J. S. 1997. "Regression Models for Categorical and Limited Dependent Variables." In: *Advanced Quantitative Techniques in the Social Sciences* Number 7. Sage Publications.

Long, J. S., and J. Freese. 2005. Regression Models for Categorical Outcomes using Stata, Second Edition. College Station, TX: Stata Press.

Moody's Investors Service. 2013. Rating Symbols and Definitions. Retrieved January 21, 2013, from http://www.moodys.com.

Nickell, P., W. Perraudin, and S. Varotto. 2000. "Stability of transition matrices." *Journal of Banking & Finance* 24 (1): 203–227.

Pagano, M., and P. Volpin. 2009. Credit Ratings Failures and Policy Options. University of Naples CSEF Working Paper No. 239.

Peretyatkin, V., and W. Perraudin. 200). "EL and DP Approaches to Rating CDOs and the Scope for Ratings Shopping." In: *Ong, M. K. (ed.). Credit Ratings – Methodologies, Rationale and Default Risk.* London, UK: 495-506.

Rösch, D., and H. Scheule. 2010. "Rating performance and agency incentives of structured finance transactions." Paolo Baffi Centre Research Paper No. 2010-78.

Sabarwal, T. 2006. "Common Structures of Asset-Backed Securities and their Risks." *Corporate Ownership & Control* 4 (1): 258-265.

Saunders, A., and M.M. Cornett. 2011. Financial Institutions Management: A Risk Management Approach. McGraw-Hill, New York.

Shumway, T. 2001. "Forecasting Bankruptcy more Accurately: A Simple Hazard Model." *Journal of Business* 74 (1): 101-124.

Standard & Poor's. 2013. Standard & Poor's Ratings Definitions. Retrieved January 21, 2013, from http://www.standardandpoors.com/ratings/definitions-and-faqs.

Standard & Poor's. 2014. S&P/Case-Shiller Home Price Indices Methodology. Retrieved June 18, 2014, from http://us.spindices.com/index-family/real-estate/sp-case-shiller.

Tavakoli, J.M. 2008. Structured Finance & Collateralized Debt Obligations. Wiley Finance, New York.

White, L.J. 2002. "The credit rating industry: An industrial organization analysis." In: *Levich, R.M., Reinhart, C. & Majnoni, G. (eds.), Ratings, rating agencies and the global financial system. Kluwer Academic Publishers* Boston: 41–63.

White, L.J. 2010. "The Credit Rating Agencies." *Journal of Economic Perspectives* 24 (2): 211-226.

CHAPTER FOURTEEN

ASSET CORRELATIONS UNDER STRESSED MACROECONOMIC CONDITIONS

CHRISTIAN THUN[1]

I. Introduction

Being exposed to credit risk, i.e. the risk that a borrower may default on its financial obligations, is an inherent element of lending. Ultimately it cannot be hedged or structured away. The impact of credit risk can only be reduced through mitigation instruments (e.g. collateral) or managed through diversification.

Banks with their large loan portfolios usually benefit the most from diversification. Their portfolios often suffer from concentrations that are the result from business activities in specific industries, client segments or geographical regions. Unexpected defaults in these concentrated areas of the portfolios can have devastating effects on a bank's overall solvency. Especially in times of stressed macroeconomic conditions being able to understand the interdependences between individual exposures is a critical element of prudent risk management.

The benefits of diversification have been known for decades since Markowitz pioneered the quantitative research in 1950. Quantitative methods for portfolio analysis have since then been developed and successfully applied to understand the contribution of individual assets (i.e. loans) to the overall portfolio risk and to estimate the amount of risk that can be reduced through diversification. The objective of such quantitative approaches has been the maximisation of the portfolio return while keeping the risk of losses within acceptable limits (Kealhofer 1998, 1).

Since the 1990s and the introduction of the capital standards by the Basel Committee of Banking Supervision the modelling of credit portfolio

[1] Dr. Christian Thun is from Moody's Analytics.

risk has become one of the most important topics in the banking industry and numerous approaches have been developed and discussed by practitioners and academics (BCBS 1999; Rösch 2003, 309). The three most important drivers in determining credit portfolio credit risk are probability of default (PD), loss given default (LGD), and default correlation. Due to regulatory focus on the first two drivers PD and LGD have been modelled quite extensively by practitioners and academics. The third one however has not received so much attention, mainly due to the lack of data. A common approach to estimate default correlation in a portfolio is to combine PDs with asset correlations. The assumption is that two firms will default on their financial obligation if both of their asset values fall below the value of their obligations. Asset correlation help to define the joint behaviour of the asset values of the two borrowers (Zhang et al. 2008).

In this abstract the approach to model PDs as well as asset correlation that the KMV Corporation (now part of Moody's Analytics) developed in the 1990s will be explained and how it can be extended to consider macroeconomic shocks for the estimation of asset correlations under stress.

I. Measuring the stand-alone default risk of borrowers

As mentioned above the primary source of risk in a bank's lending portfolio is the risk of a borrower defaulting on its financial obligations of default. The risk is expressed as the probability of default over a certain time horizon. Traditional approaches for measuring default probabilities involve a detailed examination of a company's operations including its financial statements in order to project current and future cash flows of the firm. Other estimation methods such as those used by Moody's Analytics (MA) rely on estimating default probabilities from observable equity prices. MA produces a probability of default called "Expected Default Frequency" (EDF™) based on equity prices. The benefit of this approach is that is allows not only to model default but it can also be extended to model correlations among firms. This following paragraph briefly describes the MA model of default.

The methodological foundation for the MA model of default is the "Black-Scholes-Merton" (BSM) model of default that dates back to the research published by Fischer Black, Myron Scholes, and Robert Merton in the early 1970s. While MA's approach has its intellectual roots in the BSM model, it has been significantly modified by Oldrich Vasicek and

Stephen Kealhofer that MA's model of default for calculating EDF™ values is hence called the Vasicek-Kealhofer or VK model.

This model focuses on the relationship of the firm's market value of assets and its contractual liabilities. The market value of assets however is not fixed and evolves over time as new information about the firm's ability to generate revenues become available to the market. This volatility of the asset value reflects the underlying risk inherent in the business.

The VK model is a structural model used to estimate the EDF™ value of a firm. There are three main elements that determine the EDF™ value of a firm (Crosbie et al. 2003, 6).

- *Value of Assets*: The market value of the firm's assets. This is a measure of the present value of the future free cash flows produced by the firm's assets discounted back at the appropriate discount rate. This measures the firm's prospects and incorporates relevant information about the firm's industry. This information also reflects the impact of current economic conditions on the firm.
- *Asset Risk*: The uncertainty or the risk of the asset value. This is a measure of the firm's business and industry risk. The value of the firm's assets is an estimate and, thus, is uncertain. As a result, the value of the firm's assets should always be understood in the context of the firm's business or asset risk.
- *Leverage*: The extent of the firm's contractual liabilities. Whereas the relevant measure of the firm's assets is always their market value, the book value of liabilities relative to the market value of assets is the pertinent measure of the firm's leverage, since that is the amount the firm must repay.

A firm will default when the value of assets falls below the liabilities due (i.e. the net worth becomes negative). Two firms with the same net worth will not necessarily have the same risk of default. The firm with the riskier business model (represented by a higher volatility of asset values) will have a higher risk of default. The VK-model incorporates the volatility of asset values to calculate the firm's "distance-to-default," which is the market net worth of a borrower divided by the standard deviation of the annual percentage change in asset value. In order to derive the stand alone EDF™ of a firm its distance-to-default value is mapped to observed to historical default rates (Crosbie et al. 2003, 10).

II. Modelling credit correlations

A typical loan portfolio of a bank consists of more than one single exposure but rather hundreds, if not thousands of exposures. Obviously, the overall risk of a portfolio depends not only on the risk that individual exposures may default but also on how the values of these exposures are correlated with each other. Estimating the correlation of the value of an exposure with the values of other exposures in a portfolio is crucial to understand the overall portfolio risk.

The value of a firm's debt depends strongly on the distribution of the asset returns of the firm. Consequently, the correlation in the values of two different exposures in a bank portfolio will similarly depend on the asset return correlation and the EDF™ values of their respective firms. In other words, one can compute the correlation in the values of any two exposures as long as we know the asset correlation and the EDF values for the corresponding firms.

As explained above the value of a firm's assets is not directly observable but can be inferred from equity prices. While it may be tempting not only use equity prices but also equity correlations to infer asset correlations, research has shown that equity correlations are poor substitutes for asset correlations because equity returns reflect the effects of leverage. If equity values were a linear function of asset values, the two correlations would be identical. However, empirical studies have observed nonlinear and unstable levels of leverage in many firms, particularly those with highly leveraged balance sheets such as financial institutions and utilities as well as low credit quality firms (Zhang et al. 2002, 7).

Instead of direct historical observations of asset return time series, MA uses a factor model called Global Correlation Model (GCorr™) to measure asset return correlations between firms. Factor models are accepted in almost all areas of applied finance as the best approach to estimating correlations. Large amounts of sampling error can be found in historical correlations thereby limiting their usefulness in estimating future correlations. On the other hand the predictive power of a factor model results largely from its control over these errors.

The factor model approach chosen by MA imposes a structure on the correlation of asset returns. It implies that the correlation between the asset returns of any pair of firms can be explained by the firms' relationships to a set of common factors (Huang et al. 2012, 7).

As shown in figure 13-1 there are three levels used in GCorr's factor structure

1) A composite company specific factor;
2) Country and industry factors;
3) Global, regional, and industrial sector factors

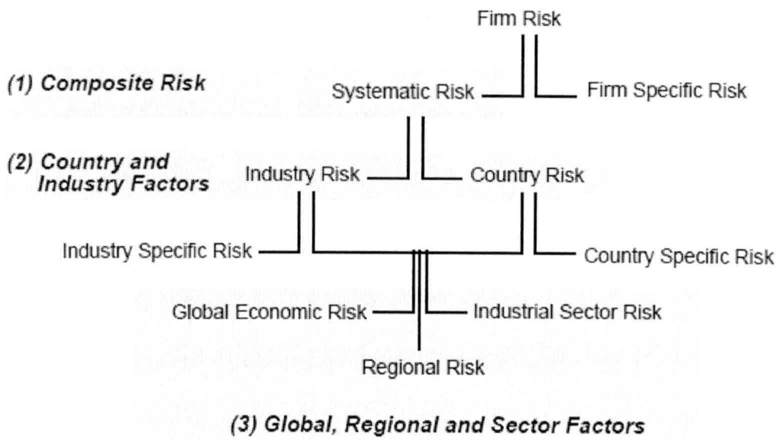

Figure 13-1: Factor model overview

At the first level the structure differentiates between firm-specific, or idiosyncratic risk, and systematic, or undiversifiable, risk. Systematic risk is captured by a single composite factor. This factor is unique to each firm and is a weighted sum of country and industry factors to which the firm has exposure.

At the second level the country and industry factors are also correlated with each other. Similar to the first level their risk can be decomposed into systematic and idiosyncratic components. The systematic component of the risk is captured by the basic economic factors in the third and last level of the structure.

There are three types of basic factors: global economic effects, regional economic effects, and industrial sector effects. The global, regional, and sector factors describe all of the common risk between countries and industries. That is, they capture all of the correlation between the country and industry factors The idiosyncratic risk components of countries and industries—the risk that is unrelated to the basic factors— is being retained as country- and industry-specific factors.

The following paragraph provide a more technical description of the MA factor model and how the asset return of each borrower in a portfolio is affected by a systematic and an idiosyncratic component.

$$r_i = \sqrt{\rho_i}\phi_i + \sqrt{1-\rho_i}\varepsilon_i$$

r_i is the asset return of borrower i,
φ_i is the composite index,
ρ_i is the R-squared of borrower i—the proportion of risk that is captured by the systematic factor,
ε_i is the idiosyncratic factor of borrower i.

The composite index φ_i (representing the systematic factor) represents the state of economy during a particular period and summarizes all the relevant systematic risk factors that affect the borrower's credit quality. The variable ε_i represents the borrower-specific risk (the idiosyncratic event or shock) that affects the borrower's credit quality or ability to repay debt (Huang et al. 2012, 7).

While the shock in the systematic factor φ_i is the same for borrowers with the same composite index, the borrower-specific shock ε_i is unique to each borrower. By construction, the systematic factor φ_i is independent of the idiosyncratic factor ε_i, and both are distributed with a standard normal distribution. Two borrowers correlate with one another when both are exposed to correlated systematic factors (with potentially varying degrees). Mathematically, the correlation between the changes in credit quality measures for any two borrowers is equal to the following formula (Lee et al. 2010, 5).

$$\begin{aligned} corr(r_i, r_j) &= corr(\sqrt{\rho_i}\phi_i + \sqrt{1-\rho_i}\varepsilon_i, \sqrt{\rho_j}\phi_j + \sqrt{1-\rho_j}\varepsilon_j) \\ &= \frac{\operatorname{cov}(\sqrt{\rho_i}\phi_i + \sqrt{1-\rho_i}\varepsilon_i, \sqrt{\rho_j}\phi_j + \sqrt{1-\rho_j}\varepsilon_j)}{\sigma_{r_i}\sigma_{r_j}} \\ &= \frac{\sqrt{\rho_i}\sqrt{\rho_j}\operatorname{cov}(\phi_i, \phi_j)}{1*1} = \sqrt{\rho_i}\sqrt{\rho_j}\, corr(\phi_i, \phi_j) \end{aligned}$$

Therefore, the only input parameters required to calculate the asset correlation between any two borrowers are the R-Squared values of borrowers and the correlation between their systematic factors.

III. Extending a correlation model to include macroeconomic variables

Following the bankruptcy of Lehman Brothers in September 2008 and the global financial crisis stress testing emerged as a preferred tool for supervisors and risk managers. Stress testing allows to estimate a bank's performance under a severe macroeconomic environment described by a set of macroeconomic variables such as change in GDP, inflation or unemployment. The Federal Reserve in the United States established stress tests with the Supervisory Capital Assessment program (SCAP) in 2009 and consequently with the Cumulative Capital Analysis Review (CCAR) since 2011 as part of its supervisory toolset (Tarullo 2010, 2; Rubinstein 2012, 6). Similar efforts have been undertaken by the Bank of England or the European Banking Authority.

During the tests banks were asked to calculate credit losses and capital adequacies under stress. Given the available research and data for PD and LGD the modelling did not present a major problem. However there is hardly a straight forward solution for stressing asset correlations. MA latest research aimed at understanding how the Global Correlation Model could be leveraged to solve this problem.

As discussed before the factors in GCorr™ perform well in decomposing the drivers of changes in asset returns and explaining the influence of the state of the economy (i.e. the systematic component) on the credit risk of a portfolio. As banks need to be able to relate real-world scenarios to credit losses in their portfolios the GCorr™ model has been expanded by linking GCorr™ systematic credit risk factors to macroeconomic variables representing the state of the economy and financial markets.

In order to implement the expanded approach two inputs are needed:

a) an expanded factor covariance matrix and a mapping between macroeconomic variables MV and
b) standard normal macroeconomic factors φMV.

Within GCorr™, systematic factors φCR are defined as weighted sums of geographical and industry factors for each asset class. As a result, the covariance matrix of GCorr factors implies correlations among systematic factors. The covariance matrix can be extended by adding macroeconomic variables to GCorr™. This expansion involves estimating parameters for two blocks of the covariance matrix: variances and covariances of the macroeconomic factors and covariances of macroeconomic factors with the GCorr factors. The expanded covariance matrix as displayed in Figure 13-2 implies the correlation matrix which links systematic credit risk factors φCR to macroeconomic factors φMV.

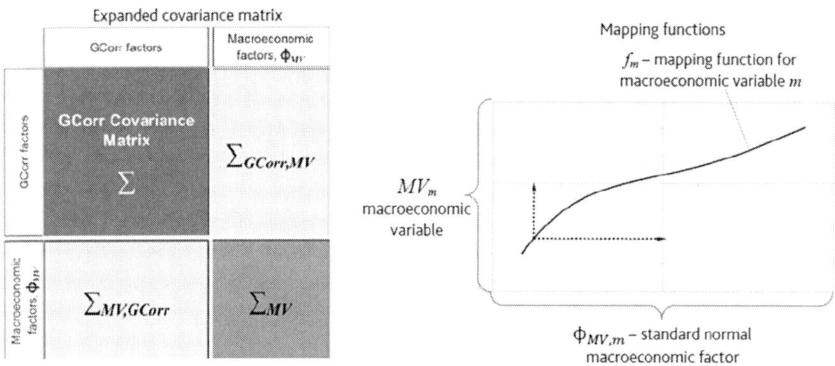

Figure 13-2: Expanded covariance matrix and mapping functions.

While the research suggests that correlations across systematic credit risk factors are reasonably stable over time some challenges remain. Stress economic scenarios are often not defined over a single period (for example, one year), but over multiple future periods. The relationships among macroeconomic variables as well as between macroeconomic variables and GCorr™ systematic factors vary over time, both in directions and in magnitude (Pospisil et al 2012, 12).

IV. Conclusion

Stress testing has become an important risk management tool for supervisors and financial institutions following the financial crisis of 2008–2009. Banks translate adverse macroeconomic scenarios into risk drivers such as PD, LGD and asset correlations and assess the impact of the losses on their balance sheets.

This article introduced the expanded GCorr™ model. The expanded GCorr™ model provides an economic interpretation of the factors by connecting them to macroeconomic variables. The expanded model allows for additional credit portfolio analyses, such as understanding relationships between portfolio losses and macroeconomic variables, stress testing and reverse stress testing analyses.

References

Basel Committee on Banking Supervision (BCBS). 1999. "Credit Risk Modelling: Current Practices and Applications." http://www.bis.org/publ/bcbs49.pdf.

Crosbie, P., and J. Bohn. 2003. "Modeling Default Risk." Moody's KMV Research Paper.

Huang, J., M. Lanfranconi, N. Patel, and L. Pospisil. 2012. "Modeling Methodology – Modeling Credit Correlations: An Overview of the Moody's Analytics GCorr Model." Moody's Analytics Research Paper.

Kealhofer, S. 1998. "Portfolio Management of Default Risk." Moody's KMV Research Paper.

Lee, J., A. Levy, and N. Patel. 2010. "Modeling Methodology – Correlations of unlisted firms including small and medium-sized enterprises." Moody's Analytics Research Paper.

Pospisil, L., N. Patel, A. Levy. 2012. "Modeling Methodology – Modeling Credit Correlations Using Macroeconomic Variables." Moody's Analytics Research Paper.

Rösch, D. 2003. "Correlations and Business Cycles of Credit Risk: Evidence from Bankruptcies in Germany." *Financial Markets and Portfolio Management* 17 (3): 309-331.

Rubinstein, S. 2012. "Putting Banks to the (Stress) Test." *Region Focus* 16 (4): 6-8.

Tarullo, D. 2010. "Lessons from the Crisis Stress Tests." *Remarks at the Federal Reserve Board International Research Forum on Monetary Policy* (http://www.federalreserve.gov/newsevents/speech/tarullo20100326a.htm)

Zhang, J., F. Zhu, and J. Lee. 2008. "Modeling Methodology – Asset Correlation, Realized Default Correlation and Portfolio Credit Risk." Moody's Analytics Research Paper.

Zeng, B, J. Zhang. 2002. "Measuring Credit Correlations: Equity Correlations Are Not Enough!" Moody's Analytics Research Paper.

CHAPTER FIFTEEN

CAPITAL STRUCTURE AND PAYOUT POLICIES: THEORY AND PRACTICE IN SWITZERLAND

CHRISTOPHE VOLONTÉ[1]

The choices of the optimal capital structure and payout policy are important topics in corporate finance. Several theories attempt to explain differences in these corporate decisions. However, empirical studies often fail to find evidence for a particular theory. Most probably, a number of factors on the managerial, corporate, legal and taxation level influence both capital structure and payout policies. In this article, we investigate the development of capital structure and payout policies of listed firms in Switzerland from 1999 to 2012. The results indicate that debt-to-capital ratios vary across industries but are relatively stable over time. Large firms have higher debt-to-capital ratios. Furthermore, firms have made stock splits in order to increase the number of shares and reduce the shares' nominal value. –Finally, large firms exhibit higher payout ratios, and payout channels vary across firms. Legal and taxation changes had an important impact on both the capital structure and payout policies.

I. Introduction

Two major topics in financial economics concern the optimal capital structure and the optimal payout policy. According to corporate finance theory, corporate decisions are optimal when they increase the firm's value. The famous articles written by Miller and Modigliani (MM) (1958; 1961), however, state that, on perfect capital markets and given the investment policy (and business risk), the capital structure and payout policy are irrelevant for the firm's value.

[1] Dr. Christophe Volonté is from University of Basel, christophe.volonte@unibas.ch.

Shareholders can replicate the firm's financing policies at no cost to their preferences (i.e., they can generate homemade leverage and homemade dividends). However, in reality, capital markets are not perfect because of market frictions (transaction costs, bankruptcy costs, and taxes), asymmetric distribution of information (adverse selection and moral hazard), and not fully rational agents.

Under these circumstances, corporate financial decisions are crucial in a firm's strategy to maximize firm value. There are interrelations between firm valuation, credit risk, capital structure decisions, and payout policies (see, e.g., Bolton, Chen and Wang 2011). In fact, a number of factors on the managerial, corporate, legal and taxation level influence the choice of the capital structure and payout policy.

The interests of managers, shareholders and debt holders do typically not fully overlap. The firm's capital structure affects the relationship between the three parties, and managers' decisions affect the investors' returns. Managers may follow their own interests and pursue value-reducing investments such as empire building (see Jensen 1986). This relates to the classical principal-agent problem (see Jensen and Meckling 1976). Shareholders are fully affected by such managerial decisions because they can only claim the residual after all obligations (including taxes and interest payments) have been paid off. As a result, they are affected by substantial risk. However, also debt holders are affected by managerial decisions. Capital structure and payout policies have an effect on credit risk and therefore the valuation of debt. The value of risky debt depends on the amount issued, the risk-free rate, the credit default spread (which is, e.g., affected by business risks, maturity of debt, and dividend policies) and taxes (see Leland 1998).

Besides the conflict between managers and investors, there is also a conflict between shareholders and debtholders (Jensen and Meckling 1976, Myers 1977, Morellec, Nikolov and Schürhoff 2012).

Agency theory deals with conflicts of interest between managers, shareholders, and debtholders (Jensen and Meckling 1976). These conflicts depend on the capital structure, that is, on the relationships between the firm's claimants. For instance, the managers' potential risk aversion may favor debtholders because their claims are fixed, while shareholders are residual claimants on the firm's net income (Easterbrook 1984). In return, shareholders, as the firm's owners, receive voting rights and have a say on some corporate decisions and the composition of the firm's board of directors. Therefore, shareholders may influence decisions that harm debtholders. Due to the agency problem associated with the conflict between debtholders and shareholders, overinvestment (e.g., empire building in negative net present value (NPV) projects) or underinvestment (not all positive NPV projects are pursued) can occur. Managers may pursue overly risky projects because the shareholder's residual claim has the characteristics of an option (risk-shifting) (Jensen and Meckling 1976). In contrast, Myers (1977) argues that debt overhang may prevent firms of pursuing all possible projects. Shareholders may bypass positive NPV projects because debtholders would benefit more from the investments. Chava, Livdan and Purnanandam (2009) find that firms that protect themselves from the market for corporate control (a corporate governance strategy that potentially harms shareholders) have lower costs of bank loans.

Managers' decisions are about investment policies, financing sources, compensation schemes, risk management and other firm strategies (i.e., acquisition strategies). Understanding the motives of (potentially self-interested) managers is therefore essential and the considerations are important in the evaluation of the capital structure and payout policies in capital markets that are not perfect.

In this article, we investigate the development of the capital structure and payout policies of listed firms in Switzerland from 1999 to 2012. Specifically, we examine the evolution of the debt-to-capital ratios, the changes in the capital structures, payout ratios and payout methods across industries.

Even though we do not explicitly test any of the theories mentioned, the figures indicate that decisions depend on firm characteristics (industry affiliation and firm size). For instance, industry-specific leverage ratios are relatively stable over time. On average, larger firms have higher debt-to-assets ratios and higher payout ratios. In addition, changes in the legal environment and in tax regimes have had an impact on corporate decisions.

The next Section 2 revises the theorems of Miller and Modigliani (MM), discusses the deviations of their assumptions and the theories emerging from these deviations. Section 3 describes the data and the evolution of the capital structure and payout policies in Switzerland. The final Section 4 concludes.

II. Miller-Modigliani and the theories on capital structure and payout policies

The choice of the optimal capital structure and payout policies in order to reduce capital costs is one of the most central topics in corporate finance. Lower costs of capital increase a firm's value. Closely linked to the choice of the capital structure is the payout policy of a firm (the amount and way of how cash is returned to shareholders).

Miller and Modigliani argued that both capital structure and payout policies are irrelevant for firm value. Firm value is only affected by the firm's ability to generate cash flows which depends on its investment policy and business risk (but not its financial risks), i.e., on the left-hand side of the balance sheet. Projects generate value if their NPV is positive. In a simple discounted cash flow-valuation model, the firm's value depends on the present value of a firm's expected free cash flows and the continuing value[2]. Expected free cash flow is discounted by the firm's cost of capital. MM claim that the firm's value is affected by the capital budgeting part of corporate finance rather than the financing part, i.e., it's the size of the pie that matters and not how the pie is sliced. Therefore, real and financial decisions can be separated (see Dammon and Senbet 1988).

Based on this reasoning, the first MM proposition suggests that a firm's debt-to-equity ratio has no effect on a firm's market value (MM 1). The value of the levered firm is the same as the value of the unlevered firm. The second proposition suggests that a firm's debt-to-equity ratio has no effect on a firm's total cost of capital (i.e., their weighted average cost of capital is constant). Hence, the cost of equity is a linear function of the firm's leverage ratio and the associated financial risks (leverage effect) (MM 2). The lower financing costs of debt are offset by higher returns required by shareholders. The total cost of capital depends on the firm's assets and activities and not its financial structure. Investors themselves can borrow or lend money in order to replicate the firm's capital structure that matches their preferences (homemade leverage). Furthermore, Miller and Modigliani (1961) formulated the dividend irrelevance proposition which suggests that a firm's dividend policy has no effect on the firm's market value. Higher payouts reduce retained gains which would cause the firm's value to increase given their investment opportunities. Investors can adjust the return of their investment by replicating cash flow streams by buying or selling shares (homemade dividends). As a result, there are no optimal capital structure and no optimal payout policies.

For capital structure and dividend policy to be irrelevant, MM show that the following assumptions have to be met: No taxes, no capital market imperfections (e.g., agency problems, transaction costs, costs of distress)

---

[2] E.g. Cash flow to investors = operating cash flow (= EBIT + depreciation – taxes) + cash flow from financing – capital spending (investments).

and homogeneous expectations.[3] In reality, markets are not perfect. They contain market frictions and information that is asymmetrically distributed. The deviation from these assumptions has led to new theories. In general, these new explanations show that managers both influence the firm's operating income and the risk profile of the firm which affects the cost of capital.

As a key driver, corporate decisions are substantially affected by taxes. For example, interest payments on debt are tax-deductible expenses and therefore firm value increases with higher debt (tax shield). In the context of payout policies, it has been argued that share repurchases should be favored over dividends because the former generate capital gains (which in some countries are not taxed or at a lower rate), while the latter are taxed as income. Hence, changes in taxes potentially have an effect on the choice of financial decisions. Agency theory has been suggested to be a powerful theory to explain corporate decisions when information is asymmetrically distributed and the interests of the economic agents do not fully overlap.

1. Capital structure theories

The capital structure of a firm consists of equity and debt or a combination of the two. The capital structure therefore defines the relationships between different providers of capital or claimants. It also shows how risky a firm's financing is (see leverage effect). Shareholders, financial analysts, rating agencies and banks integrate the capital structure as an important factor in a firm's evaluation. Furthermore, a firm's capital requirements can be met through external (i.e., share or debt issuances) or internal (i.e., retained earnings) resources.

Theories that explain capital structure decisions differ from the assumptions of perfect capital markets and the irrelevance principles of MM (see Harris and Raviv 1991, Myers 2001). An important deviation from MM's assumption is the presence of taxes. If taxes are included, debt features benefits because interest is a tax-deductible expense (tax shield). However, if the costs of financial distress which are associated with potential bankruptcy are included as well, then there exists an optimum for a firm's capital structure. In the *trade-off theory* of capital structure, the optimal capital structure is therefore determined by the trade-off between the benefits and costs of debt (Kraus and Litzenberger 1973).

---

[3] DeAngelo and DeAngelo (2006) show that even in frictionless markets, payout policy is not irrelevant when retention is allowed and not 100 percent of free cash flows have to be paid out.

The *pecking order theory* provides a hierarchical view on financing sources (Myers and Majluf 1984; Myers 1984). In a perfect capital market, firms would have no problems acquiring additional cash to finance their projects on external capital markets. However, the different financing sources are associated with different costs and information. Internal funds from retained earnings are the cheapest financing source. In contrast, equity issuance is the most expensive source of finance. Borrowings, the issuance of bonds, or hybrid financing sources are more expensive than internal finance, but cheaper than equity. Investors revalue the firm's market value when firms issue new equity securities. The decision to raise equity instead of debt is suspected to be affected by insider information of the managers. Myers and Majluf (1984) point to the problem that shareholders may undervalue equity prices when new equity should be used to finance projects. As a result, actual shareholders would lose and therefore the new project will not be financed. This underinvestment problem can be circumvented by financing through internal funds or debt. Huang and Ritter (2009) find that firms finance through external equity when the cost of capital is low.

An additional benefit of debt exists from an agency perspective. The *free cash flow hypothesis* by Jensen (1986) argues that debt repayment and interest payments decrease the managers' discretionary power and their potential to waste cash flows (see also Stulz 1990). As a result, higher leverage reduces agency costs. In contrast, higher debt levels can also lead to agency costs related to conflicts between debt holders and shareholders (see Myers 1977).

Still, other theories have been developed to explain capital structure. For instance, Ross (1977) suggests that the managers' capital structure decision is aimed to send a *signal* to investors. Under asymmetric information, managers know substantially more about their firm's condition and value than shareholders. The theory suggests that firms with pessimistic prospects have low leverage ratios. On the contrary, a higher leverage may signal a higher debt capacity, i.e., that the firm expects higher future profits and is in a good shape. Finally, the tax clientele effect suggests that investors have different preferences related to the firm's capital structure which are due to their tax environment (Zechner 1990).

From an empirical view, it has been shown to be difficult to find evidence of any single theory (Rajan and Zingales 1995, Graham and Harvey 2001). Fama and French (2002) find evidence both for the trade-off and the pecking order theory to explain leverage. However, one of the firm's highest priorities appears to be the objective to remain financially flexible (Graham and Harvey 2001).

2. Payout theories

Just as the capital structure irrelevance seems not to be true in reality, dividend policy irrelevance is questioned, as well. DeAngelo and DeAngelo (2006) argue that Miller and Modigliani's (1961) arguments do not hold even in frictionless markets if firms are not required to payout 100% of free cash flow. In addition, transaction costs obstruct, for example, homemade dividends as suggested by Miller and Modigliani (1961). The link between dividends and firm value can be attributed to Gordon's (1959) Growth Model that uses expected dividends which are discounted by the cost of capital and the dividend's growth rate to value firms.

Firms have generally two options in the use of their earnings. Either they retain earnings or they can pay out the earnings to their shareholders. Retained earnings can be used to fund future investment opportunities (positive NPV projects) which will increase a firm's value. The higher firm value will lead to capital gains or future dividends. From that perspective, dividends are irrelevant. Firms increase their value if they invest in positive NPV projects. Once all positive NPV projects have been funded and all obligations have been paid off (e.g., interest payments, taxes), this free cash flow (i.e., the shareholders' residual claim) should thus be returned to shareholders or retained for future projects.

The payout ratio is the proportion of earnings that is paid out to shareholders as dividends. However, payout ratios (in percent) and or the level of dividends paid out (in absolute terms) are often relatively stable which suggests that managers do not just follow the strategy above because firms rarely have a constant amount of investment opportunities. Rather, the fluctuation of earnings is usually higher than the fluctuation of dividends.

Lintner (1956) assumes that firms have a long term target payout ratio and try to smooth dividend payouts. Laery and Michaely (2011) find that firms that are not financially constrained, that face low levels of asymmetric information, and are most susceptible to agency conflicts are also more likely to smooth their dividends. Fama and French (2002) observe that more profitable firms and firms with fewer investments have higher dividend payouts. Hence, firm characteristics are important factors in explaining payout policies.

However, also investors may benefit from dividends. Lintner (1962) and Gordon (1963) suggest that investors have a preference for secure dividends and steady cash inflows today in contrast to unsecure capital gains in the future ("bird in the hand" theory). (In MM without transaction costs, shareholders could replicate cash flow streams and thereby they would be indifferent).

Payout policies are in the discretion of the managers and must not be optimal (see Chang 1993). Agency theory suggests that managers may pursue negative NPV projects such as in the case of empire building, consumption of perks, underinvestment due to risk aversion, etc. (see, e.g., Jensen 1986, Stulz 1990). Jensen (1986) argued that interest payments decrease agency costs because managers are bonded to interest payments. Dividends have a similar function if, for instance, the management is bound to a specific payout target (see, e.g., Easterbrook 1984; Hansen, Kumar, and Shome 1994).

Miller and Rock (1985) point to the information content of dividends which is not to be underestimated in a world of asymmetric information. Their signaling theory suggests, for example, that higher dividends signal higher future cash flows which increase firm value. Dividends certainly have information content. For example, cuts or omissions in dividends are bad signs and typically accompanied by decreasing stock prices (see, e.g., Jensen, 1986; Michaely, Thaler, and Womack, 1995). However, this dividend signaling may also be a reason for the underinvestment problem discussed earlier (Miller and Rock 1985).

If managers have decided to return earnings to their shareholders, they can choose between two main payout methods: cash dividends or share repurchases. Firms have traditionally paid out cash dividends. However, share repurchases theoretically have the same effect.[4] In the case of share repurchases, shareholders receive cash back if they sell their shares to the firm. If shares are retired, the number of shares decreases and the firm's value is thus divided by a smaller number of shares. Therefore, every single share appreciates. Besides, there exist other reasons for share repurchases, e.g., the purpose could be to change the shareholder structure, to implement a share-based executive compensation scheme or to use shares as a currency for takeovers.

It has therefore often been suggested that share repurchases and dividends are substitutes. However, in many countries dividends are less attractive because they are often taxed as income. Black (1976) refers to the „dividend puzzle" for the fact that firms pay out dividends even though they are not attractive from a tax perspective. Chetty and Saez (2005) provide empirical evidence on the importance of taxes on the decision of share repurchases or dividends.

---

[4] Various methods exist for share repurchases, e.g., open market repurchase or negotiated repurchase to just name the two most common methods.

Allen, Bernardo and Welch (2000) argue that due to tax reasons different groups of shareholders (institutional investors or private investors) have different preferences for payout types. Desai and Jin (2011) show that institutional shareholder's tax environment affects the choice of stocks they hold (low-dividend paying firms and high-dividend paying firms) and that managers consider their institutional investors' preferences. Finally, from a behavioral finance perspective, Shefrin and Statman (1984) argue that shareholder's preferences for dividends could be explained by self-control because people prefer current income through dividends and not stock sales which would reduce their investment volume. Graham and Kumar (2006) find empirical evidence for both the dividend clienteles and the self-control hypothesis.

Brav, Graham, Harvey and Michaely (2005) investigate payout policies in the twenty-first century. Their survey is based on interviews with executives. Their findings suggest that firms target a dividend level and share repurchases are made when enough cash is available. More recently, share repurchases have been favored over dividends for their flexibility. Executives do not assume that there is a clientele effect and that investors are indifferent between dividends and share repurchases. Firms with more volatile profits are more likely to use share repurchases than cash dividends (Jagannathan, Stephens and Weisbach 2000; Grullon and Michaely 2002). Dividends are thus part of a long-term strategy, while share repurchases can be used to temporarily reduce excessive cash holdings.

III. Data

For our overview on capital structures and payout policies, we target all firms contained in the Swiss Performance Index from 1999 to 2012. The final sample yields 2,443 firm-years or 175 firms per year, on average. Data for the debt-to-capital ratio and for the payout ratio is obtained from Thomson Reuters Datastream. All other data has been hand-collected from the commercial register or annual reports. Table 14-1 shows the composition of our sample according to firm sizes and industry affiliations.

	Consumer goods and services	Industrials	Health care	Financials	Others	Total
Large	42	47	48	91	38	266
Mid	153	269	79	199	213	913
Small	326	420	108	195	215	1,264
Total	521	736	235	485	466	2,443

Table 14-1: Sample firms.

1. Variables

Leverage is calculated as the ratio of book value of total liabilities over book value of total liabilities plus book value of shareholders' equity (debt-to-capital ratio). Payout ratio is defined as cash dividends divided by earnings. All information concerning the change in share capital stems directly from the statements in the commercial register.

The payout methods are cash dividends, share repurchases, nominal value repayments and repayments from contributions. Cash dividends are present if the payout ratio obtained from Thomson One Banker is positive. We identify share repurchases if both the number of shares and the share capital decrease. Nominal value repayments are present if the nominal value of the shares decreases and if it is not due to a share split. This information is derived from the capital structure changes as indicated in the commercial register. Furthermore, the fact whether firms made repayments from contributions is obtained from annual reports.

2. Major legal and taxation changes

Some major legal and taxation changes in relation to the firm's capital structure and payout policies occurred in the last years.

The capital structure has been affected by the permission to have lower nominal values attributed to shares. In Switzerland, each share has an underlying nominal value. The nominal value describes the share's proportion of share capital. If a firm has 100 shares outstanding with a nominal value of 10, the share capital has a value of 1,000. In 1991, the minimum nominal value of shares has been lowered from 100 Swiss francs to 10 Swiss francs. In 2001, this minimum nominal value has further decreased from 10 francs to 1 centime (i.e., 0.01 Swiss franc) (Swiss Code of Obligations Art. 622, para. 4). One reason for these changes was that share prices were seen to be too elevated due to the high minimum nominal value requirements. As a result, smaller shareholders would not obtain such shares and stock-based compensation cannot be optimized adequately.

In addition to the permission for lower nominal values, payout methods have also been affected by taxes. The Corporate Tax reform II had a particular impact on payout policies. Different parts of the Corporate Tax reform II have become effective between 2008 and 2011.

In 2008, the tax reform reduces the double taxation disadvantage (profit taxation for the company and income taxation for the shareholder) of dividends in some circumstances. This advantage accrues to shareholders with significant ownership (over 10%) and is therefore mostly aimed at smaller, not particularly listed, companies.

The Corporate Tax reform II allows companies to repay the shareholders' initial contributions (capital contribution principle). From 2011, the repayment of shareholders' contribution (like nominal value repayment) is no more treated as a distribution of profits. These payments out of a new capital contribution reserve, created from additional paid in capital since January 1, 1997, are now free of Swiss withholding tax to shareholders.

Dividends are subject to withholding taxes (which can be refunded) and income taxes. Share repurchases are subject to withholding taxes and income taxes on the value of repurchase value minus nominal value if the firm cancels the shares except for Swiss holding companies and tax exempt entities. If the shares are not cancelled, no taxes arise. No taxes are imposed on capital gains of trades by individuals (if they are not classified as professional traders), however, capital gains are taxed as regular income if done by businesses.

In contrast, nominal value repayments are neither subject to profit taxes nor to income taxes. Likewise and as already mentioned, repayments from contributions are not subject to taxes on the corporate or the individual level.

3. Capital structure

In this section, we investigate the evolution of the capital structure in Switzerland. We will look both at the debt-to-capital ratio and the changes in the share capital of the firms.

3.1 Debt-to-capital ratio

Frank and Goyal (2009) point to the importance to examine the evolution of the capital structure over time and to account for a firm's circumstances. The models used by Frank and Goyal (2009) show that six factors explain 27 percent in the variation of market-based leverage. Harvey, Lins, and Roper (2004) point out that the debt-to-capital ratio measured in book values is the most appropriate measure of leverage.

We classify firms into four important industries. The industry's regulatory environment, the competition and growth opportunities are likely to affect the levels of debt. We do not differentiate between different types of debt which would be important in practice (see Rauh and Sufi 2010). We use industry medians because outliers affect the leverage ratio in some years.

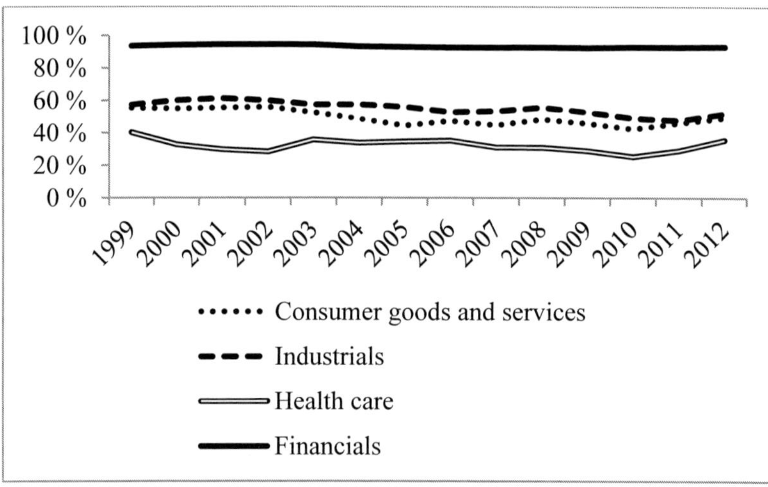

Figure 14-1: Debt-to-capital ratio (medians from 1999-2012).

Obviously and due to the corporate structure, financials exhibit the highest median debt-to-capital ratio (93%; s.d.: 0.72%). The median ratio of non-financial-firms decreased from 51% in 1999 to 39% in 2010 before it increased again in 2012 to 46%. From the non-financial-firms, industrials depict a high debt-to-capital ratio (55%; s.d.: 3.99%), followed by consumer goods and services (49%; s.d.: 4.54%) and health care firms (32%; s.d.: 3.75%). Our figures suggest that the ratios are affected by industry affiliation. The variation of leverage across time was by far the lowest within the financials (only 0.72%), in contrast to 4.54% within the consumer goods and services.

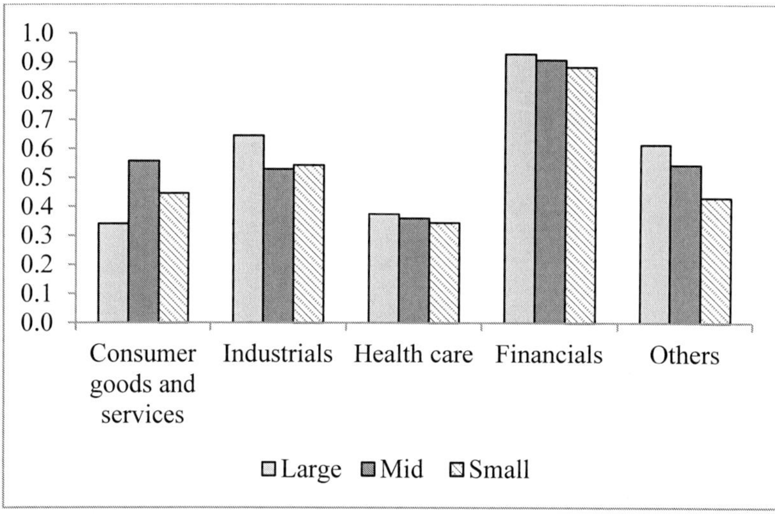

Figure 14-2: Leverage and firm sizes (averages). The results in Figure 14-2 indicate that leverage is positively related with firm size (except in consumer goods and services).

3.2 Changes in share capital

Next, we investigate the change in the share capital of Swiss firms. We calculate the average percentage change from one year to another in share capital, nominal value and number of shares as indicated in the commercial register. If we had used yearly median values, then the values would be zero since the majority of firms in each industry had no changes in their share capital in a given year. As a result, we circumvent the influence of equity structure changes of very large companies. In 2001, firms were allowed to lower the nominal value of their shares to 1 centime. In consequence, many firms made stock splits to lower their shares prices. Total share capital was only marginally changed.

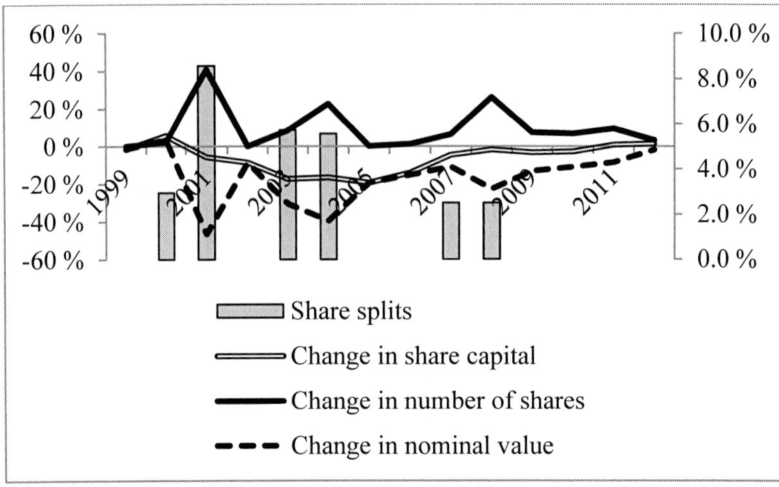

Figure 14-3: Consumer goods and services (share splits are displayed on the secondary axis).

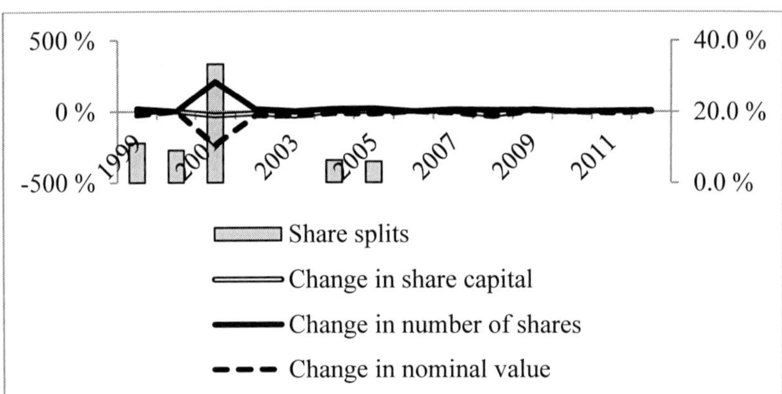

Figure 14-4: Health care.

In contrast to consumer goods and services, share capital in health care was relatively stable as indicated by the percentage changes. The positive change in average nominal value in 2009 is due to Ypsomed's increase of capital in 2009 which included a nominal value increase of the shares. This measure has been used in order to be able to repay tax-friendly dividends (i.e., nominal value repayments) in the future (Ypsomed, 24 June 2009, media release). In the same year, they also had a nominal value repayment.

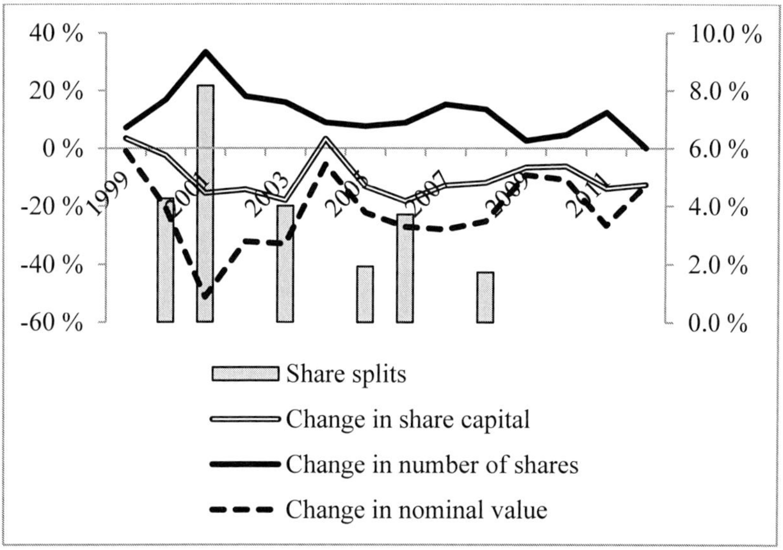

Figure 14-5: Industrials.

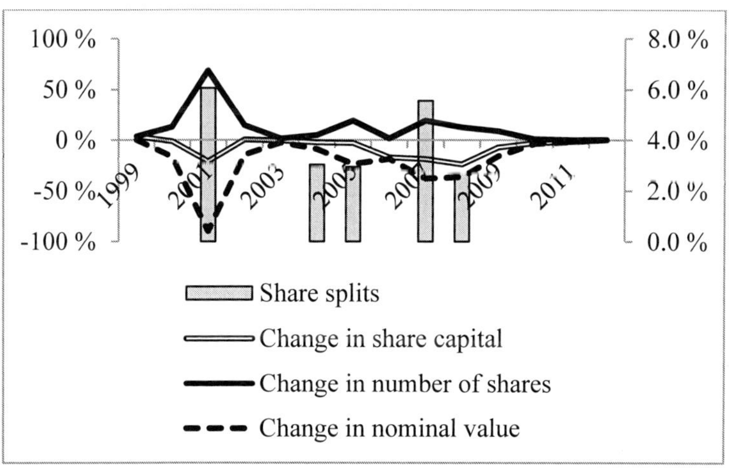

Figure 14-6: Financials.

In total, share capital on average has decreased over the whole period and every year. In 2001, share splits in every industry were en vogue. This can be ascribed to the legal change that allowed a lower nominal value. Accordingly, the number of shares has increased.

4. Payout policies

Payout policies are often investigated by analysts. Many companies target a specific payout ratio or they seek a sustainable growth in dividends.

4.1 Payout ratios

DeAngelo, DeAngelo and Skinner (2004) find that smaller firms cut dividends, while large firms increased dividend payments. These large firms constitute the bulk of dividend payers (25 dividend paying-firms account for 50% of aggregate dividends) (see also Denis and Osobov, 2008). Frank and Goyal (2009) show that industry affiliation is an important determinant of payout ratio because it reflects the competitive environment, regulation, etc. within an industry (see also Michel 1979). Therefore, the industry median ratio can work as a benchmark. In the next step, we thus analyze the evolution of the payout ratio across industries and firm sizes.

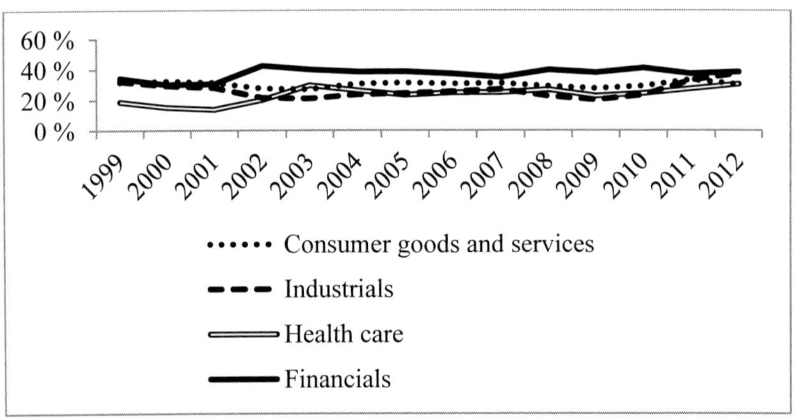

Figure 14-7: Payout ratios across industries (medians).

Over the whole period, the average payout ratio increased from 29.27% in 1999 to 34.23% in 2012. However, from 1999 to 2010, payout ratios were almost constantly at 29%. On average, financials had the highest payout ratio (av. 37.26%; s.d.: 3.5%), followed by consumer goods and services (av. 30.3%, s.d.: 1.83%), industrials (av. 26.44%, s.d.: 4.94%), and the health care industry (av. 23.53%, s.d.: 4.81%). The standard deviation of payout ratio being relatively low, investors who invested into consumer goods and services could almost be sure to receive 30% of earnings as dividends.

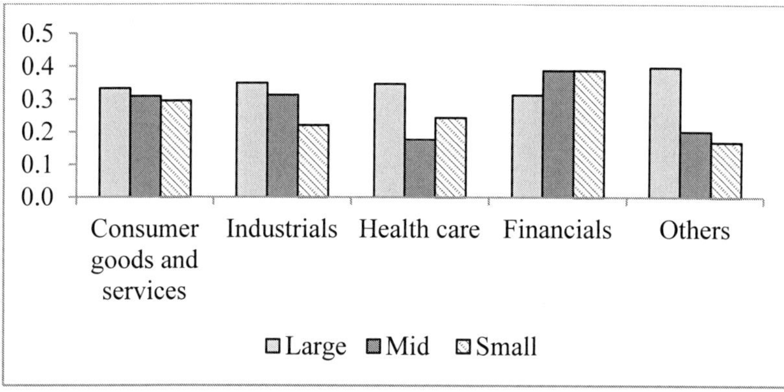

Figure 14-8: Payout ratios and firm sizes.

As Figure 14-8 indicates, similar to leverage ratios, payout ratios are positively related to firm sizes (despite financials).

4.2 Payout instruments

Firms can return cash to shareholders through four channels: cash dividends, share repurchases, nominal value repayments, and repayments from contribution. As an illustration of the different payout instruments used by Swiss companies, we take the example of Georg Fischer.

Example: Payout instruments of Georg Fischer

a l M e e	f c	a l u e	e g i s	B e a
20.03.2013	15 CHF			
21.03.2012	15 CHF			
23.03.2011		10 CHF		
24.03.2010		-		
18.03.2009		5 CHF		
19.03.2008		25 CHF		
21.03.2007		25 CHF		
22.03.2006		15 CHF		
22.03.2005		10 CHF		
17.03.2004		-		
12.03.2003		-		
19.03.2002			7 CHF	
20.03.2001			15 CHF	
21.03.2000			14 CHF	
23.03.1999			14 CHF	
31.03.1998			12 CHF	60 CHF
07.04.1997			9 CHF	45 CHF
22.04.1996			7 CHF	35 CHF
25.04.1995			6 CHF	30 CHF

The example shows that Georg Fischer changed from more classical dividend payments to the tax advantageous repayment of nominal value and repayment of contributions. Hence, legal and taxation changes led to substitution effects. The table also indicates that Georg Fischer unified their equity structure in 1998.

Next, we examine which forms of payout firms have used across industries. However, we do not account for the amount of money that has been paid out to shareholders.

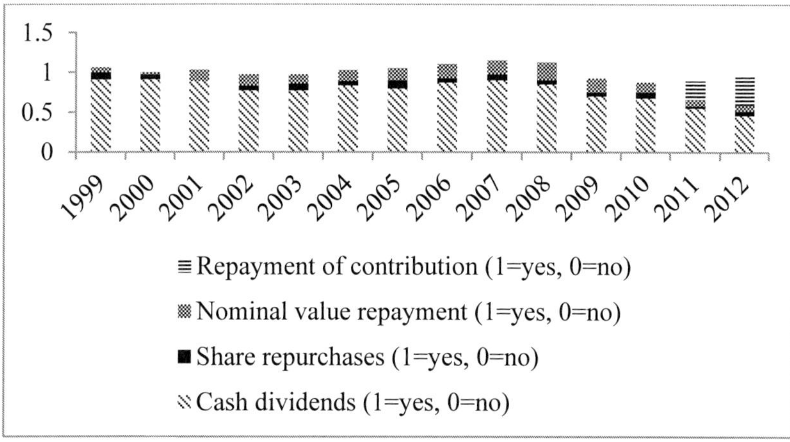

Figure 14-9: Payout instruments in the consumer goods and services industry.

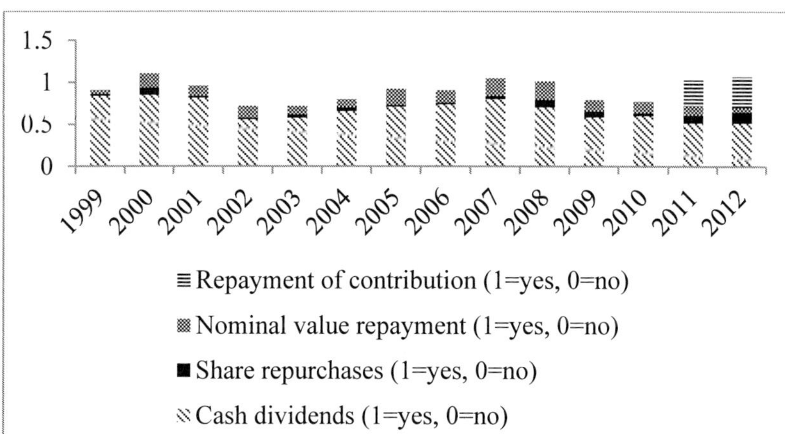

Figure 14-10: Payout instruments in the industrials industry.

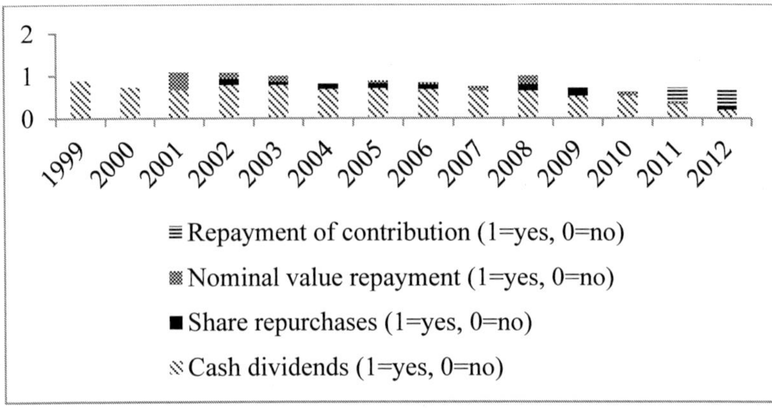

Figure 14-11: Payout instruments in the health care industry.

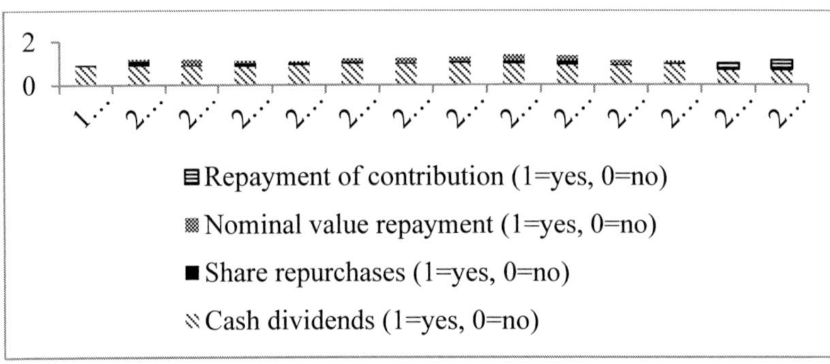

Figure 14-12: Payout instruments in the financial industry.

Across all industries, the four different payout instruments have widely been used. However, the majority of the firms used cash dividends as the traditional payout instrument. From 2011, repayment of contributions has widely been used by firms that met the legal criteria. 2000-2001 and 2007-2008 were the years when most of the firms paid out earnings. The proportion of firms that paid out cash dividends decreased in the health care industry. Interestingly, from 1999 to 2001 no firm in the health care industry made use of repayments of nominal value.

IV. Conclusions

Starting from the very useful theories of Miller and Modigliani (MM), many other concepts have been developed aiming at explaining capital structure and payout policies in situations when the MM assumptions are not met. However, also these theories failed to completely explain the corporate policies used in practice.

Our study examines the evolution of the capital structure and payout policies of listed firms in Switzerland during the past 14 years. Even though we do not explicitly test any of the theories mentioned, the figures indicate that decisions depend on firm characteristics (industry affiliation and firm size). For instance, industry-specific leverage ratios are relatively stable over time. On average, larger firms have higher debt-to-assets ratios and higher payout ratios. In addition, changes in the legal environment and in tax regimes had an impact on corporate decisions.

References

Allen, F., A.E. Bernardo, and I. Welch. 2000. "A theory of dividends based on tax clienteles." *The Journal of Finance* 55 (6): 2499-2536.

Black, F. 1976. "The dividend puzzle." *The Journal of Portfolio Management* 2 (2): 5-8.

Bolton, P., H. Chen, and N. Wang. 2011. "A unified theory of Tobin's q, corporate investment, financing, and risk management." *The Journal of Finance* 66 (5): 1545-1578.

Brav, A., J. R. Graham, C.R. Harvey, and R. Michaely. 2005. "Payout policy in the 21st century." *Journal of Financial Economics* 77 (3): 483-527.

Chang, C. 1993. "Payout policy, capital structure, and compensation contracts when managers value control." *Review of Financial Studies* 6 (4): 911-933.

Chava, S., D. Livdan, and A. Purnanandam. 2009. "Do shareholder rights affect the cost of bank loans?" *Review of Financial Studies* 22 (8): 2973-3004.

Chetty, R., and E. Saez. 2005. "Dividend taxes and corporate behavior: Evidence from the 2003 dividend tax cut." *The Quarterly Journal of Economics* 120 (3): 791-833.

DeAngelo, H., and L. DeAngelo. 2006. "The irrelevance of the MM dividend irrelevance theorem." *Journal of Financial Economics* 79 (2): 293-315.

DeAngelo, H., L. DeAngelo, and D.J. Skinner. 2004. "Are dividends disappearing? Dividend concentration and the consolidation of earnings." *Journal of Financial Economics* 72 (3): 425-456.

Dammon, R. M., and L.W. Senbet. 1988. "The effect of taxes and depreciation on corporate investment and financial leverage." *The Journal of Finance* 43 (2): 357-373.

Denis, D.J., and I. Osobov. 2008. "Why do firms pay dividends? International evidence on the determinants of dividend policy." *Journal of Financial Economics* 89 (1): 62-82.

Desai, M. A., and L. Jin. 2011. "Institutional tax clienteles and payout policy." *Journal of Financial Economics* 100 (1): 68-84.

Easterbrook, F. H. 1984. "Two agency-cost explanations of dividends." *American Economic Review 74* (4): 650-659.

Fama, E. F., and K. R. French. 2002. "Testing trade-off and pecking order predictions about dividends and debt." *Review of Financial Studies* 15 (1): 1-33.

Frank, M. Z., and V.K. Goyal. 2009. "Capital structure decisions: which factors are reliably important?" *Financial Management* 38 (1): 1-37.

Graham, J. R., and C.R. Harvey. 2001. "The theory and practice of corporate finance: evidence from the field." *Journal of Financial Economics* 60 (2): 187-243.

Graham, J. R., and A. Kumar. 2006. "Do dividend clienteles exist? Evidence on dividend preferences of retail investors." *The Journal of Finance 61* (3): 1305-1336.

Grullon, G., and R. Michaely. 2002. "Dividends, share repurchases, and the substitution hypothesis." *The Journal of Finance* 57 (4): 1649-1684.

Gordon, M. J. 1959. "Dividends, earnings, and stock prices." *The Review of Economics and Statistics:* 99-105.

Gordon, M. J. 1963. "Optimal investment and financing policy." *The Journal of Finance* 18 (2): 264-272.

Hansen, R. S., R. Kumar, and D.K. Shome. 1994. "Dividend policy and corporate monitoring: Evidence from the regulated electric utility industry." *Financial Management* 23 (1): 16-22.

Harvey, C.R., K.V. Lins, and A.H. Roper. 2004. "The effect of capital structure when expected agency costs are extreme." *Journal of Financial Economics* 74 (1): 3-30.

Harris, M., and A. Raviv. 1991. "The theory of capital structure." *The Journal of Finance* 46 (1): 297-355.

Huang, R., and J. R. Ritter. 2009. "Testing theories of capital structure and estimating the speed of adjustment." *Journal of Financial and Quantitative Analysis* 44 (02): 237-271.

Jagannathan, M., C.P. Stephens, and M.S. Weisbach. 2000. "Financial flexibility and the choice between dividends and stock repurchases." *Journal of Financial Economics* 57 (3): 355-384.

Jensen, M. C. 1986. "Agency costs of free cash flow, corporate finance, and takeovers." *American Economic Review* 76 (2): 323-329.

Jensen, M.C., and W.H. Meckling. 1976. "Theory of the firm: Managerial behavior, agency costs and ownership structure." *Journal of Financial Economics* 3 (4): 305-360.

Leary, M.T., and R. Michaely. 2011. "Determinants of dividend smoothing: empirical evidence." *Review of Financial Studies* 24 (10): 3197-3249.

Leland, H.E. 1998. "Agency costs, risk management, and capital structure." *The Journal of Finance* 53 (4): 1213-1243.

Lintner, J. 1956. "Distribution of incomes of corporations among dividends, retained earnings, and taxes." *American economic review 46* (2): 97-113.

Lintner, J. 1962. "Dividends, earnings, leverage, stock prices and the supply of capital to corporations." *The Review of Economics and Statistics*: 243-269.

Kraus, A., and R.H. Litzenberger. 1973. "A state-preference model of optimal financial leverage." *Journal of Finance*: 911-922.

Michel, A. 1979. "Industry influence on dividend policy." *Financial Management* 8 (3): 22-26.

Michaely, R., R.H. Thaler, and K.L. Womack. 1995. "Price reactions to dividend initiations and omissions: overreaction or drift?" *The Journal of Finance* 50 (2): 573-608.

Miller, M. H., and K. Rock. 1985. "Dividend policy under asymmetric information." *The Journal of Finance* 40 (4): 1031-1051.

Miller, M. H., and F. Modigliani. 1958. "The Cost of Capital, Corporate Finance and the Theory of Investment." *American Economic Review* 48: 261-97.

Miller, M. H., and F. Modigliani. 1961. "Dividend Policy, Growth and the Valuation of Shares." *Journal of Business*. 34: 411-33.

Morellec, E., B. Nikolov, and N. Schürhoff. 2012. "Corporate governance and capital structure dynamics." *The Journal of Finance* 67 (3): 803-848.

Myers, S. C. 1977. "Determinants of corporate borrowing." *Journal of Financial Economics* 5 (2): 147-175.

Myers, S. C. 1984. "The capital structure puzzle." *The Journal of Finance* 39 (3): 574-592.

Myers, S. C. 2001. "Capital structure." *Journal of Economic Perspectives* 15 (2): 81-102.

Myers, S., and N. Majluf. 1984. "Corporate financing and investment when firms have information that investors do not have." *Journal of Financial Economics* 11: 187-221.

Rajan, R. G., and L. Zingales. 1995. "What do we know about capital structure? Some evidence from international data." *The Journal of Finance* 50 (5): 1421-1460.

Rauh, J. D., and A. Sufi. 2010. "Capital structure and debt structure." *Review of Financial Studies* 23 (12): 4242-4280.

Ross, S. A. 1977. "The determination of financial structure: the incentive-signalling approach." *The Bell Journal of Economics*: 23-40.

Shefrin, H. M., and M. Statman. 1984. "Explaining investor preference for cash dividends." *Journal of Financial Economics* 13 (2): 253-282.

Stulz, R. 1990. "Managerial discretion and optimal financing policies." *Journal of Financial Economics* 26 (1): 3-27.

Zechner, J. 1990. "Tax clienteles and optimal capital structure under uncertainty." *The Journal of Business* 63 (4): 465-91.

CHAPTER SIXTEEN

CHALLENGES IN RATING MODEL DEVELOPMENT: A LITERATURE OVERVIEW

BEATRIX WULLSCHLEGER[1]

Rating model literature has a long history and, more importantly, the end of the story of rating models has not yet been written. This article gives an overview on the development of credit rating models and the different approaches put forward by a number of authors. Furthermore, it discusses potential future improvements.

The foundation for the contest in modeling the most sophisticated rating model is laid by Beaver (1966) and Altman (1968). Both tried to find a model for the prediction of bankruptcy in the industrial sector based on publicly available financial ratios. While Beaver suggested a univariate analysis, that is, he examined the predictive ability of ratios one at a time; he indicated that it might be possible that a multivariate analysis, using several different ratios and/or rates of change in ratios over time, would yield event better bankruptcy prediction. Notably, the author's intention was not to find the best predictive model for failure, but rather to assess the predictive power of different financial ratios. Two years later Altman (1968) publishes the first multivariate analysis. Using data from manufacturing corporations he strives to identify the combination of variables which best serve to explain corporate bankruptcy. Accordingly, he writes: "The theory is that ratios, if analyzed within a multivariate framework, will take on greater statistical significance than the common technique of sequential ratio comparisons. The results are very encouraging (Altman 1966, 609)." Studying a list of twenty-two potential variables Altman identifies five ratios as having the best predictive power

[1] The author is from the Institute for Finance, School of Business, University of Applied Sciences Northwestern Switzerland.

of corporate bankruptcy. In an iterative process he develops a discriminant function, the so called Z-score.

The Z-score (discriminant-ratio model) differentiates between bankrupt and non-bankrupt firms and was able to predict bankruptcy correctly in 94 per cent of cases in the initial sample.

Nevertheless he saw further need for research, as for example all the firms examined were publicly held manufacturing companies: "An area for future research, therefore, would be to extend the analysis to relatively smaller asset-sized firms and unincorporated entities where the incidence of business failure is greater than with larger corporations (Altman 1966, 609)." Nevertheless, even today the study of Altman still owns a vital function within the rating model literature. In 1977 Altman et al. refine the original model and develop the so called ZETA model. In contrast to the earlier Z-score the Zeta model (Altman et al., 1977) is based on 7 ratios and applied most recent developments in the application of discriminant analysis. The main contribution of the ZETA model is the equal accuracy of bankruptcy prediction not solely for manufacturing but also for retailing companies.

Gupta and Huefner (1972) and Mensah (1984) expand this strand of research in challenging the relationship between the predictive power of diverse financial ratios and the industry affiliation of a company. They find that bankruptcy prediction models may be improved by applying different financial ratios for different industries. The biggest drawbacks in these early studies are the lack of data about small and medium sized enterprises (SMEs) and the fact that they have to rely on publicly available accounting figures.

Only recent studies (Altman and Sabato, 2006; Ciampi and Gordini, 2008) take a closer look on the modeling of credit risk of SMEs and they find that a new foundation is necessary. Accurate bankruptcy prediction models for big companies do not have enough predictive power for SMEs. The expansion of this area of research was driven by the large share of SMEs in most economies and their relevance in the Basel II Capital Accord. The new Basel Capital Accord[2] required the calculation of the probability of default for SMEs. Indeed, Edmister (1972) was the first to focus on SMEs, but his goal was the discovery of accurate financial ratios and not the development of a new, better model of default behavior for SMEs, different from models predicting bankruptcy of large companies. Altman and Sabato (2006) therefore were on the onset of Bankruptcy prediction model literature for SMEs. Their study is based on a logit analysis, the second model used in a lot of the most cited past studies

[2] (Basel Committee on Banking Supervision, 2004)

along with the multiple discriminant analyses technique (MDA) first used by Altman. The first one applying the conditional logit model in the default prediction model context was Ohlson (1980). "The practical benefits of the logit methodology are that it does not require the restrictive assumptions of MDA and allows working with disproportional samples (Altman and Sabato 2006, 6)." Altman and Sabato (2006) use a sample of 2010 US firms including 120 defaults for the years 1994 to 2002. Based on the definition of SMEs from the Basel Capital Accord they analyze only companies with sales less than USD 65 Million because this SME definition is relevant for banks under Basel II. Applying a logit analysis they demonstrate that a specific SME model outperforms a generic corporate model (Z-Score model) in predicting defaults of SMEs. Ciampi and Gordini (2008) use a sample of 1000 small manufacturing companies (turnover in 2001 below EUR 15 Mio.) in Central and Northern Italy, of which 50 per cent of cases defaulted during the year 2005 and 50 per cent of cases did not default. By applying both a discriminant analysis and logistic regressions Ciampi and Gordini (2008) prove that separate credit rating models should be used for small enterprises. That applies especially with regard to the industry belonging as well as the stage of growth of a small company because they are crucial for the accuracy of the prediction rate of a credit rating model for small firms.

But these newer studies looking for adequate forecast models also struggle with the fact that they have to rely on publicly available data and their focus is still on the question of the best quantitative ratios to include in the models. Only at the start of the new century a new research strand begins to sprout. The focus shifts from publicly available accounting figures and the development of bankruptcy prediction models to bank internal data and the search for the best bank internal rating system. Therefore, for the first time internal data becomes available and the question of the predictive power of qualitative factors in addition to quantitative factors starts to rise.

In a detailed discussion paper the 'Models Task Force' of the Basle Committee empirically tests and classifies internal rating models of banks (Basel Committee, 2000). The research shows that there are no consistent standards for the design and application of internal rating models, but there are some common factors like the choice of risk indicators, the structuring of the rating process or the prioritization of debtor rating over the transaction rating. Beyond that Krahnen and Weber (2001) develop thirteen principals, the so called generally accepted rating principles, known as quality standards for the development of adequate bank internal rating systems. Regarding the rating process mainly the request for informational efficiency as well as the necessity to deal carefully with incentive problems in the design of the rating process are worth mentioning. Additionally, continuing control of the ratings is important. The Bank for International Settlement (BIS) follows the same arguments in a consultation paper (Basel Committe, 2006, 4 (ii) Integrity of rating process and (iii) Overrides) describing the cumulative relevant mandatory requirements for rating models to be accepted by national supervisory authorities.

2014 we see different research areas in-between the internal rating model literature. The first one strive to answer the question if anything being equal **quantitative and qualitative factors will generate the same model output** respectively how a mixture of both criteria's affects the rating of debtors. Weber et al. (1999) indicate in an early study that qualitative sub-ratings as an element of a risk classification are systematically higher than the correspondent quantitative sub-ratings and that they show less variation over time. Based on the corporate rating data from three commercial German banks, covering the time period from 1993 to 1997, Brunner et al. (2000) evaluate the extent to which non-public information determines corporate ratings. They find a positive impact of qualitative factors on credit ratings in about one third of the cases. In addition, the authors of the study come to the conclusion that qualitative criteria are systematically and significantly valued higher and show a lower variance across risk classes. Lehmann (2003) and Grunert et al. (2005) take an additional step by investigating the predictive power of a rating model with a combined application of quantitative and qualitative factors. By analyzing a credit data sample from four major German banks, Grunert et al. (2005) confirm that the concurrent use of financial and non-financial elements has a higher predictive power of future default events than the sole use of either qualitative or quantitative factors. Lehman (2003) empirically examines the role of the inclusion of soft facts (i.e. subjective judgments of credit analysts) in a bank internal credit rating model solely based on hard facts (financial ratios, checking account data). She uses a sample with 20'000 observations of German SME credit data from a commercial bank. The results reveal significant better outcomes for the model including qualitative information and therefore indicate that subjective judgments are beneficial information and improve credit ratings based exclusively on quantitative information. These results are in contrast with the study of Bernet and Westerfeld (2008), who find no empirical evidence for the superiority of models combining quantitative and qualitative factors. In addition to the explanations mentioned in the studies themselves it might be the case that the incentives driven valuation of the non-financial factors is responsible for the complimentary research result.

A second research branch of the internal rating model literature concentrates on the question of the **architecture and the application of internal rating systems**. The research of Treacy and Carey (2000) and English and Nelson (1998) is built on internal rating models of U.S. banks. While the first study concentrates on large institutions, English and Nelson (1998) explicitly use data from all US banks. They analyze data of 114 small, medium and large US banking institutions and find that smaller banks generally have a less elaborated internal rating system than larger banks. Treacy and Carey (2000) study the internal rating system of the 50 largest US banking organizations to find the relationship between different choices of the architecture of the applied rating system and the effectiveness of this system. They emphasize the role of human judgment and therefore the necessity of careful design controls and internal review procedures.

Jacobson et al. (2006) and Nakamura and Roszbach (2005) present related studies for Swedish banks. Jacobson et al. (2006) examine data from two of the 4 Swedish commercial banks to verify if banks with internal rating systems generate the same estimates of credit risk for identical loan portfolios. As the authors could not verify this fact, they undermine the study of Treacy and Carey (2000) by stating that besides the architecture of a rating system also the implementation of the rating model is crucial. Nakamura and Roszbach (2005) find that according to the Swedish data sample internal bank ratings are not fully efficient. Comparing internal bank ratings with public ratings the authors of this study conclude that internal ratings do not fully include all publicly available information.

The most recent studies in the credit model literature deal with **informational efficiency of internal credit rating processes**. Informational efficiency means in this context that there should be no possibility of predicting future ratings relying on historical data. Rather should all publicly available as well as all private information be included in the rating, therefore making the current rating the best predictor of future ratings. Thereby biases and incentive problems known from the principal-agent-theory of the unbiased decision-making in the credit market concerning key account manager and credit analysts (Leland and Pyle, 1977; Flannery, 1986; Fazzari and Athey, 1987; Goswami et al., 1995) should be addressed in the rating system. From an economic perspective the efficiency of the debtor selection in the lending process is crucial due to its influence on the supply of credit to the economy, the long-term depreciation ratio and thus the profitability of banks. Furthermore, regarding the importance of those credit contracts for the financial industry, the stability of the financial industry should be considered. Studies focusing on the informational efficiency of rating processes are Liberti and Mian (2009) and Hertzberg et al. (2008). The study of Liberti and Mian (2009) as well as the study from Hertzberg et al. (2008) is based on data from the loan approval process of a large multinational U.S. bank operating in Argentina and examine the informational efficiency of the credit assessment process. Liberti and Mian (2009) empirically test the influence of the hierarchy on the reliance of qualitative and quantitative factor and find that a greater hierarchical distance reduces the positive effect of subjective information. Hertzberg et al. (2008) examine the incentives for loan officers to use qualitative information ("soft facts") for influencing the rating of a borrower regarding a loan officer rotation-program. Their results show that anticipated rotation generates positive incentives and that the informational efficiency improves significantly. Furthermore the research of Brown et al. (2013) investigates how internal control affects the credit rating process using a proprietary data sample of 3360 credit assessments by 340 loan officers at six banks. They document a positivity bias of control, that is, they find empirical evidence for the manipulation of borrower ratings by loan officers. Additionally, Berg et al. (2013) discover in their study that a system solely based on hard information does not necessarily lead to better results but that the loan making process is crucial. Exactly, Berg et al. (2013) state: "The underlying incentives are important, and in the setting at hand, where loan officers are incentivized based on loan volumes, reliance on hard information actually leads to outcomes with worse loan performance (Berg et al. 2013, 31)." These results are consistent with the findings of Mosk (2014). He expounds that soft information has not only predictive power for corporate bankruptcy but also explains the deviations from the credit rating models. That is, loan officers rely on soft information in applying their discretionary authority. Based on a data set of a SME division of an international financial institution Mosk (2014) identifies no difference in the performance of loans where loan officers use discretion from otherwise similar loans.

We have seen the amplitude and profoundness of the credit rating model literature. Nevertheless, there is still a large amount of work to be done. According to the latest research developments in this literature area the next necessary step is to find a solution for the empirically found problem of the credit rating manipulation by loan officers. The optimal architecture and application of an internal rating model has still to be